MEDIA
ECONOMICS

Dedication

To Bruce, Carol, Deborah, Deidre, Jacqueline, and Heather

◆

We wish to acknowledge the financial support of Alberta Learning without which this text would not have been written. We would also like to thank Nicola Simpson for her able research support, Bruce Hoskins who read a draft of the manuscript and gave us valuable advice from a student's perspective, and Christine Shellska for her excellent work providing the figures in digital format.

MEDIA ECONOMICS

Applying Economics to New and Traditional Media

COLIN HOSKINS
STUART McFADYEN
ADAM FINN

University of Alberta

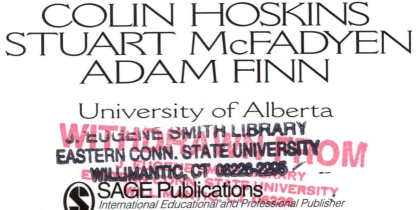

SAGE Publications
International Educational and Professional Publisher
Thousand Oaks ■ London ■ New Delhi

For information:

Sage Publications, Inc.
2455 Teller Road
Thousand Oaks, California 91320
E-mail: order@sagepub.com

Sage Publications Ltd.
1 Oliver's Yard
55 City Road
London EC1Y 1SP
United Kingdom

Sage Publications India Pvt. Ltd.
B-42, Panchsheel Enclave
Post Box 4109
New Delhi 110 017 India

Printed in the United States of America on acid-free paper.

Library of Congress Cataloging-in-Publication Data

Hoskins, Colin.
Media economics : applying economics to new and traditional media /
Colin Hoskins, Stuart McFadyen, and Adam Finn.
    p. cm.
Includes bibliographical references and index.
ISBN 0-7619-3095-7 (cloth) -- ISBN 0-7619-3096-5 (pbk.)
    1. Mass media--Economic aspects. I. McFadyen, Stuart. II. Finn,
Adam, 1946- III. Title.
P96.E25H67 2004
338.4'730223--dc22   2004003252

04   05   06   07   08   09   10   9   8   7   6   5   4   3   2   1

Acquiring Editor:	Margaret H. Seawell
Editorial Assistant:	Jill Meyers
Project Editor:	Claudia A. Hoffman
Copy Editor:	Catherine Chilton
Typesetter:	C&M Digitals (P) Ltd.
Indexer:	Molly Hall
Cover Designer:	Michelle Kenny

Contents

1

Introduction and Overview

1.1 Why Media Economics?

This book sets out the economic principles and concepts needed to understand media industries and issues. Most of the applications are real-world examples drawn from countries such as the United States, Canada, the United Kingdom, and Australia.

Media industries have customarily been defined in terms of a distinct product distributed in a particular way—books, magazines, television, radio, music, film, and video, for instance.

In the new digital economy, the content provided by many of these formerly distinct industries can be distributed via the Internet and read, viewed, or listened to on a personal computer (PC). E-mail can be read on a TV screen, and telephone messages can be routed over the Internet. With convergence, companies such as AOL-Time Warner in the United States and BCE in Canada are vertically integrated, including text, audio, and video content; an Internet portal; and distribution capability through cable or telephone wires. In this new economy, only a broad definition of what comprises media industries makes sense. Hence our applications will be drawn widely from new media, print, television, radio, film and video, video games, music recording, cable TV, and telecommunications.

These are examples of media issues and applications that will be addressed in this book. How is the Internet affecting the supply of information-based entertainment and cultural goods? Why was owning a commercial television broadcasting license, as Lord

Thomson of Fleet said, "like having a licence to print your own money" (Oxford Concise Dictionary of Quotations, 1997, p. 332)? Why did knowing that the demand for television advertising is relatively insensitive to changes in the price of advertising spots lead the Peacock Committee to recommend against permitting advertising on the BBC? Why is the benefit of subscribing to a network, such as a telephone network or Internet (e-mail) network, greater the larger the number of subscribers, and what are the implications for corporate strategy? How do economies of scale provide the United States with a competitive advantage in producing television drama and movies? Why are there so many media mergers, such as those between AOL and Time Warner in the United States and BCE's acquisition of CTV in Canada? How could Paramount claim that a movie bringing in $250 million at the box office was produced at a loss? Why are media industries inherently risky, and what can producers and distributors do to reduce this risk? How can we determine how competitive a given industry (e.g., the newspaper industry) is? How does the structure of a media industry affect its conduct and performance? Why have governments traditionally asked regulators to set the rates for telephone services? Why have many governments recently retreated from regulating long-distance rates? Why have some governments used competitive bidding to award cable television franchises or allocate electromagnetic spectrum frequencies? What has caused the "crisis" in public broadcasting? Why was it "winner takes all" in the VHS versus Betamax battle of VCR standards? Why are the prices for foreign sales of U.S. television programs so low, and does this constitute unfair competition? Why do publishers of academic journals have different subscription prices for institutions (libraries), students, and other individuals? Why do telephone companies have peak and off-peak prices for long-distance calls? Why have movie projectionists suffered big reductions in wages? Why do superstars, such as top movie directors and actors, authors, and pop stars, earn such vast salaries? Why is broadcasting, but not newspaper publishing, usually regulated and sometimes subsidized? Why is trade in television programs and films so controversial? Is protection of media industries justified?

Why study media economics? Many students in media studies, communications, radio and television, journalism, and film studies are exposed to little or no mainstream economics. Indeed, economists are often viewed with mistrust as mercenary folk who know the price of everything and the value of nothing, people who favor cost cutting at the expense of cultural development. An appreciation of the economic forces driving industry and firm behavior is, however, invaluable—not only to a general understanding of the media but to the ability to be effective in a media- or communications-related job, whether in the corporate or public sector.

If you are a student in business, economics, or political science, why should you take media economics rather than a more traditional introduction to economics? Maybe you are already pursuing a career in the media or are seriously thinking of doing so. However, the real reason to take media economics is that during the course, you will learn basic economics, and instead of worrying about widgets and whatsits, you will be able immediately to apply your learning in a dynamic and controversial sector of the economy, with interesting hands-on applications of your new skills.

Our emphasis is quite different from that of the usual media economics text, which provides a bare minimum background in economics by way of brief introductions to economic concepts and the industrial organization framework before undertaking chapter-by-chapter studies of the various media industries using that framework. The industrial organization framework has its place (we devote chapter 7 to it), but there are pitfalls in using it. Much of the industry material, such as a size ranking of the leading firms, is descriptive and soon becomes dated. More fundamentally, the traditional industry-specific perspective is increasingly outmoded, as individual industry segment distinctions are becoming almost meaningless in an era of convergence and digitization. In contrast, this text provides a much broader and deeper understanding of key economic concepts. Our approach provides a superior background for analyzing media industries and issues and functioning effectively in a job in a media company.

1.2 What Is Economics?

Economics is the science that studies how the economy allocates scarce resources, with alternative uses, between unlimited competing wants. But what does this really mean?

The *wants* reflect the desires by households or individuals acting as consumers. The wants are satisfied by consumer goods (tangible) and services (intangible). Even though most people in the developed world are able to purchase a variety and volume of goods and services undreamed of by our ancestors, very few people are able to consume everything they would like. Wants are a relative concept; there is invariably some neighbor or friend who is able to buy attractive items we would like to be able to afford but cannot.

These unlimited wants can only be provided using resources that are scarce and capable of producing many alternative products. These resources are also called *inputs* or *factors of production*. Resources can be placed in one of three categories: land (all natural resources), labor (all human employment designed to produce goods and services), and capital (all man-made aids to production).

Economics is divided into two main strands, *microeconomics* and *macroeconomics*, and an applied branch known as *managerial economics*.

- Microeconomics is concerned with the behavior of individual economic units, notably the firm and the household, and the role of relative prices in affecting behavior.
- Macroeconomics is concerned with economic aggregates, such as the overall level of employment or unemployment, the average price level, and gross national product (GNP).
- Managerial economics is the application of economic concepts, principles, and tools to managerial decisions.

This text deals primarily with microeconomics and managerial economics, as these are most relevant to media issues.

1.3 Problems to Be Solved by Any Economy

Because of scarcity, any economic system has to solve the *what, how,* and *for whom* allocation problems.

A. *What goods and services are to be produced, and how many of each?* This entails, for example, not only how many television receivers but what mix in terms of, for example, screen size, digital or analogue, flat screen or conventional, stereo or nonstereo, picture-in-picture capability or not, and so on.

B. *How are the goods and services to be produced?* Which scarce resources are to be used in their production and in what combination? Should a very capital-intensive or labor-intensive method be used? The answer will vary with the product and even within a product group. The combination of resources appropriate to production of a local television station's newscast may be quite different from that appropriate for a network newscast. How should an animated film or TV program be made? Should it be made using many graphic artists or should it be largely computer generated? In nonanimated films, should scenery and special effects be done on location or created digitally?

C. *Who is to receive the limited goods and services produced?* How are they to be allocated between consumers? Who is going to own and use the television sets, DVD players, or magazines made? Who is going to have an opportunity to watch the movie in the theater or to own a camera cell phone?

1.4 Solving These Allocation Problems Under Different Economic Systems

Under a *command economy*, such as that in the old Soviet Union, factories are state owned and allocation is made by central planners on the basis of economic forecasts. Planners may issue an edict to state-owned Factory No. 104 to produce 10,000 television receivers per month. Forecasting demand is extremely difficult, especially when economic data tends to be poor and out of date. Perhaps people would like to buy 20,000 or 5,000 television receivers from Factory 104. Perhaps they would indeed like to buy 10,000, but of a different screen size from those being produced. Perhaps they want to buy 10,000 television receivers of the size produced but would prefer to pay more for better quality. Factory 104's responsibility is to produce 10,000 units per month. Typically there is no incentive to provide an appropriate product range or to maintain the quality of output. The command economy has proved inflexible and unable to provide citizens with a rising standard of living.

In a *market economy,* allocation results from decisions made by individual households and firms interacting in the *product market* (where consumer goods and services are bought and sold) and the *factor market* (where inputs are bought and sold). Households have two roles. They are consumers of goods and services, purchasing them in the product market, and suppliers of labor (and, in some cases, investment financing for capital) through the factor market. Similarly, firms supply consumer goods and services to the product market and buy (hire) labor and other inputs in the factor market.

Money flows from households to firms in the product market and from firms to households in the factor market.

In a market economy, the *what, how,* and *for whom* allocation problems identified are solved as follows:

A. *What goods and services are to be produced, and how many of each?* This is determined by the demand for products at different prices by households (acting as consumers) and willingness of firms to supply products at different prices.

B. *How are the goods and services to be produced?* The number and combination of inputs depends on the relative prices of inputs and their productivity; that is, how effectively they contribute to making the product.

C. *Who is to receive the limited goods and services produced?* The allocation is made by rationing according to the willingness of households (which includes ability) to pay the price asked.

Economics, in examining how a market economy works, assumes that households and firms make decisions based on their own self-interest. The objective of households is assumed to be *utility maximization,* utility meaning, in this case, satisfaction. Households allocate their income among consumer goods and services in the manner that maximizes satisfaction, and they choose a line of work that gives the most satisfaction. An important element of the latter will be the level of remuneration, as this will affect the size of the basket of consumer goods and services the household can buy.

The objective of firms is assumed to be profit maximization. Profitability determines what is to be produced, the features of the product, the price at which to sell, the level of output, and the combination of resources to employ.

Households and firms weigh the benefits and costs of alternative choices in terms of utility or profits, respectively. *Incremental analysis* is important, as these choices are often not of the all-or-nothing variety but of how much or to what degree. For example, a household does not typically make a decision whether or not to buy *a* movie ticket this year but whether to buy 4 or 5 or 6. Similarly, once a company is established in the magazine business, the decision is more typically whether to produce 60,000 or 65,000 copies of next month's issue rather than whether to produce at all. Weighing the benefits and costs of relatively small changes is known as incremental or marginal analysis.

Relative prices play a crucial role in allocation decisions. Firms will find it most attractive to allocate resources to production of goods and services where the product price is relatively high and prices of inputs used in production are relatively low. Households will find low product prices attractive in their role as consumers and will prefer employment in an area where the price for their labor is relatively high. In competitive conditions, these prices themselves will be determined by the interaction of households and firms in the product market and the factor market.

Most economies today are *mixed economies,* with both a *private* and a *public* sector. However, in most of these mixed economies, the private sector, in which privately owned firms produce the goods and services, dominates. The public sector part of the economy is that in which the producing organizations, such as public broadcasting organizations, are publicly owned. In a mixed economy, the government may also assume the role of regulating and subsidizing privately owned firms in selected industries.

A classification somewhat similar to private and public is *market* and *nonmarket.* In the nonmarket sector, production may go ahead even if the revenue, if any, from selling the good or service does not cover the costs of production. An example is children's education. Normally public sector organizations supply the nonmarket sector and private sector organizations supply the market sector. For example, children's education and public broadcasting are usually provided by public organizations operating in the nonmarket sector. However, this is not always the case. Children's television programming produced in the market sector may be supplied to both private and public broadcasting organizations. In countries such as France, Canada, and Australia, some independent producers of feature films and television programs (private sector) rely partially on public funding (nonmarket sector). In other countries, such as the United States and Japan, public funding is insignificant, and film producers operate unambiguously in the market sector.

1.5 Key Concepts

Key concepts include *scarcity, choice, opportunity cost, substitutes, specialization, trade, incentives,* and *economic growth.* We will return to these concepts throughout the book, but we want to introduce them briefly here.

As we have seen, *scarcity* arises because resources are limited, but wants are unlimited. Hence there is an ongoing need to make a *choice* between desirable alternative goals or wants. There is a cost to every choice made, as satisfying one want means forfeiting another. In economic terminology, this *opportunity cost* is the best alternative foregone. Thus the public subsidy going to produce one more feature film may result in 50 fewer scholarships to university students. Supporting a public broadcasting organization may entail foregoing a tax cut; the opportunity cost here is the foregone utility from consumption of the goods and services households would choose to buy with the increase in their after-tax income. Understanding the opportunity cost concept is crucial to a sensible consideration of media issues. Arguments made often use the following faulty logic: "Public broadcasting is desirable [a list of reasons for considering it desirable is usually provided], therefore we should maintain [or increase] the level of funding." The opportunity cost concept teaches us that being desirable is not enough. *Substitutes* are always available. There are always attractive alternative goods and services that can be produced with given resources.

Both households and nations have found it more efficient to *specialize* rather than attempt to be jacks of all trades. At the household or individual level, specialization increases efficiency because talents and abilities differ. Also specialization promotes learning by doing. For example, tax accountants are very good at filing tax forms not only because they have special training but because of the learning and practice that comes from repeatedly doing this task. At the national level, it is also more efficient for a country to specialize in goods and services in which it has a comparative advantage; that is, in those goods and services that the country can produce at a lower opportunity cost.

Specialization is only possible if accompanied by *trade* that is itself facilitated by money used as a medium of exchange. Without money, barter can be the only form of trade. Specialization and trade is a very controversial topic in communications. The United States is the dominant producer of entertainment or cultural goods such as feature films, and in most countries, indigenous producers find it difficult to compete. We will return to this topic at several points in the text.

Economics assumes that people act in their own self-interest. In a market economy, *incentives* are provided by the price system. A lack of appropriate incentives was a prime reason for the collapse of communism in the Soviet Union and the Eastern Bloc. In the command economy of the Soviet Union, a common (if bitter) joke between workers that described the relationship between themselves and the state was "We pretend to work, and you pretend to pay us."

An important objective of any economy is *economic growth*. Growth permits rising standards of living and arises from technological progress and capital accumulation. Technological progress is the development of new and better ways of producing goods and services. Capital accumulation involves the production of capital goods that are then used as inputs to make consumer goods and services. In the short run, there is an opportunity cost because resources that could be used to directly produce consumer goods and services are diverted to production of capital goods. In the long run, however, production of consumer goods and services is more efficient, and growth of output occurs.

Economic growth sometimes uses up exhaustible resources and causes environmental degradation, but these are not inevitable problems. Before the collapse of communism, West Germany enjoyed higher growth rates than East Germany, but it was the East German factories that were the great polluters. It was the East German Trabant that had serious emission problems, not the clean-running Mercedes or BMW vehicles. Growth can create resources to examine and solve environmental problems. Communication improvements, by reducing the need to move goods and people, also reduce environmental problems.

1.6 Economic Methodologies

Economics employs both positive and normative methodologies. It is important to appreciate how the approaches differ because otherwise misunderstandings arise.

Microeconomics employs a *positive economics* methodology that is concerned with explaining and predicting economic phenomena that can be observed. It uses the scientific method. Definitions describe the conditions or circumstances being studied. For example, the type of industry being studied might be defined as one in which there is a single seller or, alternatively, one in which there are very many sellers. Assumptions are made about the motives of economic units. For example, as we have seen, firms are assumed to be profit maximizers. A process of logical deduction is used to discover the implications. The process of logical deduction may be made through words, graphical analysis, or mathematical techniques such as calculus. This book will use words supplemented by graphical analysis. The implications derived from the definitions and assumptions made are in the form of explanations and predictions. These explanations and predictions are tested by a process of empirical observation to see whether they are consistent with the facts. Because economics is a social science, controlled laboratory experiments are not usually possible, and the process of testing is thus difficult. Typically, testing involves statistical analysis of data generated over time (time-series data) or across economic units at one point in time (cross-section data). Consideration of such statistical techniques is beyond our scope.

Positive economics makes no value judgments. For example, a positive economic theory based on the assumption of profit maximization does not imply that firms ought to maximize profits. What it does imply is that a theory based on the assumption that firms are profit maximizers provides explanations and predictions more consistent with observed facts than theories based on alternative motivational assumptions. Noneconomists (and most people in media and communications and related fields are noneconomists) often have difficulty with this. For example, a number of years ago, we undertook a study of broadcasting for the Canada government. The completed study was reviewed by several members of the then Department of Communications. One reviewer wrote: "The assumption made [by the authors] that private broadcasters act as profit maximizers is so cynical that it undermines the credibility of the entire study." We remain unrepentant. The actions and behavior of private broadcasting organizations are explained well by a theory based on the assumption they are motivated by profits. Some may wish that private broadcasting organizations' primary motivation were more high minded, for example, promotion of cultural development, but this is another issue. Economists would be eager enough to build a theory based on such an alternative assumption if the predictions of such a theory proved to be more consistent with the facts.

Normative economics considers what should or ought to be and often involves a trade-off and judgment of what is good or bad. An example of a normative statement is: "the government should be more concerned with equity in income distribution than in economic growth." Policy decisions by governments or strategic decisions by companies (managerial economics) typically entail trade-offs and a judgment of the relative merits of competing goals.

1.7 Decision Making

When proposing a government policy, evaluating an existing policy, or considering a company strategy, six questions should be asked:

1. What is the problem?

This takes into account the question of why a decision is being considered in the first place. Context should also be considered in answering this question.

2. What are the goals?

Possible broad public policy goals include cultural goals, as well as economic goals such as efficiency, economic justice or fairness (equity), economic growth, and economic stability. A given public policy proposal may have a much narrower objective, however, such as increasing the profitability of domestic broadcasting organizations. If it is a decision of a private company, the broad goal might be profit maximization, but a narrow goal might be increasing audience ratings for the supper-hour newscast.

3. Would the proposed decision option achieve these goals?

4. Would the proposed decision option have adverse side effects?

5. Are there alternative means of achieving these goals?

6. How do the net benefits (total benefits minus total costs) of the proposed decision option compare to those for the alternatives?

Let's use these six questions to examine a government proposal to require theaters to devote at least 20% of screen time to domestic films.

What Is the Problem?

Suppose that domestic films receive about 3% of domestic cinema screen time and that the box office share is even lower (the situation in Canada).

What Are the Goals?

Assume that the government has stated the goals to be promotion of domestic film production, promotion of theatrical viewing of domestic films, and strengthening of national culture.

Would the Proposed Decision Option Achieve These Goals?

Promote domestic film production. Assured access to domestic cinemas could be expected to result in greater film production. However, will the domestic industry be able to supply enough films to meet the quota? Will these films attract an audience and be profitable? The policy would raise the need to define what constitutes a national film—cultural content or the nationality of inputs. Would international coproductions qualify? Would Hollywood films shot on location in the country qualify?

Promote viewing of national films. Making more national films available in cinemas does not ensure that people will watch them. Substitutes are everywhere. A typical person might go to the movies four times a year, and there will still be all the films from the Hollywood studios to choose from. Even if, thanks to the quota, there is no U.S. film showing at a convenient cinema at the particular time that a person feels like viewing, renting a video of a U.S. film is still an option. If exhibitors and distributors are handling national films to satisfy the quota, they are likely to keep marketing and promotion costs to a minimum; to do otherwise would be throwing good money after bad. They are also likely to relegate national films to unpopular times, such as Monday afternoons or evenings. Hence, there is ample reason to be sceptical that a screen-time quota would significantly increase theatrical viewing of domestic films.

Promote national culture. National culture can only be strengthened if more people actually watch national films. From this discussion, we can see that cinematic viewing of domestic films may not increase. Even if cinematic viewing does increase, would these additional viewers have watched the films in any case on television or video? (Films that do not get cinema release are nevertheless often shown on television.) Will the films promote national culture? To what extent will they be generic, imitating Hollywood, rather than culture specific?

Would the Proposed Decision Option Have Adverse Side Effects?

Adverse side effects that will or may occur could include:

1. The direct cost to the cinemas of providing the data with respect to screen time allocation and to the government agency or department responsible for collecting and assessing the data to see if cinemas are conforming to the quota

2. Sacrificing the best of offerings from other countries, as cinemas are going to be reluctant to reallocate screen time from U.S. to national films

3. A reduction in the number of screens because the policy can be expected to reduce the profits of cinemas (exhibitors) and distributors as they are forced to move from their preferred film portfolio

Given preferential access, domestic producers of national films may feel less pressure to produce films that will appeal to audiences.

Are There Alternative Means of Achieving These Goals?

Alternatives would include direct government subsidy of domestic film productions (which Canada already does, to some extent) and various tax relief measures.

How Do the Net Benefits of the Proposed Decision Option Compare to Those for the Alternatives?

Ideally, the benefits and costs would be quantified. Very often, such as would no doubt be the case in this example, this is impossible. Nevertheless, a benefit-cost framework is the appropriate context, and a qualitative weighing of the benefits and costs should be undertaken. This should also be done for the alternatives, such as those identified here. One alternative that should never be forgotten is *doing nothing*—that is, maintaining the status quo.

In assessing policy proposals, one should be wary of statements such as, "Our country needs to have our own cinemas showing our own films." What is wrong with this statement? The basic problem is the notion of necessity. What disaster will befall us if our cinemas are not showing our films? Does the statement imply that cinemas should only be showing our own films? Substitutes are always available. Does it change matters if our films are available on television, DVDs, or videocassettes? Is it relevant if other domestically produced cultural products, such as books, are readily available? What would be the cost of a policy ensuring that our own cinemas are showing our own films? As we have seen, resources are scarce, and hence any course of action has an opportunity cost in terms of alternatives forfeited. Would the money that would be required to attain the goal (if indeed it is attainable) be better used on day-care subsidies, health care, or left in the hands of taxpayers?

Statements of the "all or nothing" variety are suspect. An example is, "All roads in the country should be paved." The problem here is that although it may well make sense (benefits greater than costs) to pave some gravel roads, the benefits of paving some very remote, lightly travelled roads will certainly be less than the cost. Returning to our media example, even if a policy measure that improved cinema access for some of our films passed a benefit-cost assessment, it is inconceivable that this would be the case for all national films. As we have seen, using the incremental approach, economists ask, "For how many units is it worthwhile?" How many miles or kilometers of road should be paved? How many of our films should be guaranteed cinema access?

1.8 Summary

Any balanced examination of the media cannot ignore the contribution and perspective that economics provides. Unlike the traditional media economics text that provides industry-specific examinations of the media, an approach that is increasingly outmoded as convergence blurs distinctions between media, this book stresses a deeper understanding of economic concepts and the tools necessary to analyze media issues and decisions. An understanding of the economic forces driving industry and company behavior is invaluable to you if you wish to be effective in a media or communications-related job, whether in the corporate or public sector.

Economics studies how the economy allocates scarce resources, with alternative uses, between unlimited competing wants. Three allocation problems need to be solved. *What* goods and services are to be produced, and how many of each? *How* are they to be produced;

which scarce resources are to be used, and in what combination? *Who* is to receive the limited goods and services produced?

In a market economy, allocations result from decisions made by individual households and firms interacting in the product market (where consumer goods and services are bought and sold) and the factor market (where inputs are bought and sold). Households and firms are assumed to act in their own self-interest. Households attempt to maximize satisfaction or utility; firms attempt to maximize profits. Relative prices play a crucial role in allocating scarce resources.

Most economies today are mixed economies, but the private sector, where privately owned firms produce goods and services, dominates the public sector, where producing organizations, such as public broadcasting organizations, are publicly owned.

Key economic concepts are scarcity, choice, opportunity cost, substitutes, specialization, trade, incentives, and economic growth.

Economics employs both positive and normative approaches. Positive economics is concerned with explanations and predictions relating to economic phenomena that can be observed. Definitions describe the conditions or circumstances being studied, and assumptions are made about the motives of economic units. Through a process of logical deduction, explanations and predictions are made. These explanations and predictions are tested by a process of empirical observation to see whether they are consistent with the facts. The more consistent they are with the facts, the better the theory. No value or moral judgment is involved.

In contrast, normative economics considers what should or ought to be and often involves a trade-off requiring a value judgment.

When making a decision, whether it involves a government policy or a company strategy, the following questions should be asked. What is the problem? What are the goals? Would the proposed action achieve these goals? Would the proposed action have adverse side effects? Are there alternative means of achieving these goals? How do the net benefits of the proposed action compare to those for the alternatives?

2

Demand and Supply

Prices play a central role in resource allocation. In this chapter, we examine how the quantity demanded and quantity supplied of a product depend on its market price and how the interaction of demand and supply actually determines this price. We look at the sensitivity of quantity demanded and supplied to price, what is termed the *price elasticity of demand* and the *price elasticity of supply*. Aspects of demand, supply, and elasticity for media goods and services are examined.

This chapter should provide you with an understanding of the economic concepts necessary to answer the following media-related questions: How do we know that many estimates of the losses suffered by the music and video industries as a result of piracy are grossly exaggerated? Why is the quantity of telephone calls demanded more sensitive to price the greater the distance of the call? Why did a price cut by *The Times* newspaper in the United Kingdom result in a bigger increase in daily circulation 9 months later than it did 2 months later? What can we deduce about Universal's expectations of increased sales when they cut the price of music CDs by 38% in 2003? Why did some Hollywood studios cut the price of movie videos for home use from around $80 to around $25 in the late 1980s? Why did the discovery that the quantity of television advertising demanded is relatively insensitive to changes in the price of advertising spots lead the Peacock Committee to recommend against permitting advertising on the British Broadcasting Corporation (BBC)? Why did Sprint Canada, which initiated a C$20 per household per month maximum for off-peak long distance calls within Canada, subsequently amend this to add a C$0.10 per minute charge on calls after 800 minutes of calls had been logged in the month? Why did its competitors, Bell Canada and AT&T, not follow suit?

2.1 Demand

The market demand for a good or service is different from individual demand. Individual demand is how much one person or household wishes to buy. Market demand is the total amount all people in the market wish to purchase and is the sum of the demands by individuals. In this chapter, we will concentrate on market demand. Demand is not just a want; it concerns what will actually be bought at different prices and hence is a wish backed by willingness and ability to pay. Buying a product has an opportunity cost, sacrificing consumption of another good that could be bought instead. Thus wanting or even "needing" a good does not constitute demand unless this sacrifice of the next best alternative is acceptable.

The market demand for a given good or service will typically vary with the product's own price, the prices of demand-related products, the level of per capita (per person) income, the number of potential buyers in the market, expected future prices, and the tastes of consumers. In this chapter, we will examine the effect of (the product's) own price on the quantity demanded of the good, assuming for now that the values of these other determinants of demand are given and unchanged.

2.1.1 How Does the Quantity Demanded Vary With Price?

When we refer to a *price change* in this and other chapters, we are referring to a change in the price of a specific good relative to other goods. Thus an absolute increase in the price of newspapers by 5% is not a price change in this sense if the prices of all other goods increased by 5% also.

Other things being equal, the higher the price, the smaller the quantity demanded. Equivalently, the lower the price, the greater the quantity demanded. This is known as the *Law of Demand*.

The major reason for the Law of Demand is the *Substitution Effect* resulting from the change in relative prices. An increase in the price of a good will make it a less attractive purchase relative to substitute goods whose prices are unchanged. Some people will thus switch to purchasing one of the substitutes. All goods have substitutes. For example, if the price of television sets goes up 10%, a person who was about to buy a new TV might switch to buying repair service for her old set while another person might decide to buy a computer with Internet access. When we consider individual brands, rather than generic goods, even closer substitutes become available and the substitution effect greater. If the price of a particular model of Panasonic television set increases 10%, with all other prices unchanged, people will very readily switch to buying a comparable Sony or RCA television set instead, and Panasonic will suffer a large reduction in quantity demanded.

A price change also has an *Income Effect*. An increase in price, if money income is unchanged, decreases real income. As we shall see in chapter 3, for most products, but not all, a decrease in real income will reduce purchase of the good and hence operate in the same direction as the Substitution Effect. In any case, the Income Effect is typically very small and dwarfed by the Substitution Effect. For example, a decrease in the price of CDs would make people better off, as their budget goes further than before, and some would increase consumption of CDs as a result. This increase, however, would be miniscule relative to the increase in consumption of CDs caused by the substitution of CDs for downloading (both legal and illegal) music.

The implications of the Law of Demand are sometimes forgotten. For example, estimates of the piracy losses to the music, video, and computer software industries are grossly exaggerated as a consequence of ignoring the Law. Let's look at two examples that illustrate this.

In 1996, the Recording Industry Association of America (RIAA) successfully brought a case against four people for counterfeiting audiocassette tapes. The association estimated the loss to the legitimate recording industry of "up to $96 million" ("Record CD seizures," 1996). This figure was reached by taking the number of blank tapes seized and multiplying by the price of legitimate prerecorded tapes. Two assumptions were thus made in reaching the $96 million figure. The first is that all the seized tapes would have been sold after the illegal copying had been completed. The second assumption is that each pirate tape sold would displace a sale of a legitimate tape. This assumption ignores the Law of Demand. Because pirate tapes are sold at prices well below the price of legitimate tapes, the quantity demanded of pirate tapes will be greater. Successfully eliminating pirate tapes would not result in a one-for-one displacement by the higher priced legitimate tapes. Many of the buyers of low-priced pirate tapes would never have bought full-priced products in the first place. The $96 million figure is thus misleading, although the RIAA was careful to qualify it by the phrase "up to."

Similarly, the chairman of Egypt's Board of Censorship in 1996 estimated that each Egyptian film (Egypt is the dominant Arabic film producer) loses around $330,000 (converted from Egyptian pounds) as a result of video piracy (El Ibiary, 1996). For an average film, legitimate videos of the movie number only 2500, at a price of around $14.60 each, whereas pirate copies number 22,500, at a very much lower price. The estimated loss of $330,000 was calculated by multiplying the 22,500 pirate copies by the $14.60 price of legitimate prerecorded videos. Again, it violates the Law of Demand to assume that every purchaser of a low-priced pirate video would be willing, if pirate copies were not available, to purchase a (relatively) high-priced legitimate video.

Were these spokesmen unaware of the Law of Demand? We think not. It is much more likely that it was convenient to ignore it. Political purposes, such as encouraging governments to have strong copyright laws and encouraging law enforcement agencies to clamp down on violations, are best served by exaggerating the consequences of piracy. We note that in 2003 the RIAA did not use the same flawed methodology to estimate the costs of piracy from downloaded music. We suspect this is because the methodology would give a cost that would be so large as to be unbelievable. Also, it might provide fuel for those who argue that the music recording industry is being greedy by bringing legal action against individuals practicing "free" downloading.

2.1.2 Demand Schedule and Demand Curve

Economics emphasizes the importance of own price as a determinant of demand. To isolate this relationship, we assume all other determinants of demand are given and unchanged. This assumption is often known as *ceteris paribus*, which means "other things being equal." The relationship between the quantity demanded of a good and the own price of the good can be illustrated through a *demand*

Table 2.1   Number of Movie Tickets Purchased at Various Ticket
Prices

Price	$6	$8	$10	$12	$14
Quantity demanded	90,000	80,000	70,000	60,000	50,000

schedule or *demand curve.* Table 2.1 shows a demand schedule
indicating the number of visits to movie theaters in a particular city
in a month (quantity demanded) according to the ticket price.
Following the Law of Demand, the demand schedule exhibits a
greater quantity demanded at lower prices.

A demand curve is the graphical representation of this relationship and is thus negatively sloped. In Figure 2.1, the demand curve
is designated as D. A movement along the demand curve is referred

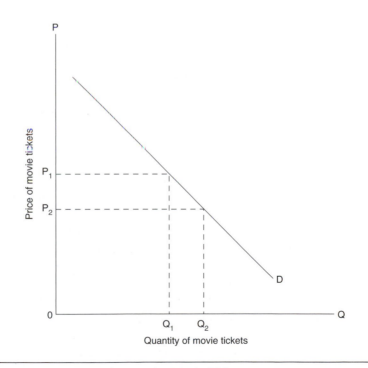

Figure 2.1   Demand Curve for Movie Tickets

Note: D indicates demand curve; P, price; Q, quantity.

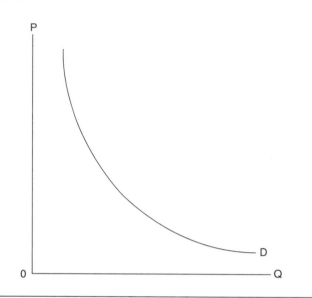

Figure 2.2   Nonlinear Demand Curve
Note: D indicates demand; P, price; Q, quantity.

to as *a change in quantity demanded.* If the price is reduced from P_1 to P_2, quantity demanded increases from Q_1 to Q_2. If the demand curve in Figure 2.1 relates to the data in Table 2.1 and $P_1 = \$10$ and $P_2 = \$8$, the increase in quantity demanded (number of movie tickets purchased), shown on the horizontal axis, would be from Q_1 or 70,000 to Q_2 or 80,000.

The demand curve we have drawn is linear; that is, a straight line. Equal dollar decreases in price result in equal increments in units of quantity demanded. In the numerical example given in Table 2.1, each $2 reduction in price results in a 10,000 unit increase in quantity demanded. What if equal dollar decreases in price result in increasing increments in units of quantity demanded? For example, suppose a decrease in price from $14 to $12 results in an increase in quantity demanded of 10,000; a decrease in price from $12 to $10 increases quantity demanded by 12,000; and a decrease from $10 to $8 increases quantity demanded by 18,000 units. In this case, the demand curve will appear convex to the origin, as in Figure 2.2. Which form of demand curve applies will vary from product to product.

2.1.3 Price Elasticity of Demand

We can see that quantity demanded will change in the opposite direction to price, but just how much will it change? This issue of how responsive quantity demanded is to price is an important one and vital to a firm contemplating a price change.

Economists measure this responsiveness by calculating the price elasticity of demand, often designated by the symbol η where

$$\eta = \text{Percentage change in quantity demanded} / \\ \text{Percentage change in price}$$

The percentages are calculated on the average (of the before and after) quantity demanded and the average (of the before and after) price.

To illustrate, let us calculate the price elasticity of demand for movie tickets for a price change from $10 to $8 based on the data in Table 2.1. This decrease in price results in an increase in quantity demanded from 70,000 to 80,000. Thus there is a 10,000-ticket change in quantity demanded on an average quantity of 75,000. This is a 13.33% (= [10,000 / 75,000] × 100) increase in demand. The change in price of $2, as a percentage of the average price of $9, is −22.22%. It is a common, although not universal, practice to ignore the minus sign. Adopting this practice gives η = 13.33% / 22.22% = 0.60. The interpretation of this result is that a 1% change in price causes a 0.60% change in quantity demanded in the opposite direction. The reason the minus sign is often dropped is that it is easier to work with positive numbers, and there is no ambiguity because it is understood that the change in quantity demanded is in the opposite direction to the change in price. The reason percentages are based on the average quantity demanded and the average price, rather than the original or before quantity and price, is so that the measure gives the same elasticity for a price increase from $8 to $10 as for a decrease from $10 to $8.

To provide another example from Table 2.1, suppose the price decrease is from $14 to $12—which, as we see from Table 2.1, would lead to an increase in quantity demanded from 50,000 to 60,000 tickets. The increase in quantity demanded is 18.18% and the decrease in price is 15.38%, giving η = 1.18.

You will notice that the elasticity is greater for a price decrease from $14 to $12 than it is for a price decrease from $10 to $8. This is because the same unit change in quantity is a greater percentage of the lower average quantity found at higher price levels, but the same dollar change in price is a lesser percentage change at the higher average price level.

The price elasticity of demand is said to be elastic if it is greater than one ($\eta > 1$) or inelastic if it is less than one ($\eta < 1$). Thus, for a ticket price decrease from \$14 to \$12 (or increase from \$12 to \$14), demand is elastic, whereas for a price decrease from \$10 to \$8 (or an increase from \$8 to \$10), it is inelastic.

Price elasticity of demand may seem to be a somewhat technical concept. But it is of critical importance. It determines whether expenditure by consumers, and hence revenue earned by the company selling the product, increases or decreases as a consequence of a price change. If demand is elastic, then the percentage change in quantity demanded is greater than the percentage change in price. The change in quantity dominates the change in price, so expenditure moves in the opposite direction to the price change. A decrease in price will thus lead to an increase in expenditure on the good, and an increase in price will lead to a decrease in expenditure.

Conversely, if demand is inelastic, meaning that the percentage change in price is greater than the percentage change in quantity demanded, then the change in price dominates, and the change in expenditure will be in the same direction as the change in price. A decrease in price will decrease expenditure on the good, and an increase in price will lead to an increase in expenditure.

In our previous example drawn from Table 2.1, in the price range of \$12 to \$14, demand is price elastic. Hence a price decrease from \$14 to \$12 would lead to an increase in expenditure on movie tickets by consumers. In fact, expenditure, equal to price × quantity, would increase from \$700,000 (= \$14 × 50,000) to \$720,000 (= \$12 × 60,000). However, in the price range of \$8 to \$10, we found demand to be price inelastic. Hence a price decrease from \$10 to \$8 would decrease expenditure on movie tickets; in fact, expenditure would fall from \$700,000 to \$640,000. Obviously, a theater would not wish to decrease price in an inelastic segment of the demand curve.

Price elasticity of demand depends on the *closeness of substitutes, the proportion of income spent on a good,* and the *length of time period* considered.

The more close substitutes for a good, the more elastic its demand. How broadly or narrowly a good is defined will have a significant effect on the number of close substitutes, and, hence, the elasticity. Television sets as a generic good have no close substitutes, so if all TV sets are increased in price by, for example, 5%, there would be only a modest decrease in demand. However, a Toshiba 27" TV set has many very close substitutes, and a 5% price increase would cause many potential buyers to switch to another Toshiba model or other brands such as Sony, Panasonic, Hitachi, or RCA.

The proportion of income spent on a good will influence its elasticity. If a product comprises a large proportion of income, people will be very price conscious and willing to search for a better price. If the price of a high-definition television (HDTV) receiver is reduced from $3200 to $2200, the difference in price is substantial relative to many people's income, and the sales at the lower price could be expected to be very much higher. At the lower price, one consumer might substitute an HDTV television receiver for a new sofa, and another might now buy it in preference to a planned vacation. If a rewritable CD (CD-RW) is reduced in price from $3.20 to $2.20, although the percentage difference in the average of before and after prices is the same as for the HDTV example at 37%, the percentage increase in sales would not be nearly as great because the monetary difference in price is miniscule relative to incomes. Consumers will scarcely notice the increase in real income and are unlikely to change their consumption as a consequence.

Because of adjustment lags, price elasticity often depends on the length of time since the price change. This adjustment can take several forms.

Price increases, where they are expected to be permanent, induce substitute products to be developed, but it can take a considerable time before these substitutes reach market. For example, increasing prices for cable TV services spurred the development and introduction of direct-broadcast satellite (DBS) and multichannel, multipoint distribution systems (MMDS). When a new substitute becomes available, some people switch to purchasing the substitute and demand becomes more elastic.

Another form of adjustment occurs when consumers have a sunk investment in a consumer durable good that is used in conjunction with software. For example, suppose the price of prerecorded movie DVD videodisks decreases dramatically. In the short run, people already owning a DVD player will increase their purchase of DVDs. But some people do not own a DVD player, and the decrease in the price of disks will persuade very few to immediately throw out their VCR and replace it with a DVD player. However, in time, existing

VCRs will need replacing. At that time, the reduction in the DVD disk price would be a factor in persuading some people to replace their VCR with a DVD player rather than with another VCR. These people will then start consuming DVDs. Hence, in the long run, the increase in quantity demanded of DVDs caused by the price decrease will be greater.

Brand loyalty may delay the reaction of consumers to a price change. We will consider an example in the next section when discussing the effects of a decrease in the price of *The Times* newspaper.

2.1.4 Estimates of Price Elasticity

Calculation of the price elasticity for a particular industry will show how sensitive quantity demanded is to price changes. Because this is a critical factor in pricing decisions, we would expect companies and policy makers to have devoted considerable time and effort to figuring out what the price elasticity of demand is for particular media industry products and brands. They have, in fact, done so, although companies usually view estimates of elasticity for their own product brands to be confidential. Let's examine some of the elasticity estimates that are publicly available.

There have been numerous estimates of price elasticity of demand for telephone calls. A survey by Albon, Hardin, and Dee (1997) reports estimates of elasticity for local calls to be 0.04 for both the United States and United Kingdom. Examples of price elasticity for within-country long-distance telephone calls include 0.38 for the United States, 0.53 for Australia, and 0.48 for Canada. Price elasticity was much higher for international calls, at 1.38 for calls from Sweden to the United Kingdom and 2.05 from Sweden to the United States. Albon et al. summarize as follows:

> Demand for services is more elastic the longer the distance of the call. The demand for local calls is very inelastic. The demand for long distance calls is much more elastic than for local calls, and, within the long distance call category, demand is more elastic the longer the distance. International calls have very elastic demand. (Albon et al., 1997, p. 42)

The explanation of why elasticity increases with distance of call is that price and, potentially, proportion of income spent rise with distance.

Researchers working for the Peacock Committee (1986), which examined the financing of public broadcasting in the United Kingdom, found the demand for television advertising to be price inelastic (the estimate of two committee researchers was 0.4).

Studies suggest that circulation demand for newspapers is insensitive to subscription prices. For example, for her sample of U.S. newspapers, Lewis (1995) found a price elasticity of only 0.20. The experience of *The Times* in the United Kingdom is consistent with an inelastic demand. In September 1993, after test marketing for one month, Rupert Murdoch's News Corp reduced the price of *The Times* from 45 pence to 30 pence. After 2 months, circulation of *The Times*, which competes in the British newspaper market with three other "serious" newspapers and about five tabloids, increased from 360,000 to 453,000 daily ("Controlling Britain's news," 1993). Assuming that it was the reduction in price that caused this increase in circulation, the price elasticity of demand over this period was 0.57 (percent change in quantity demanded / percent change in price = [(93,000 / 407,500) × 100] / [(15 / 37.5) × 100)]. However, after 9 months, the circulation had expanded further to 515,000 (Barnard, 1994-1995). Calculating the price elasticity of demand for the 9-month period gives 0.89. Thus, over the longer period, the price elasticity is higher. This can be attributed to adjustment lags caused by consumers' brand loyalty. Readers of higher priced competitive papers such as *The Telegraph* and *The Independent* were obviously reluctant to switch. It took time for some of them to give *The Times* a trial and determine that, given the difference in price, they should change their loyalties. However, even over the 9-month period, the elasticity is <1, and gross revenue from daily circulation decreased by £7500. Does this mean that the News Corp made a wrong decision? We will return to this example in chapter 11.

Crandall (1990) estimated the price elasticity for basic cable service provided by franchises owned and operated by TCI, a large U.S. cable system. He found the demand to be elastic with a cluster of estimates around 2.2.

Some of these estimates of price elasticity of demand are summarized in Table 2.2. It should be noted that these estimates are for industry products rather than specific brands. Companies do not usually make the latter information available. For individual brands, because rival brands are very close substitutes, we would expect the price elasticity of demand to be much higher. For example, we would

Table 2.2   Price Elasticity of Demand for Communication Products

Local telephone calls	0.04
Long distance calls	
Within-country long distance calls: United States	0.38
Within-country long distance calls: Australia	0.53
Within-country long distance calls: Canada	0.48
International long distance calls: Sweden to United Kingdom	1.38
International long distance calls: Sweden to United States	2.05
Television advertising in United Kingdom	0.40
Newspaper circulation in United States	0.20
Basic cable services in United States	2.20

expect the price elasticity of demand for Sprint for long-distance calls within the United States to be much higher than 0.38 because consumers can easily switch to AT&T, MCI, or any of the other competing carriers.

2.1.5 Applications: Price Elasticity and Decision Making

Firms need to know the price elasticity of demand for their products. If a firm is considering a price change, it will want to know the effect on its revenues. For example, in September 2003, Universal announced a price decrease for prerecorded music CDs, from $18.98 to $12.98. This represented a 38% decrease from the average price. This price reduction would only increase revenue if the resulting change in quantity demanded, calculated on the basis of the average quantity, were greater than 38%. To be profitable, the revenue would not only have to increase, the additional revenue would have to be greater than the incremental costs resulting from production of the additional CDs. Obviously, Universal was confident that the change in quantity demanded would be well in excess of 38%.

It is common for companies to test the market to gauge the elasticity of demand. For example, prior to decreasing the price of the Microsoft Encarta 96 Encyclopedia CD-ROM in Canada from C$139 to C$70, the company experimented with price reductions in 36 stores. Obviously, these experiments suggested that the increase in quantity demanded would be well in excess of 66%, the reduction in price.

The pricing of videos to the final consumer changed in 1989. Prior to 1989, a high price strategy of around $80 was the norm. Then in 1989, Warner Bros. broke tradition by selling the *Batman* video for $24.99. This was followed by a similar price for *Indiana Jones and the Temple of Doom*, and a trend to a low-price strategy developed. The number of prerecorded videotapes sold doubled from 1988 to 1989 (Mayer, 1990).

A very elastic demand can cause problems. In July 1998, Sprint Canada initiated a policy of unlimited long-distance calls within Canada during off-peak hours for a maximum of C$20 per month. As the rate for these long-distance calls was C$0.10 per minute, this meant that the maximum was reached after 200 minutes. Thus, after 200 minutes of calls, each additional minute was, in effect, free. But Sprint underestimated the resulting increase in quantity demanded. This pricing scheme was so popular with the public that the plan caused network congestion and frequent busy signals. Sprint responded in October 1998 by limiting calls to 800 minutes a month under the C$20 cap; additional calls beyond 800 minutes were charged at C$0.10 per minute.

Firms do not need to be passive bystanders that simply accept the price elasticity for their product. Software manufacturers build in incompatibilities with competing programs or other specific features to make switching by consumers more difficult. When consumers feel locked in to the word processing program or office suite they are currently using, demand for the product is inelastic, and firms find it much easier to raise the prices of new versions without sacrificing sales volume.

The concept of price elasticity of demand can also be relevant to public policy. One example is the work of the Peacock Committee (1986), which recommended against allowing the BBC to offer advertising. The committee predicted that permitting the BBC to sell advertising spots would lead to a decrease in the price for advertising spots. (We will examine the basis for this prediction in chapter 3). When, as we have seen, researchers commissioned by the Committee estimated the demand for television advertising to be price inelastic, the Peacock Committee recommended against permitting the BBC to sell advertising because it would reduce the aggregate revenue available to broadcasters in the United Kingdom. (The total advertising revenue received by the BBC and private broadcasters together, at the lower spot price, would be less than that received by private broadcasters alone in the absence of advertising on the BBC.)

2.2 Supply

Supply for an individual firm is the quantity that firm will supply. Market supply is the quantity that all firms making a particular good or service will supply. In the short run, defined by economists as a length of time insufficient to change capacity, the market supply is the sum of the supply of the existing firms. In the long run, the number of firms supplying the good or service can change. Allocating resources to supply a given good or service has an opportunity cost, as using the resources in this way precludes employing them to make other goods or services.

The market supply for a good or service will typically depend on own price, the prices of inputs, the state of technology, and the number of suppliers. In this chapter, we will examine the effect of own price on the quantity supplied, assuming the prices of inputs, the state of technology, the number of suppliers, and any other determinants of supply are given and unchanged.

2.2.1 How Does the Quantity Supplied Vary With Price?

Firms will wish to supply the quantity that maximizes profits. They will only be willing to supply an extra unit if the additional revenue resulting covers the incremental cost of producing the unit. In the short run, with capacity fixed, it will become increasingly costly to increase output, so firms will be willing to do so only if they can sell for a higher price. Thus the quantity supplied is positively related to price. In the long run, a higher price may also induce entry of new firms, so the increase in quantity supplied for a given increase in price will be greater.

2.2.2 Supply Schedule and Supply Curve

A *Supply Schedule* shows the number of units of the product supplied for various product prices. To return to our hypothetical example relating to movie tickets, suppose the number of tickets that theaters would supply is that given in Table 2.3.

The *supply curve* is the graphical representation of this relationship. It is positively sloped because the quantity supplied increases with movie ticket price. In this example, the quantity supplied increases by 7,000 tickets for each $2 increase in ticket price. The supply curve is designated as S in Figure 2.3. A movement along the

Table 2.3   Number of Movie Tickets Supplied at Various Prices

Price	$6	$8	$10	$12	$14
Quantity supplied	56,000	63,000	70,000	77,000	84,000

supply curve is referred to as *a change in quantity supplied.* If the price is increased from P_0 to P_1, quantity supplied increases from Q_0 to Q_1. If the ticket price $P_0 = \$8$ and $P_1 = \$10$, then the increase in quantity supplied, shown on the horizontal axis, would be from Q_0, or 63,000, to Q_1, or 70,000. It is assumed that other determinants of supply are given and unchanged.

The supply curve in Figure 2.3 is linear (a straight line), as each equal increment in dollar price results in an equal unit increment in quantity supplied. However, in some cases, each equal increment in dollar price will result in a smaller increment in units of output supplied. Then the supply curve has an increasing slope, as shown in Figure 2.4. Certainly, in the short run, as the capacity limit is approached, it will become increasingly costly to increase output. Eventually it will be physically impossible to increase short-run output further, given the capacity available, and the supply curve will become vertical.

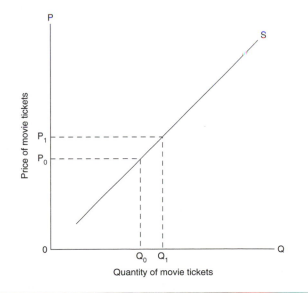

Figure 2.3   Supply Curve for Movie Tickets

Note: P indicates price; Q, quantity supplied; S, supply curve.

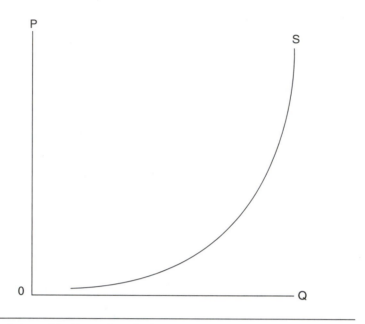

Figure 2.4   Nonlinear Supply Curve

Note: P indicates price; Q, quantity supplied; S, supply curve.

Supply curves are usually drawn for the short run. You should assume that a given supply curve is short run unless otherwise indicated.

2.2.3 Elasticity of Supply

Just as in the case with demand, it is useful to have a measure of how responsive quantity supplied is to a change in price of the service or good in question. This measure, the *elasticity of supply,* often denoted by η_s, is determined by

$$\eta_s = \text{Percentage change in quantity supplied} / \text{Percentage change in price}$$

The percentages are again calculated on the average (of the before and after) quantity supplied and the average (of the before and after) price.

To illustrate, we will calculate η_s for the increase in movie ticket price from \$8 to \$10 (or decrease from \$10 to \$8). This change in price of 22.22% (= $[2/9] \times 100$) results in a change in quantity supplied of 10.53% (= $[7,000/66,500] \times 100$). Thus η_s = 0.47 (= 10.53/22.22).

We indicated earlier that quantity supplied is more responsive to a price change in the long run than in the short run. In our example, in the short run, the number of theaters and the number of seats in them is fixed (because the capacity is given). It might appear, at first glance, that under these conditions it is impossible to increase the quantity of tickets supplied, as selling a movie ticket is actually a cinema seat rental for a particular showing of a film. However, the quantity supplied can be increased by offering more showings of the film. For example, the number of matinees offered per week can be increased, or late-night showings can be added. (When *Star Wars Episode One: The Phantom Menace* was released in North America in May 1999, many cinemas had showings on a 24-hour basis.) In the long run, if the price makes the venture appear profitable, new cinemas will be built.

2.3 The Determination of Market Price

Market used to refer only to a physical location where buyers and sellers bought and sold goods. Now it can refer to anywhere, including the Internet, where buyers and sellers reach an agreement on a transaction.

The interaction of market demand and market supply determines the market price and quantity. The *equilibrium* price and quantity, where equilibrium denotes a stable state that will be maintained unless there is a change in another (other than own price) determinant of demand or supply, is where demand equals supply. In Figure 2.5, the equilibrium price is P_1 and equilibrium quantity is Q_1. Equilibrium price is the only price for which demand and supply plans are compatible and thus sustainable.

If the current price, such as P_2, is higher than the equilibrium price, there will be an excess supply, as the quantity supplied at this price is Q_2, whereas the quantity demanded is only Q_0. The excess supply is thus $Q_2 - Q_0$. This will create a downward pressure on prices that will continue until P_1 is established.

If the current price, such as P_0, is lower than the equilibrium price, there will be an excess demand, as the quantity demanded at

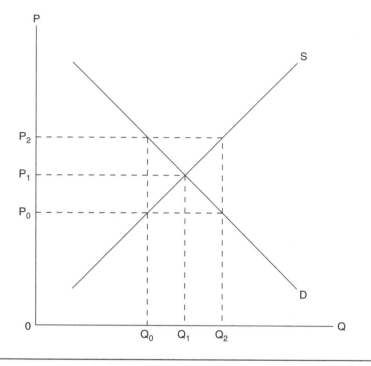

Figure 2.5   Determination of Equilibrium Price
Note: D indicates demand curve; P, price; Q, quantity; S, supply curve.

this price is Q_2, whereas the quantity supplied is only Q_0. The excess demand is thus $Q_2 - Q_0$. This will create an upward pressure on price, which will continue until P_1 is established. Price thus adjusts to effectively ration supply among consumers.

Note that for our example relating to the demand and supply for movie tickets, the equilibrium price would be $10. At a price of $10, the quantity demanded and quantity supplied are equal at 70,000.

2.4 But Aren't Prices Determined by Companies Rather Than by Supply and Demand?

The answer to this question is that it depends on the industry structure. If the industry structure is one in which there are very many firms, each with an insignificant market share, producing identical products, and no barriers to entry by new firms (this industry structure is known as Perfect Competition), then market price is indeed determined by demand and supply and firms are price takers. This is the case for commodities such as gold and wheat. It appears computers are well on the way to becoming commodities.

For most industries, even though companies have some degree of market power and set their own product price, the pressure of competition is sufficient to ensure that the price set by firms reflects the forces of supply and demand. In such cases, supply and demand analysis, as presented in this and the next chapter, provides important insights. Two examples illustrate this. The first relates to our movie seat example. Movie exhibition does not meet the criteria for Perfect Competition. Indeed, it is common to find exhibition dominated by a small number of chains, with some independent competition. Nevertheless, if exhibitors find that their theaters are often almost empty for matinee showings, they can be expected to cut back on the number of such showings and decrease price. This is precisely as predicted by supply and demand analysis. If they find their theaters are regularly overflowing, they will offer more showings, increase ticket prices, and, in the long run, build more cinemas—again, as predicted. Although exhibitors are not price takers, accepting a market price determined by the impersonal forces of supply and demand, their price changes will be consistent with supply and demand analysis.

Our Sprint Canada example provides another illustration. Long distance telephone services are increasingly competitive but do not meet the conditions necessary for Perfect Competition. Sprint Canada initiated the C$20 monthly maximum for off-peak long distance calls within Canada. It was competition that led them to try this form of price reduction. However, the move proved ill advised and had to be changed several months later. Supply and demand analysis, as illustrated by Figure 2.6, explains why. The supply curve, S, requires some explanation. It becomes vertical at Q_3 call-minutes because this is the maximum number that Sprint's capacity permits. Over much of the range in output up to Q_3 call-minutes, however, the incremental cost of additional call minutes is extremely small, so Sprint would be willing to supply at a very low price. The supply curve is, in effect, an extreme version of the one shown in Figure 2.4. When C$0.10 was charged for each minute of call, the quantity demanded, Q_1, would have been less than Q_3. After the C$20 maximum was introduced, the effective price per minute of call in excess of 200 minutes (for each household per month) became zero, as no additional money was charged. The demand curve indicates a demand of Q_2 when the price of additional calls is zero. This was obviously above Q_3 because there were customer complaints of busy signals caused by network congestion. An examination of their billing records indicated to Sprint Canada that the excess demand, $Q_2 - Q_3$, was due to a small number of customers with an apparently insatiable demand for free calls. By imposing a charge of C$0.10 per minute on calls made after 800 minutes had been logged in the month, Sprint Canada was able to reduce demand to Q_3 or below. Interestingly, although Sprint Canada's main competitors, Bell Canada and AT&T Canada, followed Sprint's move to a C$20 maximum for long distance calls within Canada, they did not follow the move to impose a charge of C$0.10 per minute on calls after 800 minutes. Presumably, for them, there was no excess demand, so Q_2 was not greater than Q_3.

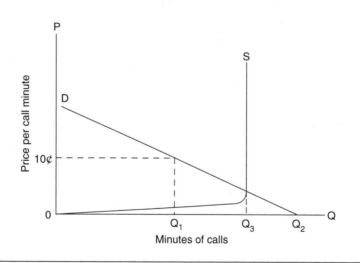

Figure 2.6   Sprint Canada's Pricing

Note: D indicates demand curve; P, price; Q, quantity; S, supply curve.

2.5 Summary

In this chapter, we examined the relationship between the quantity demanded and the quantity supplied of a good as a function of the price of that good. Price elasticity was introduced as a measure of the sensitivity of quantity demanded or quantity supplied to price. We saw that the interaction of demand and supply determined the market price under competitive conditions. Applications were drawn for media goods and services, and the relevance to company and public policy decisions was illustrated.

Individual demand is the number of units of a good a person or household wishes to buy. Market demand is the total amount all people in the market wish to buy of the good and is the sum of the demands by individuals. The wish to buy has to be expressed as a willingness and ability to pay. An opportunity cost exists because purchase of some other goods has to be foregone.

The Law of Demand states that, other things being equal, the higher the price, the smaller the quantity demanded. A change in price causes a Substitution Effect and an Income Effect. The Substitution Effect occurs because an increase in the price of a good makes it more expensive relative to other goods and causes some consumers to substitute other goods for it. An Income Effect occurs because an increase in the price of a good decreases real income and, for most goods, causes consumers to reduce the amount bought as a consequence. Thus the two effects usually work together to cause the quantity demanded to vary in the opposite direction to the change in price.

The relationship between the quantity demanded of a good and the price of the good can be shown through a demand schedule, which is a table giving the quantity demanded at various prices. The graphical representation of this data is the demand curve, which is negatively sloped.

The price elasticity of demand, η, is a measure of the sensitivity of quantity demanded to price and is determined by

$$\eta = \text{Percentage change in quantity demanded } / \text{ Percentage change in price}$$

where the percentages are based on the average of the before and after quantities and prices, respectively.

Ignoring the minus sign, if $\eta > 1$, the demand is price elastic, and consumer expenditure on the good will change in the opposite direction to a change in price. If $\eta < 1$, the demand is inelastic, and consumer expenditure will change in the same direction as price. As expenditure by consumers is revenue for companies, elasticity is important in their pricing decisions. Price elasticity depends on the closeness of substitutes, the proportion of income spent on the good, and (sometimes) the length of time for quantity demanded to adjust.

Supply for an individual firm is the quantity that firm will supply. Market supply is the quantity that all firms making a particular good will supply. In the short run, defined as a length of time insufficient to change capacity, the market supply is the sum of the supply of the existing firms. In the long run, the number of firms supplying the good or service can vary. Allocating resources to supplying a given good has an opportunity cost, as it precludes use of these resources to supply other goods.

In the short run, because capacity is fixed, it will become increasingly costly to increase output, so firms will be willing to supply more only if they can sell for a higher price. In the long run, a higher price may also induce entry of new firms, so the increase in supply may be greater.

A Supply Schedule is a table that shows the quantity supplied at various prices. The graphical representation of this data is the supply curve, which, in the short run at least, is positively sloped. The sensitivity of quantity supplied to changes in price is measured by the Elasticity of Supply, η_s, which is determined by

$$\eta_s = \text{Percentage change in quantity supplied} / \text{Percentage change in price}$$

The equilibrium price and quantity are determined by the interaction of demand and supply and are the price and quantity combination in which quantity demanded equals quantity supplied. This equilibrium is a stable state that will persist in the absence of a change in the value of nonprice determinants of demand or supply.

Even where firms have some market power, the degree of competition is usually strong enough that price and output changes can be explained and predicted using supply and demand analysis.

3

Markets

The demand and supply of goods are affected by variables other than own price. In this chapter, we will examine these other determinants and how changes in their values affect market price. This will provide an understanding of how product markets work and permit us to examine applications to media industries.

After studying this chapter, you should be able to answer the following questions: Why did a decrease in the newsstand price of *The Times* newspaper affect sales of *The Independent*? Why did the decrease in the newsstand price affect the rate *The Times* could charge for advertising? How would we expect a decrease in the price of computers to affect the demand for Internet access? Does the availability of videos and DVDs decrease or increase demand for cinema viewing of movies? How does a price reduction in television advertising rates affect demand for newspaper advertising? Why did the slump in incomes in Asia in 1998 affect Disney's sales of home videos in the region? Why does commercial advertising revenue earned by broadcasters fluctuate considerably depending on general economic conditions? Why is the U.S. market the world's largest for entertainment goods even though the populations of China and India are much greater? Why does possessing the largest domestic market provide the United States with a competitive advantage in film and television? Why did the decline in value of the Canadian and Australian dollars lead to more U.S. "runaway" productions in these countries? Why is there never a good time to buy a computer? Why don't we see many Western movies any more? Why do viewers in most countries prefer domestic television programs? Why are geographically large countries now able to support national newspapers? How is the Internet affecting the supply of information-based media goods and services? Why was owning a commercial television broadcasting license "like having a licence to print your own money" (Braddon, 1965, p. 240)? Why would a change in policy to permit the BBC to carry advertising be expected to decrease the price of television advertising spots in the United Kingdom? Why does the demand for cultural subsidies exceed the supply?

3.1 Change in Demand

If there is a change in the value of one of the other determinants of demand, such as income or the price of a substitute good, this causes a *change in demand*. Economists use this term to avoid confusion with *change in quantity demanded*, which is caused by a change in the price of the product itself. If there is a change in demand, this causes a shift of the entire demand curve. If there is an increase in demand, the demand curve will shift to the right, as more will be bought than before at any given price. If there is a decrease in demand, the demand curve will shift to the left, as less will be bought at any given price.

3.2 Effect of a Change in Demand on Price and Quantity

Before we consider further the various reasons for a change in demand, we will examine the effects on equilibrium price and quantity. Figure 3.1 shows an increase in demand, with the demand curve shifting from D_0 to D_1. Given supply curve S, the increase in demand causes the equilibrium price to increase from P_0 to P_1 and the equilibrium quantity to increase from Q_0 to Q_1.

Figure 3.2 shows the effect of a decrease in demand, a shift of the demand curve from D_2 to D_3. The equilibrium price falls from P_2 to P_3, and the equilibrium quantity decreases from Q_2 to Q_3.

To summarize, a change in demand causes both the equilibrium price and the equilibrium quantity to change in the same direction.

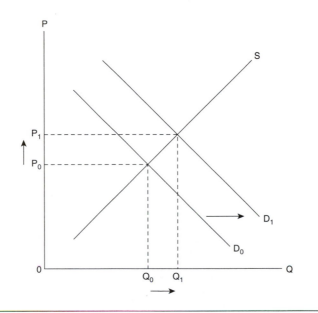

Figure 3.1   An Increase in Demand

Note: D indicates demand curve; P, price; Q, quantity; S, supply curve.

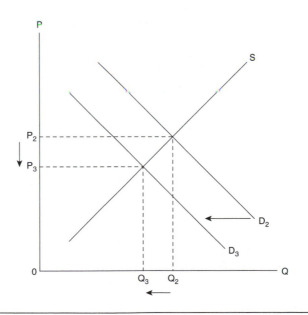

Figure 3.2   A Decrease in Demand

Note: D indicates demand curve; P, price; Q, quantity; S, supply curve.

3.3 Causes of a Change in Demand

A change in demand is caused by a change in value of any determinant of demand other than own price. Typically, these determinants will include *prices of demand-related products, income per capita, number of potential buyers, expected future price* for the product, and *consumer tastes.*

3.3.1 Price of a Demand-Related Product

Demand-related products fall into two groups, substitutes and complements. A *substitute good* is an alternative good that the consumer can purchase to fulfill the same need. A Sony television receiver is a very good substitute for a Panasonic model, as it performs exactly the same function. Stereo systems are a substitute, albeit not a close one, for TV receivers. They satisfy the same broad wants of consumers for entertainment.

There is a positive relationship between the demand for a good and a change in the price of a substitute. The demand for Sony TV receivers will increase if the price of Panasonic television receivers increases, as some people who would have bought Panasonic switch to buying Sony. If the price of Panasonic falls, then demand for Sony will decrease.

As a change in the price of a substitute causes a change in demand, it will result in a change in price and output. An increase in the price of Panasonic television receivers shifts the demand curve for Sony to the right. As we see from Figure 3.1, this will lead to an increase in the equilibrium price and quantity of Sony television receivers. Similarly, the effect of a decrease in the price of Panasonic television receivers is to shift the demand curve for Sony to the left. This is the situation depicted in Figure 3.2, which would result in a decrease in the equilibrium price and quantity of Sony television receivers.

The Times case, introduced in chapter 2, provides an application. A decrease in the circulation price of *The Times* was reported to cause sales of *The Independent*, a rival quality newspaper, to crash from 360,000 to 240,000. The effect is shown in Figure 3.3. At a circulation price for *The Times* of 45 pence (p), the demand curve for *The Independent* was D_0 and the circulation 360,000 at *The Independent*'s price of 50p. The decrease in the price of *The*

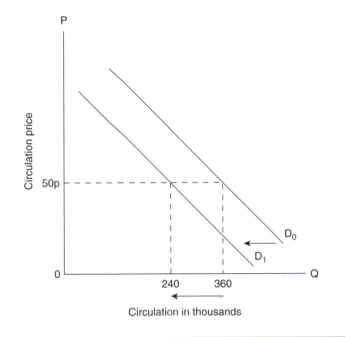

Figure 3.3   Demand for *The Independent*

Note: D indicates demand curve; P, price; Q, quantity.

Times to 30p shifted the demand curve for *The Independent* to the left, to D₁. At an unchanged price for *The Independent*, circulation was now 240,000. There was a decrease in demand for *The Independent*.

Complementary goods are those that are used in conjunction with one another. There is a negative relationship between the demand for a good and a change in price of a complement. Computers and Internet access are complementary goods. There will be an increase in demand for Internet access if the price of computers falls. How does this come about? The decrease in price for computers increases the quantity demanded of computers. With more people owning a computer, the demand for Internet access and bandwidth will increase. Thus a decrease in the price of computers shifts the demand curve for Internet access to the right and, as illustrated in Figure 3.1, this results, other things being equal, in an increase in the equilibrium price and quantity of Internet access.

Similarly, following Figure 3.2, an increase in the price of computers would shift the demand curve for Internet access to the left and decrease the equilibrium price and quantity.

The demand relationship between prerecorded movies on videocassette or DVD and theatrical exhibition of movies is an interesting one. To the extent that people watch the movie on their VCR or DVD player instead of going to the movies, they are substitutes. But there is reason to suppose that they are more complementary than substitutes. The film distributors use the VCR and DVD market as another exhibition window. Good theatrical box office for a movie feeds the aftermarket where people watch the movie at home. The demand relationship between the VCR and DVD player and television programming is also complex. To the extent that people watch a prerecorded, rented (or purchased) movie instead of watching a television program, they are substitutes. But when people use the VCR or DVD player for time shifting, this is complementary because it enables them to view programs they would otherwise miss because they are out or watching another program.

The strength of demand relationship between goods is measured by the *cross elasticity of demand,* designated by η_{xz} where

$$\eta_{xz} = \text{Percentage change in quantity demanded of good X} \, / \\ \text{Percentage change in the price of good Z}$$

η_{xz}, the cross elasticity of demand for X with respect to Z, will be positive if X and Z are substitutes and negative if they are complements. Thus for cross elasticity, unlike price elasticity, it is vital to indicate the sign.

As we have seen, a reduction in the price of *The Times* from 45p to 30p was said to be responsible for the decrease in demand for *The Independent* from 360,000 copies to 240,000 copies. Assuming this is correct, we can calculate the cross elasticity of circulation demand for *The Independent* with respect to *The Times*. The reduction in circulation of *The Independent* was 40% of the average quantity. The reduction in price of *The Times* was 40% of the average price. Hence the cross elasticity is 1.00. The products are good substitutes.

Cave and Swann, in a study commissioned by the Peacock Committee (1986) in the United Kingdom, provide another example. They estimated the cross elasticity of demand for press advertising with respect to television advertising to be 0.25. That is, a price reduction of 1% in television advertising would lead to a reduction in demand for newspaper advertising of 0.25%. As the cross elasticity is positive, the products are substitutes, although the relatively low number indicates that they are not very close substitutes. The Peacock Committee was interested in the cross elasticity because the members wanted to know the possible impact on newspapers of permitting the BBC to sell advertising.

3.3.2 Income Per Capita

An increase in income allows people to increase their aggregate expenditures on goods and services, whereas a decrease in income means they have to cut back. Hence, as one would expect, demand for most products is positively related to income per capita (per person) or income per household. Goods whose demand is positively related to income are known as *normal goods*. For example, in 1998, Disney's lower home video sales in Asia were attributed to the slump in incomes there (McClennan, 1998). Thus, as one would expect, home video is a normal good.

For normal goods, an increase in income causes more of a good to be bought at any given price. Hence the demand curve shifts to the right. As we saw in Figure 3.1, the consequence of such an increase in demand will be an increase in equilibrium price and quantity. Similarly, a decrease in income will shift the demand curve to the left and lead to a decrease in equilibrium price and quantity.

For a few goods, called *inferior goods,* demand is negatively related to income. For such goods, a rise in income and the increase in consumption expenditures this permits persuade some people to switch to purchasing a preferable alternative they previously could not afford. For example, in the early 1970s, an increase in income would probably have caused some poor families considering replacement of their old black and white television receiver to switch to the preferred color receiver, causing a decrease in consumption of black and white TV receivers.

The strength of the relationship between quantity demanded of a good and income per capita is measured by the *income elasticity of demand, η_y,* where

$$\eta_y = \text{Percentage change in demand} /$$
$$\text{Percentage change in income per capita}$$

η_y will be positive for normal goods and negative for inferior goods. Luxury goods will have a high positive income elasticity.

Most of the studies commissioned by the Peacock Committee (1986) estimate the income elasticity of demand for television advertising to be around 2.0. This is fairly high. One implication is that advertising revenues earned by broadcasters will be volatile and vary considerably with the state of the economy. Thus a disadvantage of expecting a public broadcasting oraganization to rely heavily on advertising is that this source of funds is unstable.

In the U.S. studies summarized by Wenders (1987, p. 58), the mean income elasticity of demand for long-distance telephone service was 0.39 in the short run and 1.33 in the long run.

Number of Potential Buyers

For consumer products, the population served by a market is a good indicator of the number of potential buyers. The greater the population in a market, other things being equal, the greater the demand. It should be no surprise that the United States, the developed country with the largest population, has the largest domestic market for theatrical movies, television programs, television receivers, video hardware and software, and many other media industry-related products (Hoskins, McFadyen, & Finn, 1997, p. 39). As we shall see later, U.S. market size provides a crucial competitive advantage in production of entertainment and cultural goods.

But why is it that India and China, both with much larger populations, do not comprise an even greater market for media products? The secret is differences in income levels. Recall that demand depends on income per capita as well as population. The population of both China and India may dwarf that of the United States, but the positive effect of their population size on demand is more than offset by the negative effect of their much lower per capita income.

For producer goods (goods sold to other companies), the number of potential purchasing firms, as well as population, is relevant. For example, television programs are sold to television services, such as broadcasters and cable specialty channels. In Canada, the large increase in the number of television services, mostly cable or

DBS-delivered specialty channels, is credited with stimulating demand for documentaries.

3.3.3 Expectations Regarding Future Price

If a purchase decision can be postponed (as it can be for consumer durables), demand in the current period is affected by expectations regarding future price levels. A change in expectation to reflect a lower future price (and often better reliability or features) will cause some people to delay purchase and thus decrease demand in the current period. This is certainly relevant to demand for innovative electronic hardware. When VCRs, aimed at households rather than industry professionals, were introduced by Sony and Japan Victor (JVC) in the mid-1970s, prices were well in excess of $2000, but now VCRs can be bought for as little as $50. How many people are delaying the purchase of an HDTV television now in the expectation that the price will fall by 50% or more in the next 18 months? As the saying goes, "there is never a good time to buy a computer." Early adopters, though, will value the benefits from ownership, perhaps the pride at owning the latest consumer electronic device, highly enough that they are not prepared to postpone their purchase.

3.3.4 Tastes

Consumer tastes change over time. The small number of Westerns and World War II movies now compared to the number in the 1950s can be largely attributed to changing tastes.

Tastes vary between people in different countries and regions. For example, it is well documented that viewers generally prefer domestic television programs to foreign programs, and hence demand is greater for the domestic product (Tracy & Redal, 1995). A particular television program (or other media good) rooted in one culture, and thus attractive in the home market where viewers share a common knowledge and way of life, will have a diminished appeal elsewhere, as viewers may find it difficult to identify with the style, values, beliefs, history, myths, institutions, physical environment, and behavioral patterns. If the program is produced in another language, its appeal will be further reduced by the need to employ dubbing or subtitling. Even if the language is the same, accents or idioms may still cause problems. The reduction in appeal of the foreign program relative to a domestic equivalent has been labeled the *cultural discount.*

In each country, the cultural discount provides a barrier to the entry of competing programs from foreign producers. This translates into a competitive advantage for domestic producers. Given that the United States is the country with the largest domestic market in the world, the cultural discount provides U.S.-based producers with favored access to the world's wealthiest market. This constitutes a global competitive advantage for the U.S. film and television program production industry. This is considered further in chapter 14.

3.4 Change in Supply

A change in the value of one of the determinants of supply other than own price causes a *change in supply.* Economists use this term to avoid confusion with *change in quantity supplied,* which is caused by a change in the price of the product itself. If there is a change in supply, this causes a shift of the entire supply curve. If there is an increase in supply, the supply curve will shift to the right, as more will be supplied than before at any given price. If there is a decrease in supply, the supply curve will shift to the left, indicating that less will be supplied at any given price.

3.5 Effect of Change in Supply on Price and Quantity

A change in supply causes the equilibrium price to change in the opposite direction to the change in supply. In contrast, the equilibrium quantity changes in the same direction as the change in supply. Figure 3.4 illustrates an increase in supply from S_0 to S_1, resulting in a decrease in equilibrium price from P_0 to P_1 and an increase in equilibrium quantity from Q_0 to Q_1. Figure 3.5 shows a decrease in supply from S_2 to S_3, causing the equilibrium price to increase from P_2 to P_3 and the equilibrium quantity to decrease from Q_2 to Q_3.

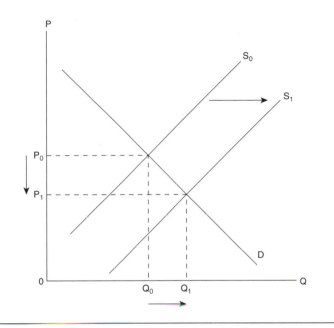

Figure 3.4   An Increase in Supply

Note: D indicates demand curve; P, price; Q, quantity; S, supply curve.

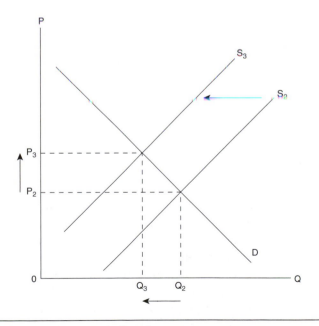

Figure 3.5   A Decrease in Supply

Note: D indicates demand curve; P, price; Q, quantity; S, supply curve.

3.6 Causes of a Change in Supply

A change in supply is caused by a change in the value of any determinant other than own price. Key determinants are the *prices of inputs*, the *state of technology*, and the *number of suppliers*.

3.6.1 Prices of Inputs

Input prices directly affect the cost of producing the industry output. A decrease in input price makes it less expensive to produce output, and firms will be willing to supply more at any given product price. Hence a decrease in input price will increase supply and shift the supply curve to the right, as in Figure 3.4. Similarly, an increase in input price will decrease supply and shift the supply curve to the left, as in Figure 3.5. As an example, the decrease in the value of the Canadian dollar and the Australian dollar (relative to the U.S. dollar) over a number of years prior to 2003 meant a decrease in input prices (in U.S. dollars) for Hollywood studios producing films and television programs in these countries. This led to an increase in supply, with more and more Hollywood "runaway" productions being shot in Canada and Australia. According to the California Entertainment Industry Development Corporation, Toronto and Vancouver are now the third and fourth largest centers in North America for U.S. film (includes television) productions, with $1 billion split almost equally between them. These cities trail only Hollywood, with $20 billion, and New York, with $2.2 billion ("California to lure," 1997, p. A14).

3.6.2 Technology

A change in technology that results in a better way of producing a product will lower costs of production by either allowing a given level of output to be produced using fewer inputs than before or by permitting substitution of a less expensive factor for a more expensive factor in the production process. Such a change in technology will increase supply, resulting in a shift of the supply curve to the right, as shown in Figure 3.4.

For example, distribution of newspapers used to involve printing copies at a central plant and then physically shipping the copies to market. The cost of shipping and time taken (there is not much of a market for day-old newspapers) was such that it was uneconomic to distribute a newspaper beyond a radius of 200 miles or so from the plant. Only geographically small countries, such as the United Kingdom, had national dailies. New technology, whereby the content is delivered by satellite to distant printing presses, changed this. Dow Jones and Company, which began distance printing of the *Wall Street Journal* in Orlando, Florida, in 1975, pioneered the technology.

The new technology meant that publishers were willing to offer many more copies at the existing price (P_0 in Figure 3.4). But to entice consumers to purchase more copies, they had to eliminate some of the "distant market" price premiums previously charged. With competition, subscription prices tended to fall from P_0 to P_1, and circulation of these now national newspapers increased from Q_0 to Q_1.

The Internet is a new information technology that offers many opportunities to increase the supply of information-based entertainment or cultural products. The innovations introduced by Amazon.com have revolutionized book retailing, bringing consumers more books at lower prices. Similar changes in the distribution of music are fast occurring with Apple's iTunes Music Store, and television programs and feature films may not be far behind, with lower costs and increased supply translating into more product in the hands of consumers at lower prices.

3.6.3 Number of Suppliers

In the long run, capacity is not fixed. Firms can enter or exit the industry. The entry of new firms will shift the short-run supply curve to the right, as, with the increased number of firms, more will be supplied than before at any given product price. Similarly, the exit of firms will shift the supply curve to the left. Entry or exit of firms usually depends on the level of profit obtainable in this industry compared to the best alternative opportunity. The profit available from the best alternative opportunity is called a *normal profit* or *zero economic profit*. A zero economic profit is just sufficient to induce existing firms to remain in the industry. If existing firms are earning positive economic profits, then opportunities are better than elsewhere and new firms will be attracted into the industry. If existing firms are earning negative economic profits, then opportunities are not as good as elsewhere and some firms will exit the industry.

Although there has been a trend toward partial deregulation, broadcasting is a regulated industry in most countries. Commercial broadcasting has been highly profitable. Lord Thomson, after being awarded the Scottish Television commercial broadcasting license, said: "It's just like having a licence to print your own money!" (Braddon, 1965, p. 240). Why is a commercial operation so profitable in a regulated environment? Don't we usually think of regulation controlling and restricting profits? We examine this question in Figure 3.6, which shows the market for advertising spots, as this is the product commercial off-air broadcasters sell. Assume that initially the supply curve is S_0, the demand curve is D, the equilibrium price is P_0, and the output is Q_0. Suppose that, at this price, broadcasters earn positive economic profits. What would normally occur under these circumstances is that these economic profits would attract new entrants. As new broadcasters entered the market, the supply curve would shift to the right and price would fall. This process would not stop until supply curve S_1 was established, where, at the new lower equilibrium price (P_1), firms would only be able to earn zero economic profits. If this had occurred, the commercial television broadcasting industry would not have been "like having a licence to print your own money."

Regulation of television broadcasting, whether in Britain, Canada, or Australia, has prevented or restricted the market entry of new television broadcasters and preserved the positive economic profits of established broadcasters. There are a number of reasons why entry of new television broadcasters, or at least sufficient entry, did not occur. So long as television signals were broadcast using the earth's electromagnetic spectrum, the limited availability of spectrum frequencies provided a rationale for restricting the number of television broadcasters. But when cable, satellite, and other delivery methods became available, these restrictions on entry continued. For example, for years the Canadian Radio-television and Telecommunications Commission (CRTC) strictly limited the number of signals cable could deliver and then delayed the introduction of direct-to-home (DTH) satellite delivery. In Australia, cable introduction was delayed until 1995, DTH satellite was licensed with limited programming, and further entry is blocked until 2005 to give existing broadcasters time to gear up for the transition to digital. In both countries, cultural rationales have often been advanced to justify protection of the economic position of existing broadcasters. As a quid pro quo, it is hoped that broadcasters will spend much of their enhanced profits on domestic programming. Perhaps an unstated expectation is that the favor will be repaid through positive news and public affairs coverage come election time. We will return to regulation in chapter 13.

In chapter 2, we promised we would explain later the basis for the Peacock Committee's prediction that permitting the BBC to carry advertising would lead to a decrease in price for advertising spots. With reference to Figure 3.6, we can now do so. In this case, the supply curve (S_0) can represent the supply, with the BBC not permitted to sell advertising spots, and the equilibrium price and output is P_0 and Q_0, respectively. If the BBC were permitted to sell advertising, it would enter this market and shift the supply curve to S_1. This would result in the market price for an advertising spot price falling to P_1.

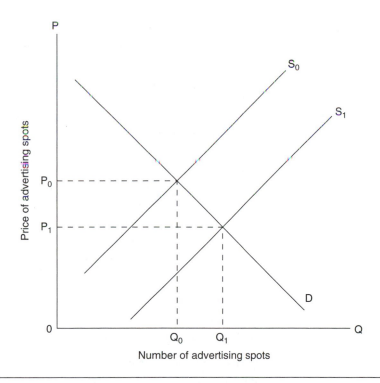

Figure 3.6   The Market for Television Advertising

Note: D indicates demand curve; P, price; Q, quantity; S, supply curve.

3.7 Further Applications

There are many additional media applications of supply and demand analysis and elasticity. Those examined here are the Principle of Relative Constancy, auctioning of the electromagnetic spectrum, and the allocation of subsidies. Other illustrations appear throughout the text. For example, in chapter 14, we use supply and demand analysis to examine the effects of domestic content regulations for television programming.

3.7.1 Principle of Relative Constancy

The Principle of Relative Constancy, put forward by McCombs (1972), states that the spending on mass media comprises a relatively constant proportion of national income. This principle has received considerable attention in the media economics field. It implies an income elasticity of demand of 1.00 because, for it to hold, any change in income must be matched by an equal change in demand. It also implies that new media growth is at the expense of old media. There is no theoretical reason why this should be the case, so the justification for the principle has to be empirical. From the 1930s to the early 1970s, there did appear to be considerable supporting evidence. The growth of spending on audio and visual media almost exactly offset the decline in spending on print media. Within the visual media, the growth of spending on television almost exactly offset the decline in spending on movies. But, as Lacy and Noh (1997) report, the share of consumer spending on the mass media increased from 2.15% of disposable personal income in 1975 to 3.69% in 1987. This increase has been attributed to the diffusion of VCR and cable TV during this period. Growing expenditure on these new media did not result in a corresponding decrease in spending on preexisting media. As we argued in section 3.3.1, there is reason to believe the demand relationship between the VCR and movies is more one of complements than substitutes.

3.7.2 Auctioning of Electromagnetic Spectrum

Communication signals transmitted through the atmosphere must be sent on different frequencies to avoid interference—such as is experienced when the signal of a distant radio station breaks up because of interference from a more powerful station. But there are only a limited number of such frequencies that are physically available in nature. Because there are many competing potential users for each spectrum frequency, they are a scarce economic resource. But the allocation of scarce resources among competing uses is what the market system of supply and demand does best. The United Kingdom and United States have recognized this by instituting an auction process for spectrum frequencies.

In the United Kingdom, a system of competitive tendering has been used to allocate new commercial television licenses for Channel 3 and Channel 5. A pure tender system would award the license to the highest bidder, that company willing to offer the highest price for the license. However, in the U.K.'s case, this was amended to the highest *qualified* bidder, and the Independent Television Commission (the regulatory authority) was delegated considerable discretion in determining whether a bid met a threshold defined in terms of programming plans, consumer protection, and financial viability (Cave & Williamson, 1991).

In the United States, auctions begun in 1994 of a relatively small portion of the spectrum yielded approximately $23 billion in 4 years, and the U.S. government received just over half of this (Robinson, 1998). Spectrum frequencies have been allocated in this way for personal communication services, direct-broadcast satellite (DBS), local multipoint distribution, and other services.

Canada (like many other countries) has been slow to use price to allocate scarce spectrum frequencies to potential broadcasters. The result has been an excess in demand, with a corresponding need for some other mechanism to decide which competing buyer wins a license. The norm has been for the CRTC (the regulatory agency) to make a choice based on its evaluation of the program commitments and financial plans submitted by the applicants. This has been likened to a beauty contest and has not been particularly successful, as program commitments are not really commitments but promises, and these promises have often not been kept. Besides this, the government has foregone an opportunity to earn considerable revenue. The government of Canada seems to have belatedly seen the light: It conducted its first spectrum auction, for wireless services, in October 1999.

3.7.3 Allocating Subsidies

Many countries, such as Canada, Australia, and France, subsidize the production of movies and TV programs. It should be no surprise that the demand for subsidies exceeds the supply. There is no price paid by the recipient of a subsidy other than the resources used in the process of applying for the subsidy. Some method of allocating funds between competing eligible projects is thus necessary. The $200 million Canada Television Cable Production Fund exhibits two alternative approaches. The Equity Investment Program component of the fund is allocated by Telefilm Canada using cultural and commercial criteria. The Licence Fee Program component, administered by a board composed predominantly of industry participants, is allocated on a first come, first served basis. (This method of allocating scarce goods was, of course, the favorite of communist regimes.) In April 1998, the strange sight of producers lining up for grants might have been seen. There was consternation when it was realized that many of the television programs widely perceived as most deserving had failed to receive any of the money.

3.8 Summary

This chapter examined changes in demand and supply and how product markets work.

A change in demand occurs when there is a change in the value of a determinant of demand other than own price. An increase in demand shifts the demand curve to the right and causes price and quantity to rise. A decrease in demand shifts the demand curve to the left and causes price and quantity to fall. Thus the change in price and quantity are in the same direction as the change in demand.

Changes in demand are caused by a change in a determinant of demand, such as the price of a demand-related good, income per capita, the number of potential buyers, the expected future price, and consumer tastes.

Demand-related goods are either substitutes or complements. A substitute is a good that fulfils the same need. The cross elasticity of demand, defined as (percentage change in demand for product X) / (percentage change in the price of Z), is positive if X and Z are substitutes. Complementary goods are those that are used in conjunction with one another. The cross elasticity of demand for complementary goods is negative.

Demand is positively related to income per capita for normal goods and negatively related for inferior goods. Income elasticity of demand, defined as (percentage change in demand) / (percentage change in income) is thus positive for normal goods and negative for inferior goods.

A change in supply occurs when there is a change in a determinant of supply other than own price. Whatever direction supply changes, the equilibrium quantity changes in the same direction and the equilibrium price changes in the opposite direction.

A change in supply is typically caused by a change in an input price, technology, or the number of suppliers.

There are a host of applications of supply and demand analysis and of the elasticity concept in the media industries. Those examined in this chapter included the effect of permitting the BBC to advertise, the Principle of Relative Constancy, the recent trend to auction the electromagnetic spectrum, and the market for subsidies.

4

Consumer Behavior

In chapter 2 and chapter 3, we examined market demand. In this chapter, we turn to analyzing demand by the individual consumer. (Consumption decisions are often made at the household rather than at the individual level. For convenience, we will continue to refer to "the consumer," but you may substitute "the household" if you wish.) Consumers have limited budgets and income, but they are presented with many goods and services that they would like to buy. They must thus choose which of the desirable goods and services to purchase. In this chapter, we will look at how the Theory of Consumer Behavior explains consumer choices in the telecommunication, movie, television, music, computer, Internet, and publishing industries.

Studying this chapter will enable you to answer the following questions: Why are more movie videos and DVDs rented than bought? Why are a higher proportion of children's than adults' movies purchased? If consumption of cultural or entertainment goods is habit forming, what are the implications for U.S. dominance of the movie industry? What are the implications for the effectiveness of film subsidy programs in countries such as Australia and Canada? What are the ramifications of a zero price per minute for local telephone calls (usual in Canada and the United States) versus a positive price per minute (the norm in Europe)? What is the relationship between the price of access and demand for usage of telephone services and vice versa? Why is the benefit of subscribing to a network, such as the telephone network or Internet (e-mail) network, greater the larger the number of other subscribers? What are the attributes of a VCR, and how did a difference in attributes between JVC's VHS format and Sony's Betamax format contribute to JVC winning the standards war? What is the distinction between search, experience, and credence goods, and what are the implications for business strategies associated with developing and selling various communications goods? What is the appropriate framework for a public broadcasting organization to use when deciding how to allocate a limited budget?

4.1 The Law of Diminishing Marginal Utility

Before studying the consumer's decision on what goods to buy with a limited budget, we must examine the *Law of Diminishing Marginal Utility*. Note that *utility* is a term used by economists to denote "satisfaction." The Law of Diminishing Marginal Utility is an empirical law that states:

> After a certain number of units of product X have been consumed in a time period, each additional unit of product X consumed yields less addition to total utility than the previous unit.

We note that the definition implies that utility can be measured. Nobody these days believes that the satisfaction a consumer gains from consumption of a unit of a good can be objectively measured, still less that the level of utility from consumption can be compared between consumers. It is convenient, though, to imagine a measure of satisfaction, known as "utils," similar to a measure of temperature. Just as the scale on the thermometer is arbitrary (there are two common scales, Fahrenheit and Celsius), so is the scale for measuring utility.

To illustrate the Law of Diminishing Marginal Utility, consider the utility Bob would get from the cinematic viewing of the movie *Terminator 3* over a 1-month period. Suppose that he quite enjoys the first viewing and, on our arbitrary scale of satisfaction, gains a utility of 20 utils. The second viewing provides Bob with an additional utility of only 5 utils, as he already knows the plot

Table 4.1   Bob's Utility From Viewing *Terminator 3* in 1 Month

Number of Viewings	Total Utility	Marginal Utility
1	20	20
2	25	5
3	26	1

and does not gain much satisfaction from seeing it again. A third viewing, within the month, yields additional utility of only 1 util. Bob's total utility and marginal utility are shown in Table 4.1, where total utility is the cumulative utility from consuming the units of the good during the month, and the marginal utility is the addition to total utility gained from consuming a given unit. Thus the total utility Bob gains from viewing *Terminator 3* once is 20 utils, twice is 25 utils, and three times is 26 utils. His marginal utility is 20 utils for the first viewing, 5 utils for the second viewing, and 1 util for the third viewing. The marginal is thus the change in total utility for each additional unit consumed.

Bob's viewing (consumption) of *Terminator 3* obeys the Law of Diminishing Marginal Utility, as the marginal utility decreases after consumption of the first unit. For the law to apply, however, it is not necessary that diminishing marginal utility set in after consumption of the first unit in a given time period, although this will often be the case. For example, Mary might gain more addition to total utility from the second viewing of *Bend It Like Beckham* after she has had time to reflect on the differences in the values and outlook of characters of different ethnic backgrounds and generations. However, her third viewing would provide less addition to total utility than the second; the law would set in after the second viewing.

It is because marginal utility usually declines rapidly for movie viewing that more videos of movies are rented rather than purchased. However, the proportion of videos purchased rather than rented is relatively higher for most movies (often animated) targeted at children. It appears that children do not tire of watching the same movie again and again. In other words, diminishing marginal utility sets in after more viewings and then is more gradual.

4.2 Consumer Equilibrium

The goal of the consumer is assumed to be to maximize his or her utility (or satisfaction) from consumption subject to the constraint arising from a limited income or budget. A consumer is in equilibrium when his or her limited budget is allocated to purchases of goods and services in such a way that utility is maximized.

Equilibrium is achieved when, subject to the budget constraint, expenditure is allocated among goods in such a way that the last dollar spent on each good purchased yields the same addition to total utility. People sometimes object that consumers do not think in this way. This may be correct, but we are not concerned with a consumer's thought processes. For consumers who wish to purchase the combination of goods that gives them maximum satisfaction, if they choose between goods and services in a manner that is consistent with this objective, then it is *as if* they are allocating expenditure such that the last dollar spent on each good purchased yields the same addition to total utility.

To state the Theory of Consumer Behavior more formally, the conditions for equilibrium are as follows:

$$MU_x / P_x = MU_z / P_z = \ldots$$

$$\text{Subject to } P_x \times Q_x + P_z \times Q_z + \ldots = Y$$

where MU_x is the marginal utility of the last unit of good X purchased, MU_z is the marginal utility of the last unit of good Z bought, P_x is the price of good X, P_z is the price of good Z, Q_x is the number of units of good X bought, Q_z is the number of units of good Z bought, and Y is the budget available.

MU_x / P_x can be interpreted as the addition to total utility from the last dollar spent on good X. For example, if Bob pays $10 for each ticket to *Terminator 3* and decides to see it twice, resulting in a marginal utility for the second showing of 5 utils (see Table 4.1), the last dollar spent on the movie adds 5/10 (0.5) utils per dollar to total utility. For the decision to view *Terminator 3* twice to be compatible with utility maximization, the last dollar spent on Z and all other goods (this is inferred by the "= . . ." at the end of the first equation) must also equal 0.5. Even this is subject to the budget constraint that Bob's expenditure of $20 (= $P_x \times Q_x$) on *Terminator 3*, plus his expenditure on good Z and all other goods, cannot exceed his budget. If Bob is allocating his limited budget in this optimal way (that is, the way that maximizes his total utility), we have an equilibrium situation because, in the absence of a change in his preferences, income, or product prices, he will wish to leave his pattern of consumption unchanged.

To further illustrate consumer equilibrium, consider the example in Table 4.2. Paula has a budget of $10 per week to spend on long distance telephone calls and/or renting videos (to simplify the example, we restrict ourselves to two products). Ten minutes of long distance telephone calls cost her $1 (she is actually charged $0.10 for a minute, but for convenience we will deal with 10-minute blocks), and videos can be rented for $2. At these prices, she can buy as many as ten 10-minute telephone calls or rent as many as five videos. Her preferences, or tastes, determine the utility she gets from each unit of consumption during the month. As can be seen from column 2 and column 4 (the column numbers are given in the first row), there is diminishing marginal utility for both long distance telephone calls and video rental, which in this case sets in after the first unit of each. The addition to total utility of the last dollar spent on each product at these prices is shown in column 3 for telephone calls and column 5 for videos. Paula would maximize utility by purchasing four 10-minute telephone calls and renting three videos in the week. With this combination of purchases, the last dollar spent on each good or service adds 15 utils to total utility, and total expenditure is $10 ($4 on telephone calls and $6 on video rentals). This is an equilibrium situation because Paula has no motivation to change this allocation. In fact, any reallocation (buying more of one product and less of another) would reduce the total utility from consumption. This combination of purchases provides a total utility of 248 utils, found by adding the marginal utility for each of the four 10-minute blocks of telephone calls and each of the three video rentals. This is higher than the utility of any other combination that could be bought for $10; for example, five video rentals would yield a total utility of 157, whereas eight 10-minute telephone calls and one video rental would yield a total utility of 198 utils.

Several typical assumptions were made in this example. We assumed that Paula's goal is utility maximization and that she is rational in pursuit of her goal. As we have seen, this does not imply that Paula consciously follows the decision process outlined earlier, but it does imply that she weighs up the merits of spending an additional $2 on another video rental or on 20 additional minutes of telephone call. Paula's preferences are given and do not change

Table 4.2   Allocation of $10 per Week Between Videos and Long Distance Telephone Calls

1	2	3	4	5	6
Quantity	Marginal Utility of 10-Minute Call	Addition to Total Utility From Last Dollar Spent on 10-Minute Call @ $1/10-Minutes	Marginal Utility of Renting a Video	Addition to Total Utility From Last Dollar Spent Renting a Video at a Price of $2	Addition to Total Utility From Last Dollar Spent Renting a Video at a Price of $3
1	40	40	66	33.0	22.00
2	30	30	45	22.5	15.00
3	22	22	30	15.0	10.00
4	15	15	10	5.0	3.33
5	10	10	6	3.0	2.00
6	7	7			
7	5	5			
8	3	3			
9	2	2			
10	1	1			

during the month. The utility she gets from consuming telephone calls is independent of her consumption level of videos and vice versa. It is usual as well to assume that the goods are infinitely divisible. If this is not the case, the equality of the addition to total utility from the last dollar spent on each good may have to be approximated. In our example, this was not a problem, but it could have been, because videos are not divisible. It is not possible to rent half or a quarter of a video. On the other hand, telephone calls are infinitely divisible. They are sold on a per-minute or even, with some long distance providers, a per-second basis.

4.3 The Effect of a Change in Price

How does a change in price of one of the goods change the consumer equilibrium? We examine this question by considering the effect of an increase in the price of video rentals to $3 on Paula's optimal pattern of purchases. The additional utility from the last dollar spent on videos at the new price of $3 is given in column 6 of Table 4.2. The increase in price has caused Paula's real income to fall, and she cannot now afford to buy the previous optimal combination of four 10-minute calls and three video rentals. Even if she could, this combination would not be optimal because at these consumption levels, the additional utility from the last dollar spent renting videos would be only 10 utils, compared to 15 utils for telephone calls. She maximizes utility after the price increase for video rental by renting fewer videos. Given the Law of Diminishing Marginal Utility, decreasing consumption increases the additional utility from the last dollar spent on videos. In this example, the additional utility from the last dollar spent on both products is equal at 15 utils when the rental of videos is reduced to two units, and consumption of telephone calls remains unchanged.

4.4 Individual Demand and Consumer Surplus

From this example, it is apparent that there is a negative relationship between an individual's demand for a good and the price of that good. Thus the negative slope of the demand curve for a consumer and, consequently, the negative slope of the market demand curve, results from the Law of Diminishing Utility.

Table 4.3   Jack's Demand Schedule for Blank Videotapes per Month

Price (in dollars)	0	1	2	3	4	5	6	7	8	9	10	11
Quantity		11	10	9	8	7	6	5	4	3	2	1	0

To illustrate further, let us suppose that Jack's demand schedule for blank videocassette tapes in a month is given in Table 4.3 and the associated demand curve, d, is shown in Figure 4.1.

Suppose that the current price is $2, and hence Jack buys nine blank tapes per month. Jack is willing to buy nine tapes because the marginal utility of the ninth tape divided by its price of $2 is equal to the MU/P ratio for the other goods he buys. At this price, he will not buy another tape because the tenth tape will have a lower marginal utility, and the MU/P would thus be less than that for

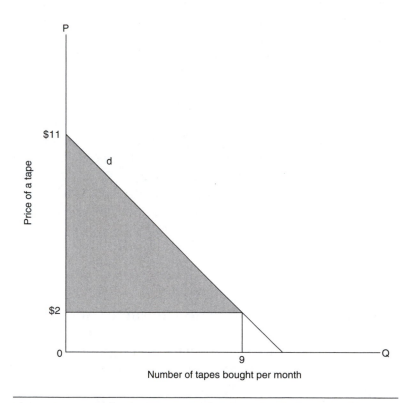

Figure 4.1   Jack's Consumer Surplus From Blank Tapes per Month
Note: d indicates the demand curve; P, price; Q, quantity.

other goods. However, if the price of the tape were reduced to $1, he would buy the tenth tape because the MU he receives from spending the dollar on the tape would now equal that from spending the last dollar on any other good purchased.

If the price is $2, and Jack buys nine tapes, he is actually paying less than he would be willing to for these nine tapes. The Law of Diminishing Marginal Utility and the resulting negatively sloped demand curve mean that for all the tapes except the ninth, Jack would have been willing to pay a higher price. This introduces us to an important economic concept known as *consumer surplus*. Consumer surplus is defined as the maximum amount the consumer would be willing to pay for the Q* units of a good he or she buys less the amount he or she actually pays for the Q* units. If Jack buys nine blank tapes at $2 each, the actual amount he pays is $18. However, Table 4.3 indicates he was willing to pay as much as $10 for the first tape, $9 for the second, $8 for the third, $7 for the fourth, $6 for the fifth, $5 for the sixth, $4 for the seventh, $3 for the eighth, and $2 for the ninth. Adding these amounts, we find the maximum he would have been willing to pay for nine tapes is $54. The consumer surplus Jack enjoys is thus $54 − $18 = $36. In Figure 4.1, this consumer surplus is approximated by the shaded triangular area below the demand curve and above the price line, as the demand curve shows the maximum price Jack would be willing to pay for each unit and the price shows what he actually pays.

Consumer surplus is an important concept, and one that we will return to. Companies view consumer surplus as "money left on the table," and in chapter 10, we will examine various pricing strategies employed by media companies to appropriate that surplus.

4.5 Demand for Access and Demand for Usage

For some goods or services, a distinction can be made between demand for access and demand for usage with access given. For example, access to making or receiving telephone calls requires rental of a line and rental (or purchase) of a telephone. Similarly, access to e-mail messaging requires an account with an Internet service provider.

An individual subscribes to a telephone service because of the utility obtained from making and receiving telephone calls. A demand curve for making calls can be drawn with the quantity (minutes) of telephone calls plotted against the price per minute. For illustrative purposes, we show Alice's demand curve for making calls in Figure 4.2. Alice has access and pays $0.10 per minute of call. At this price, she makes 200 minutes of calls in a month, which involves an expenditure of $20. However, she enjoys a consumer surplus, approximated by the area above the price and below her demand curve. If her demand curve is linear, as drawn, this can be calculated as $190. (Note that the area of the triangle representing consumer surplus is equal to half the area of a rectangle with adjacent sides of 200 and $1.90 where $1.90 = $2.00 − $0.10).

But Alice also obtains utility from most of the calls she receives (some calls from telemarketers may have zero utility). Figure 4.3 shows her demand curve for receiving calls. She receives 100 minutes of calls per month, but the telephone company does not charge her for these calls. Given a price per minute of zero, her consumer surplus is approximated by the entire area under her demand curve and amounts to $50.

Thus Alice is receiving a combined consumer surplus from making and receiving calls of approximately $240. As long as the

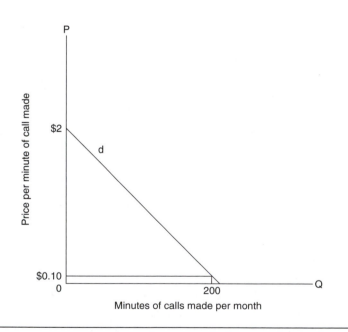

Figure 4.2   Alice's Demand for Making Home Telephone Calls per Month

Note: d indicates the demand curve; P, price; Q, quantity.

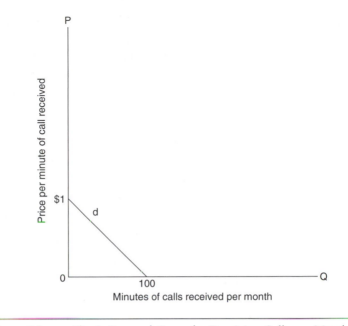

Figure 4.3   Alice's Demand Curve for Receiving Calls per Month

Note: d indicates the demand curve; P, price; Q, quantity.

price of access is less than this, Alice will choose to have access. With typical access prices around $20 per month, no increase in access price within a reasonable range will cause her to cancel access. This will not be true for some low volume users, however.

Suppose Carl is not a sociable person (he does not enjoy telephone conversations) and only gets a consumer surplus from home usage of telephone services of $22 per month, but the access price is $20 per month. An increase in the price of access to $23 will persuade him to cancel. If he does have to interact with others, he does have substitutes: He can telephone from the nearest pay phone, he may have a telephone at work he can use for personal calls, he may have e-mail at work, and he can use the post; locally, he could travel for a face-to-face meeting. As the increase in access price causes Carl and others like him to cancel their telephone service, the market demand curve for residential calls shifts to the left, with fewer calls made at any per-minute price. Carl and others who cancel make no calls, and continuing subscribers make fewer calls because they are no longer able to telephone Carl and others who no longer subscribe.

Studies estimating the price elasticity of demand for access to telephone services confirm a negative relationship between demand for access and access price, although the elasticity is very low. For example, Albon et al. (1997, p. 34) report that Cain and MacDonald estimated an elasticity of 0.096 for an increase in monthly access price from $15 to $17.50 at an initial penetration rate (percentage of households subscribing) of 95% of U.S. households.

Just as the location of the market demand curve for residential calls depends on the access price, the location of the market demand curve for access, relating the quantity of lines and telephones rented per month to the rental rate, depends on the per-minute price charged for calls. It would probably require only a small increase in price per minute of calls to reduce the consumer surplus of Carl, and others like him, below the monthly access price of $20. Thus an increase in price per minute of call will shift the market demand curve for access to the left.

This interdependence arises because the demand for access is a *derived demand*. People primarily rent telephones and lines so that they can make and receive telephone calls at home. It is thus the demand for usage that drives the demand for access. However, in some cases, a secondary reason for demanding access may be that access provides the option to make calls. For example, a senior citizen, living alone, may make or receive very few calls but values the option of being able to make a home telephone call in an emergency. This is called an *option demand*.

Analogously, the demand for hardware (such as a CD player) can be viewed as the demand for access and the demand for software (such as the CD itself) as the demand for usage.

4.6 Demand When There Is an Access Fee But No Charge for Usage

For some services, it is common to charge a fee for access but then have no charge for usage. Nonpay cable and satellite tiers and Internet accounts (at least in North America) are examples. In addition, in North America (unlike in Europe), the historical norm has been not to charge for local telephone calls. Charging a price for access but not for usage is sometimes called *flat-fee pricing* because the amount the consumer pays is not related to the quantity consumed.

Suppose Jacquie is considering subscribing to an Internet service. For $25 per month, she can enjoy unlimited hours of access. Her demand curve for usage, d, is shown in Figure 4.4. As Internet use can take several forms, including e-mail, browsing, and file transfer protocol (FTP), demand curve d is the sum of Jacquie's demand curves for these different uses. As we can see, if she decides to subscribe, she will consume 50 hours per month, given the zero price per hour of usage. The entire area under her demand curve is the value she obtains from the 50 hours of usage, her consumer surplus. She will choose to subscribe if this consumer surplus is greater than the $25 access fee. Let us suppose that Jacquie does decide to subscribe but that the Internet service provider now presents her with another option: She can choose to subscribe for $15 per month if she limits hours of usage to 20 hours per month. Note that the price per hour of usage (within the limit) is still zero. The consumer surplus she would obtain from consuming 20 hours is shown by the area below her demand curve up to that consumption level; that is the area under the demand curve to the left of the vertical line drawn down from point B on her demand curve. Jacquie will choose the option that provides the greater excess of consumer surplus over access price.

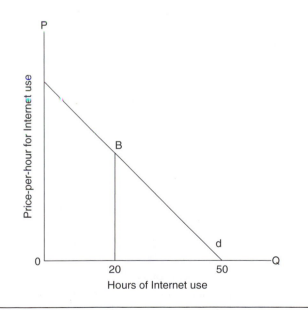

Figure 4.4   Jacquie's Demand for Internet Usage

Note: d indicates the demand curve; P, price; Q, quantity.

In chapter 10, we will examine flat-fee pricing from the perspective of the company.

4.7 Network Externalities

For most goods and services, the benefit an individual obtains from purchasing is independent of the number of others buying. One person's benefit from purchasing and consuming cheese is independent of the number of other people consuming cheese. For some goods and services, however, the benefit from consuming increases with the number of other people consuming. An extra subscriber to the network brings additional benefits to current subscribers. Similarly, the loss of a subscriber reduces benefits to continuing subscribers. In section 4.5, we saw how the telephone service cancellations by Carl and others like him reduced the value enjoyed by Alice and other continuing subscribers. In the very early days of the telephone, the utility a consumer enjoyed from having a telephone was limited because there were few other subscribers who could be contacted. Examples of recently established networks are fax and e-mail. Estimates of the number of e-mail users and the growth of e-mail use vary widely. One "educated guess" by Nua Internet Surveys (2004) is that as of September 2002 the number of Internet users worldwide was about 606 million (191 million in Europe, 187 million in Asia and the Pacific, and 183 million in Canada and the United States), whereas 10 years earlier, it would have been negligible (largely limited to a few academics and government employees). Obviously, the value of having an e-mail account has increased with the number of other subscribers.

Economists refer to this phenomenon as *network externalities*. It is called an externality because the subscription by others is not within the control of a current subscriber.

Network externalities can occur for goods and services that are not networks in the traditional sense. For example, when DVD players were in their infancy (they first became available in 1997), each additional purchaser of a DVD player added to the benefit of current owners, as an expanding base of DVD players increased the likelihood that film distributors would supply movies in the DVD format.

Another instance would be that in which an individual's enjoyment of an NFL football game on television or a movie at the cinema is affected by the number of others viewing, as part of the enjoyment results from discussing the common experience. Boardman and Hargraves-Heap (1999) make this externality the basis for supporting the U.K. government's policy of restricting the satellite service BSkyB's ability to compete with conventional over-the-air broadcasters for rights to key sporting events.

4.8 Consumption of Media Goods May Be Habit Forming

Consumer's preference, and hence utility from consumption of various goods, in one period is usually considered independent of past consumption levels. For example, Jill's utility from a visit to the laundromat in a New York suburb this month is unaffected by the number of visits she made last month. Sometimes for cultural goods, including the arts, this is not the case. Consumption of cultural goods can be habit forming in the sense that present consumption not only provides utility during this period but changes tastes through the accumulation of knowledge and appreciation for the product. Throsby (1994) makes this case. If Jill, who has not previously read widely, reads two Philip Roth novels this month, she may acquire a taste for such literature that makes future consumption still more enjoyable. If John, in Vancouver, starts watching the *Da Vinci's Inquest* television series, his future viewing of this series will provide more satisfaction as he gains knowledge about the characters, how they interact, and their work situation. He may appreciate the fact that it is easier to relate to action taking place in his own home town rather than in Chicago, New York, or Los Angeles. This appreciation may lead him to explore other Canadian television series.

If current consumption of a cultural good does change an individual's tastes, then current consumption causes an increase in the marginal utility associated with any given consumption level in the future. There will thus be an increase in the individual's demand, a shift of the demand curve to the right, in the next period. With a similar effect for other consumers, the market demand curve will shift to the right. This provides one explanation for U.S. dominance of the movie industry. Historically, the U.S. public has been exposed to very little foreign fare, especially non–English language films. As a result of consuming very little in the past, Americans have not accumulated the knowledge and experience that would increase their appreciation of future viewing. In contrast, audiences outside the United States have grown accustomed to U.S. films, and their appreciation for U.S. films has grown. One consequence is that they are not put off by subtitling or dubbing in the same way that American audiences are. Hoskins and Mirus (1988) give this as one of the reasons for U.S. dominance.

Another implication is that government measures designed to increase consumption of indigenous cultural products may have a significant carry-forward effect. For example, if an Australian government policy to subsidize Australian film results in an increased box office for Australian films, the increase in the number of movie-goers exposed to Australian films this year will change tastes or preferences (increase the marginal utility at a given consumption level) and increase demand for Australian films next year.

4.9 Attribute Theory

Attribute theory argues that consumers derive utility not from the products themselves but from the characteristics or attributes provided by the products. Hence the demand for products is itself viewed as a derived demand. The products are the means by which desired attributes are supplied to the consumption process. The attribute approach facilitates the explanation of consumer choice within groups of substitutes; for example, the choice of a Sony stereo system rather than a Panasonic, Hitachi, Toshiba, or RCA. It also permits us to incorporate new products into the analysis.

To illustrate, let us consider the service provided by an Internet service provider (ISP). Attributes related to this service include the ease of set-up, the browser and e-mail package included, the speed of the modem, the network capacity and likelihood of busy signals, the extent of the support available, the level of security, and whether using the service ties up the telephone line. Cable companies charge a premium price relative to dial-up access by emphasizing two attributes, a faster modem and not tying up the telephone line. The telecommunication companies have countered with their own high-speed asymmetrical digital subscriber line (ADSL) service with the same attributes. Both industries still try and claim superior attributes. The cable companies argue that their service is still the fastest; the telecommunications companies claim that ADSL is more secure and the speed is more consistent because the line (unlike cable) is not shared.

As another example, a computer's attributes include the speed of the processor, the type of operating system and how easy it is to use, memory size, hard drive capacity, the make and size of the monitor and whether it has a flat-panel display, the graphics card, the sound card, the speakers, the availability and characteristics of the DVD and CD-ROM drives, modem speed, the software included, whether a free trial with an Internet service provider is included, and the guarantee and support provided. For PCs, these features have become so standardized that consumers can custom order their computer with the precise specifications (attributes) they want.

For years, Apple was able to sell the Macintosh, introduced in 1984, at a premium price on the basis that its operating system was more consumer friendly than the DOS system of its rivals. With the introduction of Windows 95, much of this advantage disappeared, and the Macintosh market share fell from 11% to about 5% over an 18-month period (Picarelli, 1996). With the launch of the iMac in August 1998, Apple introduced another new attribute in the form of the futuristic styling and color of the cabinet. This attribute helped Apple to increase market share from 6.7% in the second quarter to 9.6% in the fourth quarter of 1998 (MacCentral staff, 1999), but the share has fallen substantially since then, and the model was replaced by a flat-panel iMac in January 2001.

The attributes of a television programming service cover the program mix in terms of genre, country of origin, language, and budget size. Other attributes would include the number of minutes of advertising per hour and the transmission quality. It would be difficult to support public funding of a public broadcasting organization if its mix of programming attributes were not significantly different from those of its private broadcasting counterparts.

Sony introduced the Betamax VCR for home viewing and recording in 1975, followed closely by the Victor Company of Japan (JVC) with its VHS format in 1976. The battle between Sony and JVC (and its parent Matsushita) over which format would become the industry standard was, in part, a battle between rival attributes. The Betamax picture was slightly superior, but VHS had the longer playing and recording time. When first introduced, the playing time was 2 hours for the VHS and 1 hour for Betamax; playing time was soon increased for both formats, but VHS maintained its lead. The length of playing time advantage proved more important to consumers than the picture quality, and this was one factor in the VHS victory. In the early days of the VCR, the importance of the playing time rested, in part, on the high price of a complementary product, the videotape itself. Other factors will be examined in chapter 9. For more on this case, see Cusumano, Mylonadis, and Rosenbloom (1992).

The format battle was joined by the video disk player introduced by Philips in 1978. However, the video disk player could not record. The ability to record enabled VCRs to win this battle.

The next competitor for the VCR was the DVD player, introduced in 1997. Sales of DVD players really took off in 1998, and they now outsell VCRs. The attribute responsible for this success was the strikingly better picture provided by the DVD player, which has 480+ lines of resolution in digital format, compared to 240 lines in analog format for the VCR. Although the early DVD players could not record, lack of this attribute was apparently more than compensated for by the DVD player's superior picture quality. A factor here is that over time, people were increasingly using the VCR to play prerecorded movies rather than using it to record TV programs.

One question that arises is how easy it is for consumers to discern the attributes provided by a given product. In this regard, three types of products can be distinguished: *search goods, experience goods*, and *credence goods*. Search goods are goods that consist mostly of attributes that are readily discernible by consumer search activity prior to purchase. For example, the attributes of a computer or stereo system are largely revealed by the specifications. Experience goods contain attributes that in the main can only be evaluated by the consumer after purchase through experience with the good. Examples include newspapers, magazines, books, films, and television programs. Credence goods provide mostly attributes that can be evaluated only imperfectly even after purchase. An example would be an actor's purchase of the services of an agent. If the actor is finding it difficult to land good parts, is it the fault of the agent? It is often difficult for the actor to determine how good a job the agent is doing.

In the VHS versus Betamax format war, the length of recording time was easily determined by search, whereas (small) differences in picture quality were probably only discernible through experience (although the strikingly better picture provided by the DVD player was obvious through search). Similarly, the fact that the video laser disk player, unlike the VCR, was unable to record could be determined by search.

The type of good is instrumental in determining the competitive strategy that should be adopted by the supplier. Search goods are like commodities in the sense that consumers are not willing to pay more for a given set of specifications from one supplier than from another. IBM's market share fell from 41.5% in 1985 to less than 30% in 1986 when it tried to sell personal computers at a price well above that of IBM clones. As we have seen, Apple lost market share when it continued to try to sell at a premium price after Windows 95 eliminated much of the Mac's ease of use advantage. In the case of search goods, a cost-leadership strategy (attempting to produce and distribute for a lower cost than your rivals) provides a superior (price minus cost) margin at any given price and puts the company in a strong position to meet any price competition. A cost-leadership strategy allowed Dell to rapidly become a major PC player. Direct sales to consumers, bypassing the usual wholesaler and retailer chain, resulted in large cost reductions. In addition, Dell does not build a computer until the order has been received, thus reducing inventory and storage costs.

Product differentiation is an appropriate strategy for experience goods. The aim is to provide attributes that differ from those provided by rivals and that give consumers (or at least some consumers, if a market niche is being targeted) greater value relative to price. Advertising is effective for informing consumers who have not previously bought the product about the attributes provided. A penetration price strategy is often advisable when introducing a new experience product. For example, when the *National Post* newspaper was started in Canada, it was introduced at a low price. This was to encourage people to give the newspaper a trial so they would be able to learn what attributes it provided. Several months later, the price was raised. (We expand on penetration pricing in chapter 10.)

Product differentiation through establishing a reputation is of crucial importance for a credence product. For example, agents or entertainment lawyers may establish credentials through past work, networking, and so on. Establishing a reputation can also be of great importance for those experience goods that are typically consumed only once, because marginal utility from consumption falls very sharply after the first unit. For example, after viewing *Saving Private Ryan* at the cinema, Len may conclude it was a good film, which he is glad he saw, but that he has no wish to see it again. For such goods, reputation is important to induce a single viewing. In this film, Steven Spielberg has a great reputation as a director and Tom Hanks as an actor. In addition, the large promotion budget provides a signal that the producer has confidence in the film and believes it to be a winner (otherwise why throw good money after bad?).

The competitive strategy appropriate for the different types of goods is summarized in Table 4.4.

Table 4.4   Competitive Strategy for Search, Experience, and Credence Goods

Search goods	Cost-leadership strategy
Experience goods	Product differentiation (and possibly penetration pricing)
Credence goods	Product differentiation (through reputation building)

4.10 Consumer Sovereignty

Consumer sovereignty is the notion that the consumer is the best judge of his or her own preferences. The consumer can best determine the relative utility attached to one more unit of different goods. As we have seen, under competitive circumstances, the preferences of consumers, as expressed through the market demand curve, together with the cost of producing, as reflected by the market supply curve, determine the quantity and price of each good. Consumers then have a free choice of which goods, and how many units of each, they will purchase.

Cultural development and industry protection arguments have led many countries (the United States being an exception) to introduce cultural industry policies that are at variance with consumer sovereignty. The very term "cultural industries" as opposed to "entertainment industries" reveals the nature of these concerns. These policies range from the outright prohibition of public exhibition of feature films in Saudi Arabia to trade restrictions on books, magazines, and music.

The media industry where these restrictions are most prevalent is television. In many countries, there is a government agency that regulates required levels of domestic programming and sometimes the mix of program genre. These agencies are thus playing a role in determining the viewing options available. We will consider in chapter 13 whether there are sound reasons for such regulation, but at this stage, note that consumer sovereignty is not a principle that should be dispensed with lightly.

4.11 The Equimarginal Principle

Recall that the consumer's objective is to allocate a limited budget among purchases of different goods and services in such a way as to maximize his or her utility from consumption. This is an example of a more general problem involving maximization of an objective subject to a constraint. The constraint is often budget, but time constraint is also common. As we have seen, in the case of the consumer, the solution is to allocate expenditure among goods in such a way that the last dollar spent on each good yields the same addition to total utility. The general solution to problems of this type is to allocate units of constraint in such a way that the marginal contribution of each activity toward achievement of the objective is the same, per unit of constraint, for all activities. This is known as the *equimarginal principle*.

Students regularly face a problem of this type. There is a week to go before final examinations in three subjects, Cultural Studies, Media Economics (Media Econ), and Communications Theory (Comm Theory). The objective is to maximize the percentage grade point average (the same as maximizing the sum of the percentage grades in the three courses), subject to a constraint of 7 days available for study. The percentage grade that would be earned for the courses, according to the number of days of study allocated, is shown in columns 2, 3, and 4 (the column numbers appear at the top) of Table 4.5. The solution is to allocate study days (or hours) between subjects in such a way that the last day (or hour) spent on each subject yields an equal addition to grade. The addition to total percentage grade from spending another day of study is described as "marginal grade" in the table and is shown for the courses in columns 5, 6, and 7. Note that for each course, there is a diminishing marginal grade for additional days of study. Given the 7-day constraint, the marginal grade is equated at 5% when 2 days are allocated to Cultural Studies, 3 days to Media Economics, and 2 days to Communications Theory. Another way of looking at the solution is that the first day of study should be allocated to Media Economics, where the marginal grade is highest at 30%; the second day to the same subject, where the marginal grade is 20%; the third day to Communications Theory, where the marginal grade is 15%; the fourth day to Cultural Studies, where it is 10%; and then one extra day (in no particular order) to each subject, where the marginal grade is 5%.

Table 4.5   A Student's Study Decision

1	2	3	4	5	6	7
Number of Days of Study	Cultural Studies Grade	Media Econ Grade	Comm Theory Grade	Marginal Grade Cultural Studies	Marginal Grade Media Econ	Marginal Grade Comm Theory
0	70	30	50			
1	80	60	65	10	30	15
2	85	80	70	5	20	5
3	87	85	72	2	5	2
4	88	87	73	0	2	1
5	88	88	74	0	1	1
6	88	88	74	0	0	0
7	88	88	74	0	0	0

Note: All grades shown in percentages. Econ indicates economics; comm, communications.

A book salesperson faces a similar problem. Suppose Latonya is responsible for representing the publisher in Washington State, Oregon, and Idaho. Her objective is to maximize sales revenue (she may well be paid a commission based on sales revenue). Columns 2, 3, and 4 could represent the total sales revenue (in hundreds of dollars) in Washington, Oregon, and Idaho, respectively, according to how she allocates the next 7 weeks. If this is the case, she should devote 2 weeks to Washington, 3 weeks to Oregon, and 2 weeks to Idaho. Of course, her time allocation decision will be more complex than this. Latonya must decide what mix of face-to-face meetings, telephoning, and e-mailing is optimal for the various independent bookstores and chains. Amazon.com is based in her territory, so how much time should she spend dealing with this company, and what form should her involvement take? The task she has is a difficult one, but the form of the solution is straightforward. She should allocate weeks (or hours) in such a way that the last (week or hour) spent on each activity in a period yields the same addition to total sales revenue.

A public broadcasting organization has to decide how to allocate a budget, derived from a government grant or television license fee, among competing uses. The problem is made more difficult because public broadcasting typically has multiple objectives. For example, the mandate of the Canadian Broadcasting Corporation (CBC) states that programming should be (this is not a complete list) "predominantly and distinctively Canadian," "reflect Canada and its regions to national and regional audiences," "be in English and in French," "contribute to shared national consciousness and identity" and "reflect the multicultural and multiracial nature of Canada" (Broadcasting Act, 1991). How the CBC should allocate what has been a dwindling budget has been a source of continual controversy in the last decade. The CBC has continued to spread itself thinly, operating multiple stations, exhibiting programming covering a wide range of genre, and catering to local as well as regional and national audiences. Many have argued that it could better achieve its objectives by concentrating its efforts on national programming of the sort undersupplied by commercial broadcasting (see, for example, Hoskins & McFadyen, 1996).

It is often difficult to quantify the effect of an expenditure on objectives, so the equimarginal principle may not give an unambiguous answer. However, it provides a way of thinking about and analyzing a problem and a framework for the decision-making process.

4.12 Summary

In this chapter, we examined consumer behavior in allocating a limited income among many desired goods and services. An understanding of consumer behavior is essential to an appreciation of the nature of demand by an individual. Important concepts are highlighted here.

The Law of Diminishing Marginal Utility states that after a certain number of units of product X have been consumed in a given time period, each additional unit of product X consumed yields less addition to total utility than the previous unit. It is because of this law that people generally see movies only once. It also explains why more movie videos are rented than purchased.

The objective of the consumer is assumed to be to maximize utility from consumption. A consumer is in equilibrium when, subject to budget constraints, he or she allocates expenditure between goods in such a way that the last dollar spent on each good purchased yields the same addition to total utility. To state the Theory of Consumer Behavior more formally, the conditions for equilibrium are as follows:

$$MU_x/P_x = MU_z/P_z = \ldots$$

$$\text{Subject to } P_x \times Q_x + P_z \times Q_z + \ldots = Y$$

An increase in the price of X leads to MU_x/P_x being less than MU_z/P_z. To regain equilibrium, the consumer decreases the quantity of X demanded, which, as a consequence of the Law of Diminishing Utility, increases MU_x until the last dollar spent on each product again yields the same addition to total utility. There is thus a negative relationship between price and the quantity the consumer demands.

Because of the Law of Diminishing Utility, a consumer who buys multiple units of a product at the same price enjoys a consumer surplus. The consumer surplus is the maximum amount the consumer would be willing to pay for the quantity bought minus what he or she actually pays. Graphically it is represented by the triangular area below the demand curve and above the price line.

For some goods or services, such as telephone services, a distinction can be made between demand for access and demand for usage. A person will desire access to the telephone network if the consumer surplus from usage, including both making and receiving calls, is greater than the charge for access. Due to the interdependence of demand for usage and demand for access, a higher price for usage will decrease demand for access and a higher price for access will decrease demand for usage.

There are network externalities if another subscriber to a network brings a benefit to current subscribers. Subscribing to an Internet service provider to access e-mail is more valuable now than it was 5 years ago because the number of people who can be reached through an e-mail message has exploded.

Consumption of cultural goods may be habit forming. If current consumption changes tastes, then it will cause an increase in demand in the next period. One of the reasons non-U.S. viewers generally appreciate U.S. movies is that they have been exposed to so many in the past. This addictive quality also suggests that government measures designed to increase consumption of indigenous cultural products may have significant carry-forward effects.

Attribute theory argues that consumers derive utility not from the products themselves but from the characteristics or attributes provided by the product. The attribute approach facilitates the explanation of consumer choice within a group of competing brands. For example, in the battle of VCR standards, the VHS advantage of a longer recording time was more important to consumers than the slightly superior picture quality provided by Betamax.

How easy it is for consumers to discern the attributes provided by a given product depends on whether the product is a search good, an experience good, or a credence good. Search goods are goods that consist mainly of attributes that are readily discernible by consumer search activity prior to purchase. Experience goods contain attributes that in the main can only be evaluated after purchase through experience with the good. Credence goods provide mostly attributes that can be evaluated only imperfectly even after purchase. The type of good is instrumental in determining the competitive strategy that should be adopted by the supplier.

The consumer's decision on how to allocate a limited budget between an unlimited number of desirable goods is an example of a more general problem involving maximization of an objective subject to a constraint. The constraint is often budget, but time constraint is also common. The general solution to problems of this type is to allocate units of constraint in such a way that the marginal contribution of each activity toward achievement of the objective is the same, per unit of constraint, for all activities. This is known as the equimarginal principle. An example of such a problem is the decision a public broadcasting organization has to make about how to allocate a budget, derived from a government grant or license fee, among competing uses. Although the equimarginal principle does not provide a cut and dried answer, it nevertheless provides a useful guide to how such decisions should be approached.

5

Production and Cost

Why is packet switching used for the Internet rather than circuit networks? What are economies of scale, and how do they provide the United States with a competitive advantage in producing movies and many other cultural or entertainment goods? What are the implications of economies of scale for trade disputes such as that between Canada and the United States over so-called split-run productions of U.S. magazines? Why is international coproduction of television programs and feature films growing in importance? Why do most studios produce both movies and television programs? Why are there so many entertainment industry mergers, such as Disney's acquisitions of Miramax and ABC, AT&T's acquisition of the cable company TCI, AOL's merger with Time Warner, and Bell Canada's (BCE's) acquisition of the CTV television network and the Toronto *Globe and Mail?* As we will see in this chapter, these and other communication questions can be answered through an understanding of how cost varies with output. We have to know how varying the level of factor inputs affects output and what determines the optimal combination of inputs.

We assume the objective of firms is to maximize profit. For profits to be maximized, the total cost of producing the selected output of the good must be minimized. That is, the production must be *economically efficient;* there must be no other method available that is capable of producing the output for a smaller total value (cost) of inputs. Total cost depends on the number of each factor employed and the price per unit that the firm has to pay.

5.1 Short Run, Long Run, and Very Long Run

Production opportunities—ways of combining inputs to change output—differ according to the length of time considered. The quantities of some inputs can be changed very rapidly, whereas a considerable time is needed to change others. For example, energy use can be changed by the turn of a switch, whereas building a plant or installing machinery is likely to take months or even years.

The *short run* is defined as a time period insufficient to change the input level of items such as capital equipment and plant. Such capacity factors are *fixed* in the short run. However, quantities of inputs such as labor and raw materials can be changed and are thus *variable* factors even in the short run.

The *long run* is a period of sufficient length that all factors of production are variable, but the basic technology of production is given.

The *very long run* is a period during which the technological possibilities available to the firm may also change.

5.2 Production in the Short Run

A *production function* shows the maximum quantity of a product that can be produced in a time period for each set of alternative inputs. In the short run, the production function is governed by the *Law of Diminishing Returns*. This law states that after a certain level of input of the variable factor, each additional unit of the variable factor, employed in conjunction with a fixed quantity of another factor, adds less to total product than the previous unit. (In production theory, economists use the word "product" to mean "output"; the words are used interchangeably).

The law is stated as if there were only two factors, one variable and the other fixed, but this is a simplification; the law applies for any number of variable and fixed factors. Also, note the similarity between the Law of Diminishing Returns and the Law of Diminishing Marginal Utility.

If it were not for the Law of Diminishing Returns, all the wheat sold in the world could be produced on one acre of land (fixed factor) if enough labor and fertilizer (variable factors) were employed.

To illustrate the Law of Diminishing Returns, consider the Small DVD Company, which produces DVD-R discs. With capital

Table 5.1   Small DVD Company's Short-Run Production Function

Labor input	0	1	2	3	4	5
Total product	0	2	10	20	25	26
Marginal product	0	2	8	10	5	1
Average product	0	2	5	6.67	6.25	5.2

equipment fixed at one machine, suppose the total product or output per hour for various levels of labor input (the variable factor) is shown in row 2 of Table 5.1.

The machine is designed to be operated by three people and to produce 20 units of output per hour. When only one person is employed, that person finds it almost impossible to perform all the tasks necessary to run the machine and is consequently only able to produce 2 units per hour. Adding a second person increases total product to 10 units. The two people are able to get the machine operating about half of the time. With a third person added, operating the machine goes fairly smoothly. A fourth person is useful to give the others a break, and total product is 25. With a fifth person, each can take longer breaks, but total product increases very little, to 26.

Marginal product is defined as the addition to total product from employing one more unit of the variable factor. Marginal product is shown in row 3 of Table 5.1. For example, adding a fourth worker would increase total product from 20 to 25, so the marginal product is 5.

Average product (row 4) is total product divided by the number of units of the variable factor employed.

5.3 Costs in the Short Run

Cost functions indicate how the minimum cost of producing varies with cost. We will start by defining various cost concepts.

Total Variable Cost (TVC) is the total cost associated with employing the variable factors. For example, referring to Table 5.1, the total variable cost of producing 25 units of output would be the cost of employing four units of labor. If the wage rate paid is $10 per hour, then the total variable cost is $40. This is shown in Table 5.2. To produce 26 units, five people have to be employed, so that the TVC is $50.

Table 5.2   Small DVD Company's Short-Run Costs

Labor input	0	1	2	3	4	5
Total output (Q)	0	2	10	20	25	26
TVC	0	10	20	30	40	50
TFC	20	20	20	20	20	20
TC	20	30	40	50	60	70
AVC		5.00	2.00	1.50	1.60	1.92
AFC		10.00	2.00	1.00	0.80	0.77
ATC		15.00	4.00	2.50	2.40	2.69
SMC		5.00	1.25	1.00	2.00	10.00

Note: AFC indicates average fixed cost; ATC, average total cost; AVC, average variable cost; SMC, short-run marginal cost; TC, total cost; TFC, total fixed cost; TVC, total variable cost.

Total Fixed Cost (TFC) is the cost associated with factors that are fixed in the short run. In our example, the machine is the fixed asset. If the machine has been obtained on a long-term lease at an hourly rate of $20, then TFC is $20 irrespective of output.

Total Cost (TC) is TVC + TFC, so the TC of producing 25 units of output is $40 + $20 = $60, and the TC of producing 26 units is $70.

Short-Run Marginal Cost (SMC) is the change in TC for a one-unit change in output. As the only component of TC varying with output is TVC, SMC can also be defined as the change in TVC associated with a one-unit change in output. For example, the SMC of the 26th unit of output is $10 as TC increases from $60 to $70 or as TVC increases from $40 to $50.

Average Variable Cost (AVC) is TVC/Q, where Q is the output. The AVC of producing 25 units is $40/25 = $1.60.

Average Fixed Cost (AFC) is TFC/Q. As TFC is constant, the larger Q is, the smaller the AFC will be. For example, the AFC for 2 units of output is $20/2 = $10.00, whereas for 25 units it is $0.80.

Average Total Cost (ATC) is AVC + AFC, or TC/Q. For an output of 25 units, it is $1.60 + $0.80 = $2.40.

The short-run costs for Small DVD Company are shown in Table 5.2. The amounts shown for SMC in Table 5.2 require explanation. We defined SMC as the change in TC or TVC for a one-unit change in output. But in the example, adding another person prior to the sixth person added more than one unit to the total output. If the

Small Company could hire people by the minute at a rate of 16.67 cents per minute ($10/60), then we could tell the true increase in cost of increasing output from 2 units to 3 units, 3 units to 4 units, and so on. If this is not possible, SMC can be approximated by $\Delta TC/\Delta Q$; that is, the change in total cost divided by the change in output. Thus the SMC of $1.25 shown for an output of 10 really represents an averaging of SMC for outputs from 2 to 10 units, which would increase TVC from $20 to $30 ($1.25 = $10/8).

Alternatively, SMC can be calculated as the wage rate or price paid for the variable factor, divided by the marginal product of the variable factor. For example, in Table 5.1, we can see that the second person employed had a marginal product of 8 units. Given a wage rate of $10, SMC is $10/8 = $1.25. This method of calculation makes it clear that SMC varies inversely with marginal product; thus the Law of Diminishing Returns entails increasing SMC.

Let us consider another example. Table 5.3 shows the short-run costs of the New Sound Company for producing up to 8 units of output per hour. Given the total variable costs shown in row 2 and the total fixed costs in row 3, the other costs have been calculated using the relationships presented earlier in this section. As SMC increases after an output of three units, we can infer that the Law of Diminishing Returns sets in after the input level associated with this output.

A relationship between SMC and AVC and between SMC and ATC should be noted. SMC equals AVC where AVC is at a minimum. SMC for the fourth unit is $70. This is equal to the AVC at

Table 5.3   New Sound Company's Short-Run Costs

Output	0	1	2	3	4	5	6	7	8
TVC	0	90	160	210	280	370	490	690	1,010
TFC	540	540	540	540	540	540	540	540	540
TC	540	630	700	750	820	910	1,030	1,230	1,550
AVC		90	80	70	70	74	82	99	126
AFC		540	270	180	135	108	90	77	68
ATC		630	350	250	205	182	172	176	194
SMC		90	70	50	70	90	120	200	320

Note: AFC indicates average fixed cost; ATC, average total cost; AVC, average variable cost; SMC, short-run marginal cost; TC, total cost; TFC, total fixed cost; TVC, total variable cost.

three units. Hence, adding the fourth unit leaves AVC unchanged. Whenever SMC is less than AVC, AVC is falling. Whenever SMC is more than AVC, AVC is rising. Only if SMC = AVC will AVC be unchanged. Similarly, SMC equals ATC where ATC is at a minimum.

To illustrate the relationship between marginal and average, suppose you are a rock star part way through a North American tour. The crowds at your concerts steadily declined until your last concert, in Minneapolis, which was an improvement over the previous one. However, the crowd at your last concert was still less than your average crowd, as the average includes the large crowds at the beginning of the tour. Your next three concerts are in Vancouver, Portland, and Seattle. Assume the crowd in Vancouver (marginal) is higher than it was in Minneapolis but still lower than the average crowd at the end of the Minneapolis concert. As a consequence, the size of your average crowd decreases after inclusion of the Vancouver concert. Suppose the Portland crowd is greater than that at Vancouver and equal to the post-Vancouver average. The inclusion of the Portland concert will leave the average unaffected. If the Seattle crowd is greater than that in Portland, after the Seattle concert, the average will increase.

In Figure 5.1, we show the SMC, AVC, AFC, and ATC curves for the New Sound Company. Note that the SMC is drawn with the SMC for the fourth unit plotted midway between the third and fourth units because it applies to the increase from three to four and so on for the rest of this cost curve. SMC starts to increase after the Law of Diminishing Returns sets in when the fourth unit is added. Prior to that output, the New Sound Company exhibited increasing marginal product (decreasing marginal cost). This resulted in the U-shaped SMC curve shown and also explains the U-shape of the AVC and ATC curves. However, for some producers, the Law of Diminishing Returns sets in after the first unit of the variable factor is employed, which would mean that the SMC (and AVC) curves would not have a negatively sloped portion.

An Internet service provider (ISP) is the type of organization that would have to be very clear on the distinction between fixed and variable costs in the short run. ISPs need to invest in network infrastructure such as the installation of fiber optics, routers, and software. This large investment is a fixed cost in the short run; it does not vary with output. On the other hand, customer service and maintenance costs vary with usage.

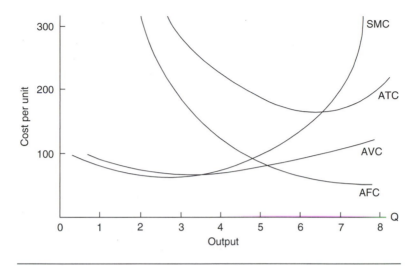

Figure 5.1   The Short-Run Cost Curves for the New Sound Company

Note: AFC indicates average fixed cost; ATC, average total cost; AVC, average variable cost; SMC, short-run marginal cost; Q, quantity (output).

5.4 Long-Run Production and Cost

The long run is a period of sufficient length that all factors of production are variable, but the basic technology of production is given.

5.4.1 The Choice of Factor Mix

The firm wishes to produce any given output at minimum cost or, equivalently, maximize output for any given level of total cost. This is achieved by employing an input mix such that the last dollar spent on each factor yields the same addition to total output. More formally:

$$MP_L/P_L = MP_K/P_K = \ldots$$

where MP_L is the marginal product of factor L (L could represent labor), MP_K is the marginal product of factor K (K could represent capital), P_L is the price of factor L, and P_K is the price of factor K.

This should look familiar. It is another example of the equimarginal principle.

A change in price of one factor will result in factor substitution. Suppose the price of input L increases. If employment levels of both factors are not changed, then the last dollar spent on L will now yield less addition to total output than the last dollar spent on K. Hence the firm will substitute K for L until equality is reestablished. In other words, it will substitute the factor that is now relatively cheap for the one that is more expensive.

The recent increased volume of animation films, such as *The Prince of Egypt, A Bug's Life, Antz, The Hunchback of Notre Dame,* and *Finding Nemo* (aimed at adults as well as children), can be explained, at least in part, by the escalating salaries of top movie actors. The increase in the price of movie actor labor has resulted in a substitution of animation characters for movie stars.

As MacKie-Mason and Varian (1994, p. 81) explain, the Internet uses packet switching rather than circuit networks because of a fall in the price of switches and routers relative to lines. Packet switching uses many more switches and routers than circuit networks but economizes on the number of lines needed.

5.4.2 Returns to Scale and Production in the Long Run

The key long-run production concept is returns to scale. Returns to scale relate to the effect on output of an equal percentage increase in all inputs.

We have *constant returns to scale* if an X% increase in all inputs increases output by X%—if, for example, doubling all inputs exactly doubles output.

Increasing returns to scale apply if an X% increase in all inputs increases output by more than X%—if, for example, doubling all inputs more than doubles output. Increasing returns to scale are also called *economies of scale*. Possible reasons for increasing returns to scale include:

A. *Technical economies.* These arise because some capital equipment is not divisible. For example, assembly line production only becomes possible when the firm has achieved a certain size. A firm cannot use half an assembly line or a quarter of a robot. Production of most consumer electronics products would be subject to technical economies.

B. *Dimensional relations.* Capacity (output) of goods like oil tankers and beer vats increases more than external size. The capacity of a concert hall or stadium increases more than proportionally to the size of the parcel of land on which it is built.

C. *Specialization.* Increases in size permit greater specialization of factors of production. Specialization of labor on the factory floor enabled Ford to reduce the time needed to assemble a Model T from 14 hours to 93 minutes. Growth of firm size also facilitates specialization of managerial tasks. For example, suppose Jock runs a one-man desktop publishing business. Although he is very good at the production side of the job, he is poor at dealing with customers and finds this part of the job is taking up considerable time. If he hires Jill, who is experienced and successful in sales and customer relations, this would enable Jock to specialize on the production side. Doubling personnel and, as necessary, equipment could be expected to more than double output.

D. *Managerial economies.* Some managerial functions do not increase in proportion to output. For example, a movie studio that distributes 40 films a year does not need a distribution arm that is twice as big as one distributing 20. A publisher with 100 titles does not need twice the sales staff as a publisher with 50 titles. Similarly, research and development does not usually have to be increased in proportion to output.

Decreasing returns to scale apply if an X% increase in all inputs increases output by less than X%. Decreasing returns to scale are also known as *diseconomies of scale.* Problems of coordination and communication are often encountered with larger size. With increasing scale, a firm can grow more bureaucratic and lose the flexibility necessary to respond quickly to changes in the external environment. Fraser (1986) provides the example of IBM's failure to recognize the potential for PCs in the 1970s. To finally respond, IBM had to set up a separate division in 1980 and give it 1 year to create and market a PC. The danger of becoming inflexible should be borne in mind by the large media conglomerates such as AOL-Time Warner, Disney, and Newscorp.

5.4.3 Returns to Scale and Long-Run Costs

The returns to scale experienced by a firm determine how long-run average cost (LAC) and long-run marginal cost (LMC) vary with output. To illustrate this, suppose the Communications Corporation is currently producing 200 units of output per hour by employing 100 units of labor and 300 units of capital. The price of these factors is $20 per hour for labor and $25 per hour for capital. Thus the long-run total cost (LTC) of producing 200 units of output is $9500 (= 100 × $20 + 300 × 25). The LAC of producing this output is LTC/Q = $9500/200 = $47.50. From this starting point, we will examine three scenarios (representing constant, increasing, and decreasing returns to scale) concerning the increase in output resulting from a 1% increase in labor from 100 to 101 and in capital from 300 to 303 units.

Suppose the 1% increase in inputs increases the output of the Communications Corporation from 200 units to 202 units per day. This represents a 1% increase in output. Hence the production function exhibits constant returns to scale. The LTC of producing the new output level is $9595 (= 101 × $20 + 303 × $25). The LAC is $9595/202 = $47.50. Thus LAC is unchanged; it does not vary with output, and the cost curve is horizontal. LMC is the increase in LTC resulting from a one-unit change in output. If the increase in output is more than one unit, LMC is approximated by ΔLTC/ΔQ. The LTC of producing 202 units of output is $9595, compared to $9500 for 200 units. Hence the LMC is $95/2 = $47.50, the same as LAC.

If the 1% increase in all inputs increases the output of the Communications Corporation from 200 units to 204 units per day, this represents a 2% increase in output, and the production function will thus exhibit increasing returns to scale. The LAC is $9595/204 = $47.03. Thus LAC decreases. LMC is ΔLTC/ΔQ = $95/4 = $23.75. LMC decreases also but at a faster rate than LAC.

Finally, if the 1% increase in all inputs increases the output of the Communications Corporation from 200 units to 201 units per day, this increase of 0.5% is less than proportional. Hence the production function exhibits decreasing returns to scale. The LAC is $9595/201 = $47.74. LAC increases with output. LTC increases from $9500 for 200 units of output to $9595 for one extra unit. Hence LMC is $95. LMC increases and at a faster rate than LAC.

There is no reason to suppose that a production function exhibits the same returns to scale throughout the entire output range. Economies of scale, especially technical economies, are often exhausted after a certain output level is attained. Diseconomies of scale are usually found only at high levels of output. As a consequence, the LAC (and LMC) curve drawn in many textbooks is usually a shallow U shape, as in Figure 5.2, with increasing returns to scale at low output levels, decreasing returns to scale at high output levels, and an intermediate range with close to constant returns to scale. Note that decreasing returns to scale at high output levels, if in fact they occur, are not due to the Law of Diminishing Returns. Decreasing

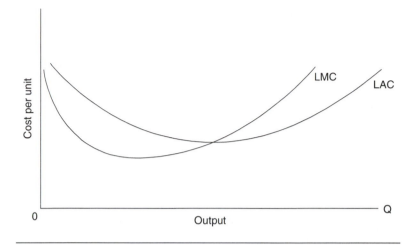

Figure 5.2   The U-Shaped, Long-Run Average Cost Curve

Note: LAC indicates long-run average cost; LMC, long-run marginal cost; Q, quantity (output).

returns to scale is a long-run concept in which all inputs can be increased in proportion, whereas the Law of Diminishing Returns is a short-run concept that applies where at least one factor is fixed.

Empirical studies estimating the cost functions of real companies suggest that an L-shaped LAC curve, as shown in Figure 5.3, is more common. Increasing returns to scale are found up to output Q^*, with constant returns to scale thereafter. Output Q^* is the *Minimum*

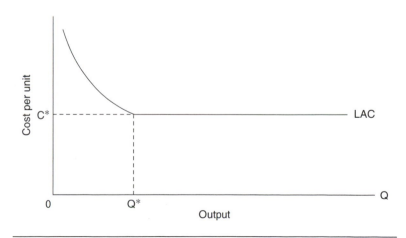

Figure 5.3   The L-Shaped, Long-Run Average Cost Curve

Note: LAC indicates long-run average cost; Q, quantity (output).

Efficient Scale, as any firm producing at a lower output will be at a cost disadvantage by producing at an average cost in excess of C*.

The relationship between average cost in the long run and in the short run is shown in Figure 5.4. The LAC curve shows the minimum average cost of producing any given output using the optimal combination of factors. A short-run ATC curve shows the average total cost of producing any given output in the most efficient manner when at least one factor is fixed. Different ATC curves (we have drawn three, but any number could be shown) can be drawn for different levels of the fixed factor. Each ATC curve is tangent to the LAC at the output level where the level of the fixed factor available is optimal. For any output above or below this, ATC > LAC because output can only be varied by adjusting the input of the variable input; in the short run, the firm will have too little of the fixed factor for larger outputs and too much for smaller outputs.

To illustrate, returning to our Communication Corporation example, let us assume that the current output is 200 units, made using the optimal mix of 100 units of labor and 300 units of capital, and assume that increasing returns to scale apply. As the quantity of capital (the factor fixed in the short run) is optimal for this output of 200 units, ATC = LAC = $47.50. As we saw, to increase output to 204 units in the long run, the firm increases labor input

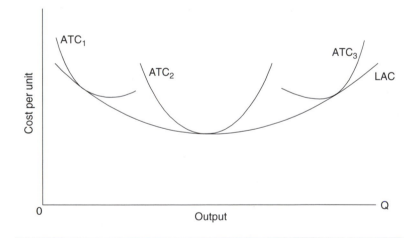

Figure 5.4   Relationship Between Average Cost in the Long Run and in the Short Run

Note: ATC_1, ATC_2, and ATC_3 indicate short-run average total cost curves for different levels of the fixed factor; LAC, longer-run average cost; Q, quantity (output).

by one unit and capital input by three units, and the LAC of this higher output level is $47.03. However, in the short run, capital input is fixed at 300 units, and output can only be increased to 204 by employing more labor. Suppose six more units of labor would be necessary. Short-run total cost becomes $9620 and ATC = $47.15. Thus, at the higher output level, ATC > LAC. The same applies to lower output levels. In the short run, a lower output level can only be achieved by employing less labor, in conjunction with too much capital. The ATC_1 curve drawn in Figure 5.4 is consistent with this example.

5.4.4 Returns to Scale in Media Goods

Many media goods exhibit increasing returns to scale. For telecommunication and cable companies, this follows from the indivisibility of the capital equipment used.

Economies of scale for entertainment and cultural goods arise from the unusual nature of the economics of their production. Production costs for an hour of U.S. drama (such as an episode of a U.S. network series) are usually quoted at $1 million or more. This is the cost of the first copy and must be borne even if only a single film or tape is made for one broadcast organization. Much of this cost can be regarded as akin to research and development, as it involves the creation of a new product. If another copy is made, so that exhibition rights can be sold to, say, the BBC in the United Kingdom, the marginal cost of this copy is the cost of replication and distribution. This may amount to around $100 (this is the price paid by the Caribbean island of Aruba, and it is unlikely that U.S. producers would be willing to sell at a price below marginal cost). If a third copy is produced for sale to CTV in Canada, the additional cost would again be around $100. This can be viewed as an extreme case of managerial scale economies, with expenditure on research and development being independent of output level. Huge economies of scale are experienced with an increase in output from one unit to two units, and constant returns to scale are experienced thereafter.

An implication is that the sale of additional copies of a television program is extremely attractive as the incremental cost is so low. Hoskins et al. (1997) report that sale of a typical hour of U.S. drama to the BBC in the United Kingdom takes place at a price of around $100,000 and to CTV in Canada at $60,000. (We consider a pricing strategy for selling TV programs in chapter 10). Thus exports are very attractive and, indeed, worthwhile at any price above the marginal cost of supplying. This helps to explain why television programs are widely traded.

The returns to scale for movies, videos, videogames, compact disks, and DVD video and audio disks are essentially the same as for television programs. Large economies of scale, although the difference in cost between the first copy and subsequent copies is typically less, also occur in book, newspaper, and magazine publishing in print form. With digital downloading from the Internet available, or becoming available, for all these goods, the marginal cost of additional copies is fast approaching zero. This has resulted in a huge piracy problem for recorded music and is becoming an issue with movies. To counter this, the RIAA has instituted legal action targeting the makers, and very recently users, of share-swapping software. Napster Inc., in its original incarnation, was put out of business, and in September 2003, copyright infringement lawsuits were initiated against hundred of individual users.

Economies of scale also provide the background to the continuing trade dispute between Canada and the United States over Canadian attempts to protect its magazine industry from so-called split-run productions of U.S. magazines. U.S. magazines, even those with a small amount of added Canadian content, would enjoy a huge cost advantage over Canadian magazines because the cost of all or most of the content is, in effect, provided free to the copies sold in Canada. Canadian governments have feared that, without protection, the Canadian magazine industry would be decimated. Whether this presumed consequence is inevitable is open to debate, but successive Canadian governments have acted on this basis. Since 1965, Section 19 of the Canadian Income Tax Act has not permitted Canadian advertisers to claim the cost of advertising in foreign magazines as a tax-deductible expense. In 1993, *Sports Illustrated* tried to get around this by beaming a Canadian edition electronically across the border to a printing press in Ontario. The Canadian Parliament then passed a law imposing an 80% tax on the Canadian income of split-run publications not previously exempted (*Time* and *Reader's Digest* had been exempted under a grandfather clause.) The U.S. government argued that this was a restraint of trade, and in 1997 the Word Trade Organization agreed. Canada was about to counter with legislation that would make it illegal for Canadian companies to buy advertising space in split-run magazines when a compromise was reached in mid-1999.

The same returns to scale advantage, and potentially the same trade issue, apply to new media. Daniel Roseman, who served from 1988 to 1993 as Canada's negotiator on telecommunication and cultural services during the Uruguay Round of GATT, points out:

> The differences between Yahoo.com and Yahoo.ca are like the differences between *Time Magazine* and *Time Magazine Canada*. Yahoo.ca is a split-run in electronic format; there is an American core with some Canadian content and Web links added on . . . traditionally Canada's restrictions in the cultural industries have focused on control and manipulation of distribution channels, but such measures are becoming untenable. New technologies and applications make restrictive regulations unworkable; that is why no one is proposing [that] the prohibition on split-run magazines apply [to this situation]. (Roseman, 1999, p. A13)

An additional reason that no one is proposing a prohibition on split-run portals is that there is no well-established Canadian industry forming an effective lobby group.

5.4.5 International Coproductions and Returns to Scale

International coproduction has become an increasingly popular mode for producing television programs and films. It involves forming an alliance with one or more foreign partners to jointly develop and produce a program or film with attributes that make it attractive to audiences in more than one national market. In effect, the partners pool financial resources to share the high cost of the first copy of the program or film and then are able to produce additional copies for the other national market(s) at a very low marginal cost because of the huge economies of scale identified earlier. Surveys by Hoskins, McFadyen, and Finn (1999) of producers indicate that in most countries, the pooling of financial resources is by far the most important reason for choosing the international coproduction route.

5.4.6 Mergers and Returns to Scale

Mergers, unlike coproductions that are temporary alliances typically for just one television program or film, are permanent amalgamations of formerly distinct firms. Increasing returns to scale are an important motive for many mergers involving firms producing the same class of product. For example, in 1987 (prior to its own acquisition by Sony), Columbia, a major Hollywood studio, merged with TriStar Pictures, an independent studio, and in 1998, Alliance and Atlantis, Canada's two largest studios, merged. Such mergers are designed to ensure sufficient market share to sustain a substantial, and costly, distribution structure.

5.4.7 Economies of Scope

Economies of scope exist if the total cost of producing two (or more) products within the same firm is less than producing them separately in two (or more) nonrelated firms.

Reasons for economies of scope are:

- The products are produced jointly. One may be essentially a by-product of the other.
- Factors of production are present that are shared by the processes used to make several different products.

When a movie is produced, there are many "by-products," or different windows of exhibition, that can be exploited. After cinema exhibition, the film can be produced in DVD and VHS video format for direct sale or rental to consumers, and it can be sold to individuals through pay per view and, later, to broadcast organizations for non–pay television exhibition. Revenues from DVD and video are typically larger than the box office from cinematic exhibition. Some films lend themselves to merchandising of items such as toys, games, and T-shirts, and film producers can sell the license for manufacturing these products. It is this license that can be thought of as the by-product. For example, Hasbro produces the Star Wars toys under license from Lucasfilm. Merchandising normally begins after exhibition of the movie has created a demand. However, merchandising of toys associated with the fourth Star Wars movie began in time for Christmas 1998, some 6 months before the movie opened in North America. Which product can be thought of as the "by-product" is becoming harder to distinguish. The first three Star Wars movies are reported to have resulted in merchandising sales far in excess of their box office, but a far smaller percentage of merchandise sales than gross box office revenue would flow back to the movie studio.

Most studios produce both feature films and television programs. Both products share labor with the same skills and use the same capital equipment and distribution infrastructure. There are economies of scope from producing both of these products within the same company because of these shared inputs.

No doubt Matsushita (brand names include Panasonic, JVC, Technics, and Quasar) obtains cost savings from producing the whole range of television sets, VCRs, DVD players, stereo equipment, camcorders, and other consumer electronic hardware. The same distribution channels would apply, many of the component suppliers would be common and quantity discounts would be greater, and the production would involve some common labor and capital equipment. The diversified product line means that the company's fortunes are not tied to one product line. For example, if it only produced VCRs, a big drop in demand caused by customers switching to DVD players would hit the company hard. But if the company produces DVD players as well, many resources can easily be transferred from VCR to DVD player production.

Economies of scope are often the motive for mergers or joint ventures involving companies making different products, in some cases at different vertical levels of the same industry. Perhaps most typically, they involve mergers between software providers and distributors or exhibitors. Examples include the $10 billion acquisition of Paramount by Viacom, whose interests include cable systems and extensive international cable and satellite channels (e.g., MTV), and Disney's purchase of Miramax, the independent film distributor, and its $19 billion takeover of Capital Cities/ABC, a U.S. TV network. The $158 billion merger of AOL and Time Warner in 2000 was also of this type.

Some mergers have involved purchases by Japanese hardware producers of Hollywood producers. Sony Corporation acquired Columbia Pictures, and Matsushita acquired MCA (Universal). No doubt prominent in Sony's motives was a desire to ensure software for its own hardware standards; software shortages had contributed to Sony's Betamax video standard losing out to the rival VHS standard. When Matsushita acquired MCA (Universal) in 1990, Matsushita bought not only a Hollywood studio and its extensive film library but also MCA Records. Economies of scope probably exist between movies and music recordings, as the soundtracks of some films earn more revenue than that obtained from the box office.

Other acquisitions serve to expand the company's activities into other media that are competing for the advertising dollar or the consumers' entertainment dollar. Thus, Murdoch's News Corporation, traditionally in publishing, has expanded into television, notably satellite TV channels such as BSkyB in the United Kingdom and Star TV, based in Hong Kong. In 1985, the corporation purchased a Hollywood studio, Twentieth Century Fox, for $575 million. To ensure a continuing source of very popular live sports television programming, Murdoch bought the Los Angeles Dodgers and, in September 1998, bid over £623 for Manchester United. (The takeover bid was blocked by the U.K. government in 1999.) *Time,* another entity that started life as a publishing company, although it had already spread into cable and satellite, acquired Warner Bros., the Hollywood studio, in 1990 for $14 billion to form Time-Warner. In 2000, the Canadian broadcaster CanWest Global Communications acquired most of Hollinger's Canadian newspapers.

Some recent merger activity is related to the convergence, resulting from digital technology, between television, cable, telecommunications, and computers. For example, convergence permits cable companies to offer local telephone services (about half of U.K. cable subscribers now use cable for local telephone services) and telecommunications companies to deliver video on demand and related television services. The ability to be able to offer a comprehensive bundle of services and to spread risks by not being totally committed to one method of distribution has sparked the merger interest between telecommunications companies and cable companies in the United States. Early in 1999, AT&T acquired Tele-Communications Inc. (TCI), a large cable TV company, for $55 billion. In May 1999, it outbid Comcast (a cable company) to purchase MediaOne Group, another large cable company, for $54 billion. With this purchase, AT&T became the biggest cable company in the United States. A Canadian example illustrating the effects of convergence between telecommunications, broadcasting, and computers is the year 2000 C$2.3 billion acquisition by BCE, Canada's largest telecommunications company, of CTV, Canada's largest private television network. BCE's primary motive seems to have been to obtain content for Sympatico, its Internet portal.

While economies of scope, often described by the buzzword "synergies," are the motive for many media mergers, it is not obvious that cost savings are always achieved. Obviously, Matsushita was disappointed with the results of its acquisition of MCA (Universal), as, after a few years, it sold 80% of its stake. With some mergers, not only do the expected synergies fail to occur, but merging different company cultures introduces new problems. The merger between AOL and Time Warner in 2000 to form

AOL–Time Warner Inc. is now widely regarded as unsuccessful, and the September 2003 decision to change the name back to Time Warner Inc. can be regarded as an acknowledgment of this.

5.4.8 Learning Curve

As companies gain experience making a product, they often learn on the job. For example, employees (both managerial and shop floor) gain familiarity and expertise in the task they are performing, and small design modifications may be made that facilitate production. Where such learning occurs, average cost decreases with cumulative output, as it is the cumulative output that is an indicator of the experience making the product. *The learning curve,* sometimes called *the experience curve,* thus relates average cost to cumulative output.

Figure 5.5 shows a learning curve. When cumulative output doubles from Q^* to $2Q^*$, average cost decreases from AC_1 to AC_2. The learning progress ratio is AC_2/AC_1, so learning has taken place if this ratio is less than one. Empirical studies suggest a fairly typical ratio is around 0.80, indicating a reduction in average cost of approximately 20% as output is doubled. This will vary according to the nature of the product, however. The learning will be greatest, and the learning progress ratio least, for complex, sophisticated, labor-intensive products. For very simple manufactured products, learning may be minimal.

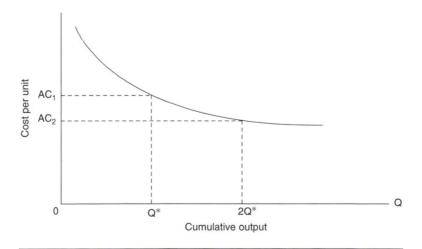

Figure 5.5   The Learning Curve

Note: AC indicates average cost; Q, cumulative output.

We would expect new media products, computer animation, and the development of computer games to be subject to considerable learning benefits. For example, Disney's movie *Dinosaur*, released in 2000, was the first time that the company meshed computer-generated images with film of real-life backgrounds and landscapes. Inevitably, the lessons the company learned from making this movie will decrease the cost of producing the next similar movie, and so on.

It is important to be clear about the distinction between the learning curve and increasing returns to scale. Suppose a company is producing 1000 units of a product per month and that by May 2001 it has been producing at this output rate for 2 years. The company's average cost at this time is $100. Returns to scale would determine the average cost of producing more or less than 1000 units in May 2001. For simplicity, we will assume constant returns to scale, so average cost would still be $100 if output in the month were 900 or 1100 units. By May 2003, cumulative output will have doubled from 24,000 units to 48,000 units. If we assume that the learning progress ratio is 0.70, then average cost in May 2003 will be $70. But, because of the constant returns to scale, if output in May 2003 is 900 or 1100 rather than 1000 units, average cost would still be $70. Between the two dates, learning would have caused the long-run average cost curve, relating average cost to the monthly output rate, to shift downwards by $30.

5.4.9 Transaction Costs and the Organization of Production

A transaction entails an exchange of a good or service. Many transactions take place in markets, but there are costs associated with finding someone to do business with, of reaching an agreement on price and terms, and of enforcing the resulting contract. These costs tend to be particularly high if both parties do not have easy and equal access to information concerning the transaction. Transactions also take place within organizations. These transactions involve costs too, but in some cases, the costs of coordination and enforcement may be less than for market transactions. Ronald Coase (1937) made transaction costs the basis for a theory explaining why firms exist and what transfers and activities take place within them.

Firms face "make or buy" decisions; that is, they produce within the firm or buy from an external supplier. For example, the success of computer animation in the 1991 movie *Terminator 2: Judgment Day* and the development of user-friendly, reasonably priced software caused many animation studios and boutiques to conclude that their animation artists needed computer skills. The decision that arose was whether to provide skill training internally or buy such training in the form of college or other external courses or programs. Initially, most chose to train within the organization, but this has changed to a primary reliance on external training through a market transaction.

In the 1930s and early 1940s, the movie industry operated through large, vertically integrated studios in Hollywood employing industrial mass production methods similar to those employed by Henry Ford. Since 1945,

> Activities that had been within the studio framework gradually moved to the external market. Eventually, this meant the complete end of the "term contract," under which writers, actors, and skilled production people worked exclusively for one studio for a specified period of time. It was replaced by a film-to-film contract. (Christopherson & Storper, 1986, p. 309)

Studios now maintain a very lean operation, bringing together teams of specialists as needed to perform the various required production functions. Many expect the role of the studios to continue shrinking, with the studio slowly "assuming the role of a sort of super banker, marshalling resources, arraying projects and orchestrating the negotiations" (Bart, 1999).

The two examples cited both exhibited a move away from internal transactions to market transactions. This is typical of a more general trend in the economy that can be expected to continue as transactions costs associated with acquiring, processing, storing, and transmitting digital information progressively decline with the improvement in compression technologies and the expansion of Internet bandwidth. The substantial drop in transaction costs between buyers and sellers who are geographically separated can be expected to lead to a movement away from production centralized near important creative centers or distribution centers, such as Hollywood, to more widely scattered locations providing unique character or creative convenience, such as Queensland (Australia) or British Columbia (Canada). There is a potential for disintermediation (doing away with the use of a middle man) as producers and consumers are more able to economically conduct transactions directly without the intervening role of distributors and exhibitors. Amazon.com and other virtual bookstores have already revolutionized book retailing. Napster and its successors have enabled people (illegally and legally) to share and download music in the MP3 format. Movies over the Internet are becoming a reality. Consumers with strong preferences are able to seek out the specific products or services they wish to acquire and complete a low-cost economic transaction, reducing the power of the traditional hierarchical distribution channel.

5.5 The Very Long Run

The *very long run* is a period during which the technological possibilities available to the firm change. This change can take the form of a new production technique or a new product. A change requires both invention and innovation. Invention is the act of creating something new. Innovation is development of the idea into a new production technique or new product that works and that can be produced at a cost which makes it viable. An example of invention is the realization that moving pictures could be captured and then transmitted over the air to a screen in people's homes and the theoretical underpinnings of how this could be achieved. An example of innovation is the development of cameras, transmission equipment, and television receivers that made this a reality.

The days of the accidental invention have largely passed. Most invention and innovation takes place in the research and development (R&D) departments of firms and government organizations and in research laboratories at universities. If universities are involved, it is usually at the invention stage. Research and development is very expensive and will only be undertaken by firms if it is likely to be profitable. The direction such research takes will reflect market signals in the form of current and expected factor and product prices. The R&D that went into the development of computer-generated imagery was primarily motivated by the creative limitations of "traditional" special-effects technology, but it was also influenced by the escalating cost of traditionally shot and edited special effects and stunts.

It is impossible to overemphasize the importance of technological change. This is illustrated by considering the products that we take for granted now but that were not available in, say, 1950. There was no color TV, no cable TV, no direct-to-home satellite TV, no VCRs, no DVD players, no high-definition television, no camcorders, no cassette players, no compact disk players, no home computers, no video games, no cell phones, no modems, no Internet, and so on. These are all new products, but the development of new techniques has been just as important. Earlier in the chapter, we mentioned the introduction of computer animation. The Sony Handicam has transformed news reporting from the field, as well as some types of documentary shooting. One individual can act as reporter, producer, and cameraperson, whereas a few years ago a whole television crew would have been necessary. Robot cameras have similarly reduced staffing needs in news studios. Musical instrument digital interface technology, which eases the transfer of sounds to computers, is transforming the music industry. Recording quality that a few years ago could only be produced in a professional recording studio with $500,000 of equipment can now be produced in a home basement with a top of the line Macintosh computer and software packages for $10,000 or so (Waxer, 1998).

5.6 Summary

We assume that firms wish to maximize profits. This requires that production be economically efficient; that is, the method used produces any given output for the least possible total cost.

Production opportunities, ways of combining inputs to change output, differ according to the length of time considered. The short run is a period of insufficient length to change the input level of factors such as capital equipment and plant; these factors are called fixed factors. Production and cost in the short run is governed by the Law of Diminishing Returns, which states that after a certain level of input of the variable factor, each additional unit of the variable factor, employed in conjunction with a fixed quantity of another factor, adds less to total product or output than the previous unit. This law explains why short-run marginal cost, the change in total cost for a one-unit change in output, increases after a certain output level. Given the relationship between marginal and average costs, the law is also the reason for the increasing portion of the U-shaped average variable cost and average total cost curves usually drawn.

The long run is a period of sufficient length that all factors of production are variable, but the state of technology is given. In the long run, the factor mix selected will be that which results in the last dollar spent on each input yielding the same addition to total output. The optimal mix thus depends on relative factor prices, as well as factor productivity (indicated by the marginal product). It is the price of switches and routers relative to lines that explains why the Internet uses packet switching rather than circuit networks.

A key long-term concept is returns to scale. We have increasing returns to scale if an X% increase in all inputs increases output by more than X%, constant returns to scale if it increases output by X%, and decreasing returns to scale if it increases output by less than X%. The shape of the long-run average (and marginal) cost curve depends on the returns to scale. Most media goods exhibit increasing returns to scale (also known as economies of scale) because the cost of the second copy and additional copies is very much less than the cost of producing the first copy. This helps explain why the United States can sell television programs to foreign countries for as little as $100. This cost structure is fundamental in understanding the origins of the Canada–United States magazine trade dispute. Similarly, it provides a motive for coproduction of television programs and films. Mergers between companies making the same product, for example Columbia Pictures and TriStar Pictures, permit economies of scale to be realized.

Economies of scope exist if the total cost of producing two (or more) products within the same firm is less than producing them separately in two (or more) nonrelated firms. This occurs when products are jointly produced or where there are factors that are shared by the processes used to make different products. This explains why most studios produce both movies and television programs. Economies of scope provide a motive for many mergers, such as that between AT&T and TCI, between companies making different products.

A learning curve may apply in the long run. As the cumulative output of a company increases, on the job learning may occur, and average cost decreases as a consequence. Such learning benefits are no doubt significant for new media products, such as computer animation and the development of computer games.

A transaction (the exchange of a good or service) bears costs whether the transaction is made through the market or within an organization. We noted a general trend away from internal transactions to market transactions. The Hollywood studios provide an example. The trend to market transactions is largely a result of the improvements in communications technology that have stimulated the movement of many business-to-business transactions to the Internet.

The very long run is a period during which the technological possibilities available to the firm change. Technological change results from invention, the act of creating something new, and innovation, the development of an idea into a new production technique or new product. A comparison of the consumer electronic products available now compared to what was available in 1950 illustrates the importance of technological change.

6

Revenue, Profit, Risk, and Managerial Decisions

Should a broadcaster schedule expensive programming with lots of audience appeal or cheaper programming? How should Bell Atlantic have decided which supplier to award with a $3 billion order for digital switches in the late 1980s? Why have U.S. broadcasters been reluctant to use the additional spectrum provided for a high definition television signal for this purpose rather than for multiple new analogue signals? How should a decision be made as to whether to establish a small Internet-based business? How can a movie make $100 million at the box office without making a profit? Why are many media industries inherently risky, and how do producers and distributors try to reduce this risk? Why are block booking and blind bidding selling practices attractive for film distributors? The economic concepts and managerial decision techniques explored in this chapter will enable us to answer these questions or explain how the decisions should be approached.

In this chapter, we begin the examination of firm and industry behavior, a topic encompassed by the *Theory of the Firm*. Firms are assumed to maximize profits. Profits are equal to total revenue minus total cost. Thus a firm chooses to produce at the output level or price that maximizes the difference between total revenue and total cost. In the last chapter, we examined how cost varied with output. The first topic we examine in this chapter is how revenue varies with output and price. By bringing together the revenue with the cost side examined in the last chapter, we are able to explore the level of output and price that maximizes profits and the use of marginal analysis in determining these. Incremental analysis and discounting are introduced as managerial techniques firms can use to identify the most profitable option in real-world situations. We examine in detail how the economist measures profit, how this differs from the accountant's concept of profit, and the implications for decision making by firms. Two managerial decision techniques, incremental analysis and net present value, are explored. The implications of risk for business decisions are considered.

6.1 Revenue

We need to distinguish between total revenue, average revenue, and marginal revenue, and examine the relationship between these revenue concepts. We will do this assuming that each unit of output sold is sold at the same price.

Total revenue (TR) is equal to the quantity (Q) sold of a good or service multiplied by the price (P) at which it is sold:

$$TR = Q \times P$$

Average revenue (AR) is the revenue per unit of output. It equals total revenue divided by quantity:

$$AR = TR/Q$$

But as $TR = Q \times P$, substituting for TR in this equation gives $AR = Q \times P/Q = P$. Hence AR is equal to price. This relationship implies that a firm's demand curve is also its average revenue curve. The demand curve shows the quantity demanded at any given price. The average revenue curve shows the average revenue, equal to price, for any quantity demanded. Hence a firm's demand curve often has an AR label attached to it as well as a D.

Marginal revenue (MR) is the change in total revenue resulting from the output of one more unit of the good or service:

$$MR = \Delta TR/\Delta Q$$

where ΔTR is the change in total revenue and ΔQ is the (one unit) change in output.

If the firm can sell the additional unit at an unchanged price, then the demand curve for the firm is horizontal, and marginal revenue equals price. As we will see later, however, this only holds for perfect competition, a very competitive situation in which many companies sell an identical product.

More usually, the firm faces a negatively sloped demand curve, which implies that price must be reduced to increase the number of units sold. In these cases, marginal revenue is less than the price of all units beyond the first. This will be illustrated by the numerical example that follows for the Forthright Company.

Another relationship between total revenue and marginal revenue is that the total revenue for a given output is the sum or the addition of the marginal revenues for each unit comprising this output:

$$TR = \Sigma\ MR$$

where Σ is the summation sign.

Table 6.1 shows the TR, AR, and MR for the Forthright Company. Given the relationship between price and quantity demanded per day, indicated by the numbers in the first two rows (these numbers are for the demand curve $Q = 5 - P$), TR is calculated as $P \times Q$, AR as TR/Q, and MR as $\Delta TR/\Delta Q$.

The AR and MR curves for the Forthright Company are plotted in Figure 6.1. As the marginal revenue of \$4 for the first unit relates to a change in output from 0 to 1, it is plotted midway between 0 and 1, and so on for the other units. MR is less than price because to sell an extra unit, the price must be reduced not only for the additional unit but for the previous units that could have been sold at the higher price. The change in total revenue is thus the price received for the additional unit less the revenue foregone from selling the previous units at a lower price. For example, to sell the

Table 6.1   Revenues for the Forthright Company

P	5	4	3	2	1	0
Q	0	1	2	3	4	5
TR	0	4	6	6	4	0
AR		4	3	2	1	
MR		4	2	0	-2	-4

Note: AR indicates average revenue; MR, marginal revenue; P, price; Q, quantity demanded; TR, total revenue.

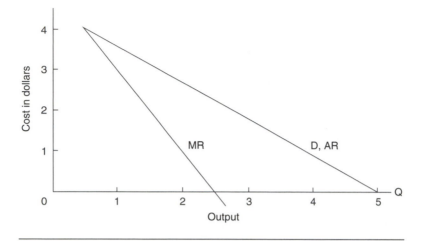

Figure 6.1   Revenue Curves for the Forthright Company

Note: AR indicates average revenue; D, demand; MR, marginal revenue; Q, quantity.

second unit, the price must be reduced from $4 to $3. Three dollars is gained, the price received for the second unit, but $1 is lost from selling the first unit for $1 less. The net addition to revenue is thus $2. The greater the number of previous units (the lower the starting price), the greater the difference between P and MR.

In chapter 2, we noted that the price elasticity of demand (η) varies along a linear (straight-line) demand curve. We also showed that a decrease in price resulted in an increase in total revenue if demand is price elastic, no change in total revenue if there is unitary elasticity, and a decrease in total revenue if the price is inelastic. It follows that if marginal revenue is positive, the demand is price elastic; if it is zero, there is unitary elasticity; and if marginal revenue is negative, then demand is price inelastic. Calculations of price elasticity for the Forthright Company confirm this: $\eta = 9.00$ for a price change from $5 to $4, 2.33 for a price change from $4 to $3, 1.00 for a price change from $3 to $2, 0.43 for a price change from $2 to $1, and 0.01 for a price change from $1 to $0.

A firm faced by a negatively sloped demand curve can make a price decision or an output decision; it cannot make both. That is because the price selected will determine the quantity that can be sold, or the output selected will determine the price at which this volume can be sold. Usually, the active decision firms make is with respect to price.

6.2 Identifying the Profit Maximizing Output and Price: Marginal Analysis

Now that we understand how revenue varies with output and price, if we combine this knowledge with that from chapter 5 on how costs vary with output, we will be able to explore the level of output and price that maximizes profit. In Table 6.2, we have added cost information assumed for the Forthright Company to the revenues reported in Table 6.1. Given the assumed level of total variable costs (TVC) in row six and total fixed costs (TFC) of $1 in row seven, total cost (TC = TFC + TVC), average variable cost (AVC = TVC/Q) and marginal cost (MC = ΔTVC or ΔTC for a one-unit change in output) are calculated. Note that as there is a fixed cost, we are examining a short-run example. Also, as marginal cost increases throughout, this is a case in which the Law of Diminishing Returns sets in immediately.

The most straightforward way to determine the profit maximizing output and price is to calculate the profit directly as total revenue (TR) minus total cost (TC). The results of this calculation are shown in the last row. Profits are maximized at $2 by producing either 1 or 2 units, consistent with a price of $4 or $3, respectively. This is shown graphically in Figure 6.2. Profits, denoted by π, are

Table 6.2   The Forthright Company's Profit Maximizing Price and Output

P	5	4	3	2	1	0
Q	0	1	2	3	4	5
TR	0	4	6	6	4	0
AR		4	3	2	1	0
MR		4	2	0	−2	−4
TVC	0	1	3	6	10	15
TFC	1	1	1	1	1	1
TC	1	2	4	7	11	16
AVC		1	1.50	2	2.50	3
ATC		2	2	2.33	2.75	3.20
MC		1	2	3	4	5
Profit	−1	2	2	−1	−7	−16

Note: AR indicates average revenue; ATC, average total cost; AVC, average variable cost; MC, marginal cost; MR, marginal revenue; P, price; Q, quantity; TC, total cost; TFC, total fixed cost; TR, total revenue; TVC, total variable cost.

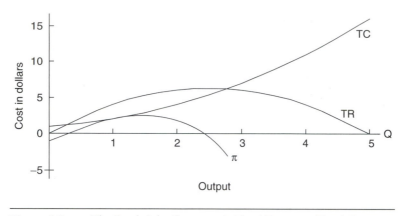

Figure 6.2   The Forthright Company's Total Revenue, Total Cost, and Profit

Note: Q indicates quantity; TC, total cost; TR, total revenue; π, profit.

maximized at the output level, where TR > TC and the vertical distance between the two curves is greatest.

One drawback with Figure 6.2 is that price is not explicitly shown. Yet it is price that is typically the active decision. The Forthright Company will maximize profits by setting a price of $4 or $3. It is partly to conduct the analysis explicitly in terms of price as well as output and partly because the marginal approach facilitates the use of calculus (a mathematical technique that does not concern us in this text) that economists usually employ the alternative marginal approach to identifying the profit maximizing output and price.

Marginal analysis compares the additional revenue (MR) and additional cost (MC) of producing an extra unit of output. If MR > MC, the unit adds to profits and should be produced; if MR = MC, the firm is indifferent to production of this unit; if MR < MC, the firm should not produce it, as to do so would decrease profits. As we have seen, MR either decreases with output, if the demand curve of the firm is negatively sloped, or is constant if the firm's demand curve is horizontal. Marginal cost in the short run, at least after a certain output level, increases with output because of diminishing increments to total output as more units of the variable factor are employed in conjunction with the fixed factor (the Law of Diminishing Return). Thus, typically, MR > MC up to a certain output level when MR = MC, and beyond this, MR < MC. The profit maximizing decision is to set a price such that the quantity demanded will equal the output, where MR = MC.

In the context of the Forthright Company, the first unit should be produced because the additional revenue (MR) is $4 and additional cost (MC) is $2. The firm would be indifferent to producing the second unit, as the additional revenue of $2 is equal to the additional cost, and the third (and certainly the forth and fifth) should not be produced, as the additional revenue is $0 and additional cost $3. Thus the Forthright Company should select a price of $4 or $3.

Figure 6.3 shows the Forthright Company's profit maximizing decision in terms of marginal analysis, represented by the MR and MC curves. Again, marginal data is plotted midway between the output units shown on the horizontal axis. Only the positive section of the MR curve is shown, because a firm will never wittingly produce in the negative portion. Also shown is the AR curve, which, as explained earlier, is also the demand curve (D) and thus enables us to identify the profit maximizing price.

Notice that MR = MC at an output of 1.5 and a price of $3.50. Because this is a discrete case, we are assuming that half a unit cannot be produced. The interpretation is that the firm should sell one unit at a price of $4 or two units at a price of $3.

However, in diagrams of this type, it is usual to make the assumption that products are infinitely divisible, like oat bran in a bulk food bin at the supermarket. Then the profit maximizing price

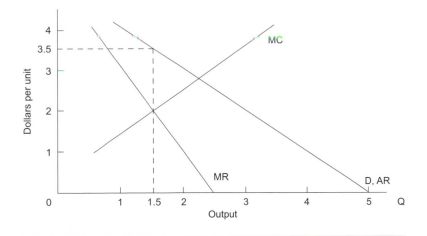

Figure 6.3   The Forthright Company and Profit Maximization

Note: AR indicates average revenue; D, demand; MC, marginal cost; MR, marginal revenue; Q, quantity.

and output is exactly that shown by MR = MC. In any case, the distinction between the discrete and the infinitely divisible cases almost disappears when output is large.

The typical diagram drawn is illustrated by Figure 6.4. This diagram also shows a U-shaped MC curve, which implies increasing marginal product for the variable factor prior to the input level where the Law of Diminishing Returns kicks in. Profits are maximized at price P* and output Q*, where MR = MC. (Note that with a U-shaped MC curve, it is possible that MR = MC at two output levels, although this is not the case in Figure 6.4. If this occurs, profit maximization is found at the larger output, and profit minimization occurs at the smaller output). Also shown are the average total cost (ATC) and average variable cost (AVC) curves. Profit per unit is equal to AR – ATC. As we shall explore later in chapter 8, it is useful to show AVC, as a comparison of AVC with AR is central to a short-run shut-down decision.

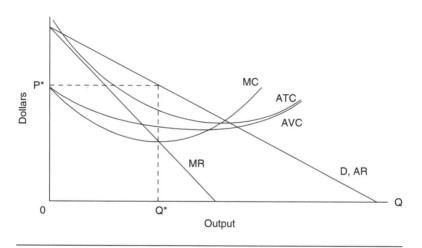

Figure 6.4   Profit Maximizing Price and Output

Note: AR indicates average revenue; ATC, average total cost; AVC, average variable cost; D, demand; MC, marginal cost; MR, marginal revenue; P, price; Q, quantity.

In chapter 5, we noted that Internet transmission of music, text, images, or computer software is made at zero marginal cost. If the marginal cost is zero, then profit is maximized at output Q_1 in Figure 6.5, the output where marginal revenue is also equal to zero. The profit maximizing price is P_1.

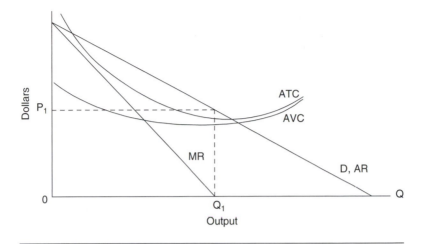

Figure 6.5   Profit Maximizing Price and Output When Marginal Cost
is Zero

Note: AR indicates average revenue; ATC, average total cost; AVC, average variable
cost; D, demand; MC, marginal cost; MR, marginal revenue; P, price; Q, quantity.

6.3 Incremental Analysis

Incremental analysis is a managerial decision technique derived from
marginal analysis. As we have seen, marginal analysis is concerned
with the effect of one-unit changes in output on total revenue and
total cost. Business decisions usually do not fit this mold. Often they
do not involve price and output at all. For example, the decision
could concern whether to replace the firm's existing capital equipment with a new type of capital equipment now available or whether
to introduce a new product. Even where price and output are
involved, one unit or even small changes in output may not be an
option. A television program production company pitching a drama
or animated series to a broadcasting organization may, if successful,
get a commitment for six or 13 episodes. A book publisher deciding
whether to order a reprint of an existing title may be looking at a
minimum print of an additional 500 copies for a scholarly book or
a book of poetry, 1000 for a novel, and 2000 for trade nonfiction.

Incremental analysis can be adopted for all such decisions. It
uses the same basic approach as marginal analysis, as it asks the
same basic question: "What difference does it make?" Incremental

analysis examines a specific decision option by identifying the incremental revenue and incremental cost that would result. The option being evaluated is preferable if

$$\text{Incremental revenue} - \text{incremental cost} > 0$$

where incremental revenue is the change in total revenue relative to the other alternative and incremental cost is the change in total cost relative to the other alternative. The other alternative or base is normally the option of doing nothing—of continuing to operate in the same way as before.

Decisions may involve several alternatives to the status quo. For example, there may be several types of new equipment being considered as a replacement for the existing equipment. In this case, incremental analysis would involve the estimation of incremental revenue minus incremental cost for each of the new alternatives relative to the existing equipment. The alternative with the greatest excess of incremental revenue over incremental cost should be accepted. However, if incremental revenue minus incremental cost is negative for each, the firm should decide to continue to use the existing equipment.

A good way of incorporating the incremental approach is to estimate the cash flows of the firm if the option being evaluated is accepted relative to the cash flows of the firm if the option is rejected. This "with versus without" framework calculates incremental revenue and incremental cost as

Incremental revenue = Cash inflows of the firm if option is accepted – Cash inflows of firm if option is rejected

Incremental cost = Cash outflows of the firm if option is accepted – Cash outflows of firm if option is rejected

Thus another way of expressing the incremental approach is to say an option should be accepted if:

(Cash inflows of the firm if option is accepted – Cash inflows of firm if option is rejected) – (Cash outflows of the firm if option is accepted – Cash outflows of firm if option rejected) > 0

Some decisions, such as those involving durable capital equipment, affect cash flows for a long time (any period longer than

1 year can be thought of as qualifying). If this is so, the incremental approach should entail estimates for each year affected. However, discounting is essential to a comparison of cash flows occurring in different years. Discounting is examined in the next section, 6.4. In section 6.5, we will apply incremental analysis and discounting to an illustrative case study.

Many decisions made by media companies are amenable to incremental analysis. Broadcasters' choice and scheduling of programs, for instance, involves incremental analysis. Suppose a broadcaster plans a 2-hour special beginning at 11:00 p.m. on December 31, 2003, and the choice is between a program that is costly to produce and exhibit and another program that is inexpensive. The expensive program is likely to attract a large audience and associated advertising revenue, whereas the cheap program is likely to attract a small audience and modest advertising revenue. The decision would be based on incremental analysis: The program selected would be that with the greater excess of incremental revenue over incremental cost.

The FCC provided U.S. broadcasters with extra spectrum for the introduction of digital HDTV. The reluctance of the broadcasters to use the spectrum for this purpose rather than multiple additional analogue signals no doubt reflects incremental analysis that shows the latter to be more profitable.

All decisions involving capital equipment should be made using incremental analysis. For example, Shapiro and Varian (1999, p. 105) examined the decision by Bell Atlantic, in the late 1980s, concerning whether to replace its analogue switches with new digital switches and, if so, which digital switch to choose. Three companies, Siemens, Northern Telecom (now Nortel Networks), and AT&T (the division involved was later split off to become Lucent Technologies) could supply digital switches. Bell Atlantic's decision to place the $3 billion order with AT&T would have been based on incremental analysis.

6.4 Discounting and the Time Value of Money

If a decision has implications for the cash flows of a company over a year or more, the time value of money must be taken into account. For example, if a decision involves spending $1000 now and getting back $1550 in 5 years, the firm cannot sum these amounts and conclude it would be better off by $550. This would not be valid, because the $1000 could be invested elsewhere to obtain a return. Foregoing this return is an opportunity cost. Having $1000 now is better than having $1000 in, say, 2 years, and it may be better than having $1550 in 5 years. Whether it is will depend on the return that could be obtained elsewhere at similar risk. Similar risk is stipulated because, as we shall see in section 6.6, the expected return from investments is positively related to risk exposure.

In Table 6.3, we show the value of $1 invested now at 10% interest at different dates in the future and how these values are calculated. Note that today is the end of year 0 or the beginning of year 1, and 1 year's time is the end of year 1 or the beginning of year 2, and so on. The $1.00 invested now, at the end of year 0 (or the beginning of year 1), will earn interest (or a return) of $1.00 \times .10 = 0.10 by the end of year 1, giving a value at the end of year 1 of $1.10. As the interest earned is not withdrawn, this is a compound interest example, with the principal at the beginning of year 2 being $1.10. The interest earned during year 2 on this principal is $1.10 \times .10 = 0.11. The value at the end of year 2 is thus $1.21, which equals $(1.10)^2$. This becomes the principal at the beginning of year 3. There is a pattern here, and we find the value at the end of year 3 is $(1.10)^3$ and the value at the end of year n, where n can take on any value, is $(1.10)^n$.

We are now in a position to consider whether investing $1000 now and getting back $1550 in 5 years' time is a good deal. Suppose the return or interest available elsewhere at similar risk is 10%. At the end of 5 years, $1 will be worth $(1.10)^5$, or $1.61 rounded to the nearest cent, so $1000 will be worth $1000 \times (1.10)^5$, or $1611. Hence, the opportunity to invest $1000 now to obtain $1550 after 5 years should be rejected, as it is not as good as earning a return of 10% elsewhere.

Table 6.3   The Time Value of Money at an Interest Rate of 10%

	Principal (beginning of year)	*+*	*Interest (earned during year)*	*=*	*Future Value (at end of year)*	*Present Value Factor*
Year 1	1.00	+	$1.00 \times .10$	=	1.10	$1/(1.01)$
Year 2	1.10	+	$1.10 \times .10$	=	$1.21 = (1.10)^2$	$1/(1.10)^2$
Year 3	1.21	+	$1.21 \times .10$	=	$1.33 = (1.10)^3$	$1/(1.10)^3$
Year n	$(1.10)^{n-1}$	+	$(1.10)^{n-1} \times .10$	=	$(1.10)^n$	$1/(1.10)^n$

An alternative to comparing the values of a future receipt and the future value of the principal invested elsewhere, as we did just now, is to compare the sum invested and the present value of the future receipt. For example, from the Future Value column in Table 6.3, as the future value of $1.00 at the end of year 3 is $(1.10)^3$, or $1.33, the present value of $1.33 received in 3 years' time must be $1.00. To return to our earlier example, to find the present value of $1550 at the end of year 5, we multiply $1550 by $1/(1.10)^5$, where $1/(1.10)^5$ equals .62092 and is known as the *present value factor*. This calculation, which is called *discounting*, gives $962 (rounded to the nearest dollar). The interpretation is that if $962 were invested at the rate of 10% available elsewhere, it would have a future value of $1550. The opportunity to invest $1000 now to obtain $1550 at the end of 5 years should thus be rejected because the present value of $1550 is less than the $1000 investment. The comparison of the present value of the future cash inflow with the current investment is taken care of by the *net present value* (NPV) criterion. The net present value is the present values of future cash flows minus the initial cost or principal invested. For our example:

$$NPV = 1550/(1.1)^5 - 1000 = -\$38$$

An interpretation is that investing $1000 now to obtain $1550 at the end of 5 years would reduce wealth, in current dollars, by $38.

NPV is an appropriate technique to use to evaluate any decision involving an initial cost outlay and one or more (usually positive) future cash flows. The net cash flow in any year is the incremental cash inflow (revenue) in the year minus the incremental cash out-flow (cost) in the year. All company purchases of durable capital equipment are of this type. The general formulation is as follows:

$$NPV = B_1/(1 + i) + B_2/(1 + i)^2 + B_3/(1 + i)^3 + \ldots + B_n/(1 + i)^n - C$$

where B denotes a net cash flow and the subscript attached denotes the end of the year in which the net cash flow occurs, C is the cost outlay or investment (assumed immediate), and i is the return available elsewhere at similar risk.

We will calculate NPV for a realistic example in the next section. At this stage, we will just note that present value tables exist (refer to http://www.infoUSA.com, or they can often be found at the back of accounting and finance textbooks) that calculate the present value of $1 for a range of combinations of interest rates and years. However, these tables are now largely obsolete, as computer spreadsheets, such as Excel, have built-in present value and NPV functions.

6.5 Economic Profit Versus Accounting Profit

We will define economic profit and accounting profit and then examine these definitions to see how the economist's concept of profit differs from that of the accountant:

Economic profit = Total revenue − Total economic costs

Accounting profit = Total revenue − Total accounting costs

There is no difference in view concerning revenue. The difference arises over what constitutes a cost. Thus the first step is to define what constitutes economic costs and what constitutes accounting costs.

Economic costs = Explicit costs + Implicit costs

Accounting costs = Explicit costs + Accounting depreciation

Explicit costs are costs of factors of production that are paid for in the period they are employed. Explicit costs involve a money transaction, with funds flowing from the firm to the owner of the factor. These costs include the salaries or wages paid to hire labor, the expenditure on raw materials used in the production process, the cost of leasing computers and vehicles, and so on. Explicit costs are recognized by both economists and accountants.

Accounting depreciation is a method accountants use to spread the historic cost of acquiring a long-lived capital asset over time. For each type of asset, there is a conventional depreciation rate. Suppose Bruce of the Bruce Film Studio buys a videocamera for $5000. The accounting convention may be to depreciate this class of asset at 20% on a straight-line basis; that is, write off one fifth of the original purchase price in each of the 5 years. In this case, the accounting depreciation would be $1000 per year for 5 years. Accounting depreciation is included as a cost by accountants but not economists.

Economic cost is made up of explicit costs plus implicit costs. If using a resource or factor in one way precludes an alternative use, the resource's value in the next best use is an opportunity cost. Opportunity costs that are not matched by accounting entries are called implicit costs. Implicit costs include economic depreciation, normal profit, and other imputed opportunity costs.

Economic depreciation is the decline in the value of long-lived capital equipment over time. This decline results from wear and tear and, in some cases, obsolescence. In any given year, the economic depreciation is the decline in market value during the year; that is, the purchase price (or resale price available if the asset is not new) at the beginning of the year minus the resale price available at the end of the year. Returning to our videocamera example, suppose Bruce purchased it 2 years ago. During the first year, a videocamera manufacturer came out with an innovation that led to introduction of a new model that was smaller, lighter, and provided a better quality picture. As a consequence, Bruce's videocamera suffered obsolescence (as well as the usual wear and tear) and could be resold for only $2000 at the end of the first year. Economic depreciation was thus $3000 in the first year. In the second year, there was no further breakthrough, but normal wear and tear meant the price at which the videocamera could be resold at the end of the year fell to $1600. Economic depreciation was $400 in the second year. As this example illustrates, there is no reason to suppose that economic depreciation equals accounting depreciation.

At the beginning of the second year (end of year 1), the economic depreciation for the second year is an opportunity cost, as the decline in value of $400 could have been avoided by selling the videocamera for $2000 and using the proceeds for some alternative purpose. However, in contrast, by the beginning of the second year, the economic depreciation for the first year is a *sunk cost*. A sunk cost is a cost incurred in the past that involves no current opportunity cost. Bruce may deeply regret buying the videocamera new for $5000 and suffering economic depreciation of $3000 during the year, but this is now a bygone and cannot be retrieved. Sunk costs are irrelevant to current decisions. At the beginning of the second year, Bruce's decision about whether to retain the videocamera for another year should not be influenced by this past economic depreciation.

Normal profit is the return owners could have obtained by investing their funds elsewhere at similar risk. It is an opportunity cost because investment in the firm entails foregoing the return available from the best alternative.

Other imputed costs vary from situation to situation, but two common ones are implicit salary and implicit rental rate. If a person sets up and operates a small business, he or she foregoes the opportunity to work elsewhere and receive a salary from that employment. This is an economic cost associated with the operations of the small business. Similarly, if the person owns a physical asset (for example, a truck), using this asset within the business precludes the opportunity to rent or lease the asset to someone else.

Transfer payments are the value assigned to products or services provided by one division of a vertically integrated company to another division of the same company. This type of payment is another source of difference between economic and accounting treatment. The relevant cost to the economist is the opportunity cost, so the value attached should be the price that would have to be paid to an external supplier of the product or service. To the accountant, it is the actual payment made, but this price can be manipulated to serve the interest of the company as a whole. Major Hollywood studios provide a case in point. They are vertically integrated and are in distribution as well as production. It is the profits of the studio as a whole that are important, and if the contract of the director or a lead actor stipulates a share of the profit on the production, then it may be better that the distribution arm realizes all the profits on a particular project. Prindle (1993, pp. 22-23) provides an example. The worldwide box office receipts for *Coming to America* were $250 million. The theaters retained half of this, leaving Paramount, which produced and distributed the film, with revenues of $125 million. Nevertheless, the production arm of Paramount showed a net loss of $15 million after deducting production costs of $57 million, distribution and marketing costs of $36 million, interest of $5 million, and (and this is the key) a distribution fee of $42 million to its own distribution arm.

Multinational companies have another reason for distorting transfer payments. This is to reduce taxes by reporting more of the company's accounting profit, on which tax is based, in subsidiaries located in low-tax countries.

To illustrate the calculation of economic profit and how it differs from accounting profit, consider the case of Carol, who is evaluating whether to set up a small Internet-related business. Her situation is as follows. She is confident that she has the expertise necessary because she has good experience working for the university, where she currently earns $45,000 per year. Establishing the business would involve spending $90,000 on computer equipment. She has the $90,000 available because she recently inherited this sum, together with office space that would be suitable. The $90,000 is currently invested in liquid financial assets (assets that can be easily and quickly sold), yielding an expected return of 10%. The office space is vacant, but Carol knows that office space is in short supply, and similar space in the area rents for $15,000 per year. The accounting convention in the jurisdiction where Carol resides is to depreciate computer equipment at a rate of 33.3% on a straight-line basis. The potential vendor of the computer equipment tells Carol that, if things do not go well, he would be willing to buy the equipment back for $55,000 after 1 year. Besides working full-time herself in the business, Carol would have to hire two assistants, each at $30,000 per year. Other expenses for software, office supplies, and utilities are $18,400 per year. Carol expects to bring in annual revenues of $185,000 from supplying this service.

Carol's explicit costs are:

Salaries to assistants	$60,000
Software, supplies, and utilities	$18,400
Total explicit costs	$78,400

Accounting cost is explicit costs plus accounting depreciation. Accounting depreciation is 33.3% of $90,000, or $30,000 annually. Carol's annual accounting cost is thus:

Total explicit costs	$78,400
Accounting depreciation	$30,000
Accounting cost	$108,400

Economic cost is explicit costs plus economic depreciation plus normal profit plus other imputed costs. We will calculate economic cost for the first year of Carol's proposed business. The economic depreciation is the decline in market value of the computer equipment. The equipment is to be bought for $90,000 and could be sold back to the vendor at the end of the year for $55,000. Unless there is reason to suppose Carol could get a better resale price elsewhere, economic depreciation is thus $35,000.

Carol expects a return of 10% on the $90,000 invested in financial assets. This amounts to $9000 in the first year. If she sells these financial assets to invest the $90,000 in buying computer equipment for her business, she foregoes this $9000. Assuming the risk of investing in her business is the same as the risk associated with her financial assets, the normal profit is $9000.

If Carol operates her own business, she will have to give up her university job and forego her employment salary of $45,000. Her implicit salary cost is hence $45,000. Similarly, if she uses the office space she owns, she foregoes an opportunity to rent it out for $15,000. This is the implicit rental cost.

Carol's economic cost for the first year is thus:

Explicit costs	$78,400
Economic depreciation	$35,000
Normal profit	$9,000
Implicit salary cost	$45,000
Implicit rental cost	$15,000
Economic cost	$182,400

As total revenue is $185,000, the alternative profit figures are:

Economic profit = $185,000 – $182,400 = $2600

Accounting profit = $185,000 – $108,400 = $76,600

There is a difference of $74,000. Economists would say that the new business is only just profitable; accountants would say it looks lucrative. The difference would have been smaller if circumstances had been somewhat different. If Carol had not received her inheritance, she would have had to borrow $90,000 to invest in computer equipment. If she had borrowed at 10%, the interest payment would be $9000. As this would involve a transfer of funds, it would be an explicit expense and, as such, recognized as an accounting cost. Also, she would not have owned suitable office space and would have to rent office space at $15,000; this would again have been an explicit cost.

The economic concept of cost is the one that makes sense when the purpose is to make decisions on the basis of profit. If economic profit is positive, then Carol should go ahead with her new business, as she will be better off. Accounting profit is not a reliable guide in this respect. For example, suppose the university learns that Carol is about to leave their employment, and this makes them realize how much they value her contribution. To try and persuade her to stay, they offer her a salary of $56,000, an $11,000 pay raise. This would increase the economic cost associated with operating her own business by $11,000 and lead to economic profit in the first year being –$8400. If she is making the decision on purely monetary grounds, Carol should now reject the new business and stay in employment with the university. Accounting profit would be a misleading guide, as it would still be $76,600.

However, there is one difficulty associated with Carol using economic profit in the first year as the basis of her decision. Economic profit may differ from year to year. We have already seen that there is no reason to suppose economic depreciation will be the same each year. Other costs and revenue may also vary. For example, Carol may believe that she will have to increase the salaries of her employees by $3000 each at the end of the first year. Depending on the economic depreciation during the second and third years, this might result in a negative economic profit in the second year or third year or both. What does she do when faced with these conflicting signals? In fact, we laid the groundwork for the solution in the last section: Any decision affecting cash flows over a period of a year or more should be based on NPV.

To calculate the NPV for the decision to set up her own business, Carol will have to estimate her revenue and costs for years 2 and 3 in addition to year 1. A 3-year horizon is chosen because the computer equipment is expected to have a 3-year life. The NPV calculation will actually indicate whether she should invest the $90,000 in this capital equipment, but this is equivalent to setting up her business.

Let us suppose that Carol believes that revenue and economic costs (omitting economic depreciation) will remain unchanged in years 2 and 3 and that she believes the computer equipment will have a zero resale value at the end of the 3 years. To calculate NPV, we have to make two adjustments to the economic costs identified to obtain the net cash flow. First we ignore annual economic depreciation. The reason for this is that NPV allows for the economic depreciation over the life of the capital equipment rather than on a year-by-year basis. It does this by deducting the purchase price when the asset is bought—this is the initial cost (C)—and then adding any resale value at the end of the asset life. Second, the normal profit is not included as an annual cash outflow because the discounting process itself allows for the time value of money. Adding these two items (amounting to $44,000) to annual economic profit (of $2600) gives annual net cash flows of $46,600 for each of the 3 years. The NPV, given an alternative investment opportunity at similar risk of 10%, is

$$NPV = 46,600/(1.1) + 46,600/(1.1)^2 + 46,600/(1.1)^3 - 90,000 = \$25,887$$

Carol should set up her own business because, by doing so, she is $25,887 better off (in today's dollars) over the 3-year horizon. Another way of looking at it is that if the university wanted Carol to stay in its employment for the next 3 years and offered her an immediate one-time bonus to stay, the bonus would have to be at least $25,887 to make it worth her while.

The method we used of adjusting economic cost and profit to arrive at annual net cash flows (NCFs) was somewhat cumbersome. The easiest way to identify the NCFs is using the incremental approach of comparing the "with" and "without" options. For Carol, the "with" option is with her new business, and the "without" option is remaining in employment at the university. Table 6.4 shows this approach to determining the net cash flows for each of the years 1 through 3. The table is largely self-explanatory, but we will illustrate by discussing two of the items. In row 2, salaries are paid (negative cash flow) by Carol to assistants in the "with" business option (shown in column 2) but not the "without" business option. The component of the net cash flow attributable to this item is "with" minus "without" and equals –$60,000. In row 5, the cash flow Carol receives from owning her own office space is zero for the "with" business option because she will use the space for her business. The cash flow is $15,000 for her "without" business option because under these circumstances she can receive $15,000 from renting the space out. The "with-without" is thus –$15,000. In the last row, the "with-without" cash flows are summed to give the annual net cash flow of $46,600. If the years had differed in respect to any of the items, the net cash flow would have to be calculated in this way for each year. The net cash flow for the end of year 0 is, of course, the initial cost.

Changes in estimates or assumptions are easily handled by recalculating the NCFs and reapplying the NPV formula. For example,

Table 6.4 The Incremental Approach to Identifying Carol's Net Cash Flow From Her Business

	"With" Cash Flow	*"Without" Cash Flow*	*"With-Without" Net Cash Flow*
Revenue from business	185,000	0	185,000
Salaries paid to assistants	−60,000	0	−60,000
Software, supplies, and utilities	−18,400	0	−18,400
Carol's university salary	0	45,000	−45,000
Rent received from owned office space	0	15,000	−15,000
Annual net cash flow			46,600

if Carol believes she will have to increase the salary of both of her assistants by $3000 at the beginning of the second year, then paid salaries will increase to $66,000 for years 2 and 3 and NCF will decrease to $40,600. Hence

$$NPV = 46,600/(1.1) + 40,600/(1.1)^2 + 40,600/(1.1)^3 - 90,000 = \$16,421$$

NPV is still positive, so Carol should still set up her business.

Another alternative scenario we introduced earlier is that of the university, where Carol is currently employed, increasing her salary to $56,000 to try to persuade her to stay. This would decrease her NCFs from her business to $35,600 for years 1 through 3, and

$$NPV = 35,600/(1.1) + 35,600/(1.1)^2 + 35,600/(1.1)^3 - 90,000 = -\$1,468$$

As NPV is negative under this scenario, Carol should not set up her business.

In summary, NPV is the decision tool that is appropriate for any decisions involving cash flows for a year or more. As we have seen, it involves incremental analysis and an appreciation of economic rather than accounting concepts of cost and profit, and it incorporates a method for comparing cash flows occurring in different years. It applies to Carol deciding whether to establish a small Internet-based company, Bell Atlantic in its $3 billion decision on digital switching equipment, U.S. broadcasting organizations assessing whether it is more profitable to use extra spectrum for multiple analogue signals or a single HDTV signal, and film distributors determining the length and sequencing of exhibition windows (for example, cinema, video, and pay TV) for movies. It would not be the basis for a broadcasting organization's decision about what program to air at 11:00 p.m. on December 31, 2003, as this decision does not involve cash flows a year or more apart. Thus NPV incorporates incremental analysis, but incremental analysis for decisions with a very short time horizon does not involve NPV.

6.6 Uncertainty and Risk

When we have referred to the opportunity cost of funds as the return available elsewhere, we specifically added at *similar risk*. This is because people in general are risk averse. They prefer $10,000 with certainty to a .5 (or 50%) probability of $20,000 and a .5 probability of $0. This is even though the latter has the same *expected value*, where the expected value is the sum of each outcome multiplied by its probability of occurrence. For our example, the calculation is

$$\$20,000 \times .5 + \$0 \times .5 = \$10,000$$

Because people are risk averse, a return-risk trade-off is established through supply and demand in financial markets. A higher expected return can only be obtained by accepting a higher risk. An expected return of 10% might be available from a risky growth stock, but a return of only around 3% might be available from risk-free government treasury bills. The difference between the return expected on a risky stock and that on a risk-free asset is known as the *risk premium*. The greater the risk, the larger the risk premium.

6.6.1 Risk and Business Decisions

Carol's Internet-related business would be risky. The net cash flow of $46,600 in each year would itself be an expected value. She would not be certain what sales she would be able to obtain. The cost of software might be more or less than she anticipates, and so on. If Carol believes the risk inherent in her business would be similar to the risky stock with an expected return of 10%, she should use 10% as the discount rate in the NPV calculation (and in the calculation of normal profit, if she wishes to determine economic profit for a given year). The repercussions from using the wrong discount rate can be serious. If we take the last scenario for Carol's business, where the expected net cash flow was $35,600 in each of the 3 years, the NPV was –$1468 using a discount rate of 10%. However, if the risk-free rate of 3% had been used,

$$NPV = 35,600/(1.03) + 35,600/(1.03)^2 + 35,600/(1.03)^3 - 90,000 = \$10,699$$

This NPV is positive, which suggests that Carol should go ahead and establish her business. But this is misleading because Carol would only get an actual return of 9.07% from investing in her new business, whereas, at similar risk, she can enjoy an expected return of 10% from purchasing a growth stock. (Note that the actual return of 9.07% Carol would get from her business is the discount rate that would result in NPV = $0. A rate of return calculated in this way is sometimes known as a *discounted cash flow rate of return* or as an *internal rate of return*.)

Risk depends not only on the type of business—an Internet-related business is likely to be inherently risky—but also on the type of decision. Decisions tend to be more risky the more innovative they are, as the past provides less guidance with respect to the likely outcome. Using new technology to produce a product is risky. New product decisions tend to be very risky unless they involve only minor changes to an existing product. The film industry, television program production industry, music recording, and book publishing are risky lines of business because they involve the continual introduction of a stream of new products. Every new movie and every new book are new products. We will return to these new product decisions in the next section.

Company size can be an important factor in the degree of risk exposure. A rule of thumb in the movie industry is that 1 in 10 movies succeeds, and the huge profits from the single success make up for the losses from the other nine. This gives a big advantage to the Hollywood studios, who produce and distribute some 20 movies per year. Among 20 movies, on average, we would expect two successes. The probability of no successes at all is only 12%. (For there to be no successes, there must be a sequence of 20 movies without a success. Where for each movie the probability of not being successful is 90%, the likelihood, in percentage terms, of a sequence of 20 failures is $0.9^{20} \times 100$.) Compare this to a small film producer making two films a year. The probability of this small producer failing to produce a hit in a given year is 81%. Unless the small producer is lucky and hits the jackpot very early on, in the absence of government support, he or she is unlikely to survive long enough to produce a hit. Even Goldcrest, a British studio that initially had hits in *Chariots of Fire*, *Gandhi*, and *The Killing Fields*, went under after *Revolution* and *Absolute Beginners* bombed (see Eberts & Ilott, 1990). The reduction in risk resulting from the diversifying effect (not having all your eggs in one basket) associated with increased numbers of films, stocks, or whatever the asset is, is called the *portfolio effect*.

The portfolio effect provides an explanation for the attraction of two trade practices used by film distributors, block booking and blind bidding. Block booking occurs when exhibitors are required to take a group of films, including a number of films they would not normally choose to exhibit, to secure rights to some other film that is believed to have high market potential. Blind bidding occurs when exhibitors are required to bid on forthcoming films before they are available for viewing. Despite being outlawed in more than 20 U.S. states, these practices continue because they provide a method of market control for distributors and security of supply for exhibitors. They ensure that the distributor can reach the market with sufficient films each year to be confident that some will be successful. Another reason for the attraction of block booking will be given in chapter 10.

Coproductions reduce risk through a portfolio effect by pooling resources. For a given total budget, coproductions enable a producer to be involved in more projects, thus reducing risk through the diversifying effect of greater numbers.

The portfolio effect, together with risk aversion, explains why there is a market for insurance. Suppose Jill owns a house worth (not including the land) $200,000. If it burns down, an outcome with a probability of .001 (1 in 1000) in any given year, the value would be $0. Thus Jill has a .001 probability of losing $200,000 (the difference between owning a house worth $200,000 and a burnt-down house worth nothing). The expected value of the loss is $200,000 \times .001 = \$200$. If she is risk averse, Jill will be prepared to pay more than $200 to insure against this loss. Let us suppose she is willing to pay $220 per year for this peace of mind. But insurance companies are owned by risk averse people too, so why would an insurance company be willing to offer Jill fire insurance for $220? The portfolio effect provides the clue. The insurance company will be issuing hundreds of thousands of similar policies. In aggregate, the number of claims will be very close to 1 in every 1000 policies issued, and the aggregate profit will be very close to the expected profit per insurance policy issued of $20 (equal to the premium paid of $220 less the expected value of the pay-out of $200) multiplied by the number of policies issued.

A special form of insurance in the movie industry is the completion guarantee. In the event that a producer runs out of money before completion of shooting, the completion guarantor contracts to deliver a finished film at no additional cost to investors. This is required by banks and investors. The guarantor has considerable powers, such as the right to take over production and fire the director. The completion guarantor also spreads risk over a portfolio of film projects.

6.6.2 Risk and the Value of Information

As we saw in chapter 4, search goods are goods whose attributes can be assessed before they are bought through gathering and analyzing information about the product. For example, a small independent film producer might conduct a search for a video camcorder. Is it analogue or digital? Are the tapes or disks currently in use compatible with this new camera? What is the price of the tapes or disks? Is this camera readily connected to the existing editing equipment? The search would involve examining the characteristics of various brands, and the implications of these attributes for ease of use, quality of output, reliability, and so on. Search thus reduces uncertainty about these attributes and reduces the risk of buying the wrong camcorder for the purpose. But search costs money (including any adverse effect from delaying the decision). At some point, search should end and a decision be made. This should be when the benefit from additional search is offset by the additional cost of search. That is, the marginal benefit of search equals the marginal cost of search.

Consideration of the optimal (best possible) level of search is relevant to a Hollywood studio looking for a shooting location for its next film. How many alternatives—for example, Hollywood itself, a low-cost state such as Texas, Canada, Australia—should it examine and in what depth?

But many media goods are experience goods, whose attributes can only be assessed through use. Movies and books are examples. This presents a problem for both the consumer and the producer. The potential moviegoer does not know whether he or she will like the film. The producer and distributor find it very difficult to predict the demand for a given movie. The producer and distributor try to reduce risk by making the moviegoer's decision easier and more predictable. Various approaches are used. One way of reducing the uncertainty when developing a new film, television program, or book is the use of sequels that continue with the same characters and format of storyline that have proven successful in the past. Examples abound in feature films and books. Feature films based on the James Bond books of Ian Fleming were so successful that other authors were commissioned to write sequels after Fleming's death. The original *Star Wars* was an unprecedented success and has so far been followed by four sequels (one of these, *Star Wars Episode One: The Phantom Menace*, is more accurately described as a prequel, as it is set in an earlier time than the original *Star Wars*), with more to follow. *Harry Potter and the Sorcerer's Stone* was the first Harry Potter movie in 2001, and the third was filmed in the summer of 2003. Robert Jordan wrote the *Wheel of Time* series of books. The television equivalent of the sequel is the series itself. Colin Dexter wrote a line of books featuring Inspector Morse, and these books became the basis for an extremely successful series of television programs.

Film producers and distributors try to promote demand for their films and reduce risk through the use of popular actors or directors. The Hollywood star system is an attempt to establish brand loyalty and promote high, stable revenues. Another approach is for the distributor to signal, through a large promotional budget for a given film, to potential moviegoers that it is committed to the film and has confidence in its quality and appeal.

The formation of media conglomerates through vertical and horizontal integration serves to reduce risk by providing preferential access to other exhibition windows and other media. For example, Disney has preferential access to the Disney Channel, a U.S. cable channel, and to the U.S. television network ABC, which it acquired. Time Warner produces and distributes not only films but also magazines, audio recordings, and books, and its operations encompass cable television franchises and AOL.

6.6.3 Moral Hazard and Adverse Selection

When transactions take place between parties with different levels of information, problems of moral hazard and adverse selection may occur.

Moral hazard occurs if, after the contract is in place, one party to an agreement uses private information to act in a manner that benefits that party at the expense of the other party. For example, a television producer may fail to report certain project revenues to his or her coproduction partners.

Adverse selection occurs if one party enters an agreement because he or she has private information that the contract will work to his or her advantage. For example, a movie producer who knows that he or she will have difficulty collecting film rentals in home territory will have a particular incentive to enter into an international coproduction agreement with a partner who is not aware of the problem.

Public policy makers need to be aware of potential moral hazard and adverse selection problems and try to avoid subsidy and regulation schemes that provide the wrong incentives. We will return to this in chapter 13.

6.7 Summary

This chapter examined revenue, profits, and managerial decision techniques that are consistent with profit maximization, which is assumed to be the goal of companies.

If the same price is charged to each customer, average revenue is equal to price. In the case of marginal revenue, the change in total revenue resulting from a one-unit change in output, it is equal to price so long as the firm can sell more of its product without lowering the price. If the price must be lowered to sell more, then marginal revenue is less than price, as price has to be reduced for all units to sell an additional unit.

Profits are maximized at the output/price where total revenue minus total cost is at a maximum. Profit maximization can alternatively be found at the output/price where marginal revenue equals marginal cost. If there are two outputs in which this condition is satisfied, profit maximization is found at the larger output (and profit minimization occurs at the smaller output).

Marginal analysis looks at the effect of one-unit changes in output on revenue and costs. However, most managerial decisions are not of this nature. They may involve large changes in output and often do not involve price and output at all. Incremental analysis is a useful way to approach these real-world decisions. It asks the same basic questions as marginal analysis; that is, "What difference does it make?" Incremental analysis examines a specific decision option by identifying the incremental revenue and incremental cost that would result. The "with versus without" framework is a good method for operationalizing the incremental approach.

If a decision has implications for the cash flows of a company over a year or more, incremental analysis requires discounting and the calculation of net present value. The general formulation is

$$NPV = B_1/(1+i) + B_2/(1+i)^2 + B_3/(1+i)^3 + \ldots + B_n/(1+i)^n - C$$

where B denotes a net cash flow and the subscript attached denotes the end of the year at which the net cash flow occurs, C is the cost outlay or investment (assumed immediate), and i is the return available elsewhere at similar risk.

Incremental analysis (and NPV) requires an understanding of the economic concepts of cost and profit, which differ from accounting cost and profit. A key difference is that economic cost includes opportunity costs, such as the return that owners could obtain from investing their funds elsewhere at similar risk (normal profit), the return available elsewhere from owned property or equipment, and, for an owner-manager, the salary that could be earned elsewhere.

Business decisions are risky and people are risk averse. Financial markets establish a risk premium in terms of a higher expected return. The discount rate used in calculating NPV should reflect this risk premium by being equal to the return available elsewhere at similar risk.

Risk is related to the line of business and type of decision. Media industries are inherently risky because they involve the continual introduction of a stream of new products. Every new film, television program, and book is a new product.

The portfolio effect, the reduction in risk associated with increased numbers, gives the Hollywood studios an advantage. The portfolio effect also provides an explanation for block booking and blind bidding, the popularity of coproduction, and insurance.

For some decisions, such as where to shoot a movie, search can provide information that reduces risk. However, search comes at a cost, and should only be undertaken up to the point where the marginal benefit of search equals the marginal cost of search.

Many media goods are experience goods, whose attributes can only be assessed through use. Producers try to reduce demand uncertainty by making the purchase decision more predictable. Various approaches are employed: For example, film approaches include the use of sequels, large promotional budgets, the star system, and vertical and horizontal integration to provide preferential access to other exhibition windows and other media.

Problems of moral hazard and adverse selection may occur when parties to a transaction have different levels of information.

7

Market Structure, Theory of the Firm, and Industrial Organization

W hy is the market power of cable television franchises less today than it was 10 years ago but nevertheless still much greater than that enjoyed by radio stations or magazine publishers? How can we determine how competitive a given industry (e.g., book publishing) is? How should we go about analyzing media industries? How does market structure affect firm and industry conduct and performance? What competitive strategies do companies use to compete, and how does this vary with the market structure of the industry? What are the dimensions of industry performance? How has digitalization affected competition in media industries? This chapter will provide insights into these and other questions.

In this chapter, we introduce the *Theory of the Firm*, which is the subject matter of chapters 8 and 9. We also examine the *industrial organization framework*, a framework based on the Theory of the Firm, and how this framework is used to analyze the real-world structure, conduct, and performance of industries.

7.1 Introduction to the Theory of the Firm

The Theory of the Firm assumes that the objective of companies is profit maximization. The theory explains and predicts firm and industry behavior (or conduct) and industry performance. We will describe elements of conduct and performance later in the chapter but note here that conduct includes pricing behavior, and performance includes profitability and technological progress. Economists have come to recognize, however, that firm and industry behavior and performance differ depending on the market structure. As a consequence, there are four variants of the Theory of the Firm, depending on market structure. The four market structures distinguished are, in decreasing order of competition, *perfect competition, monopolistic competition, oligopoly,* and *monopoly.*

The terms *market* and *industry* are used interchangeably here. An industry is a group of firms supplying substitute goods or services to a common group of buyers. In addition to a product dimension, a market has a geographic dimension. For example, a cable television franchise in Seattle is not competing with a cable television franchise in New York to serve the same group of customers.

Many companies produce multiple products that sell in different markets. For example, prior to the merger with Vivendi, Seagram was selling in the liquor, movie, and music recording markets. A few products, but important in the media field, have elements that sell in different markets. For example, magazines sell information and entertainment through subscriptions and newsstand sales to individuals, but they also sell advertising space, primarily to corporations.

The characteristics of the alternative market structures identified in the Theory of the Firm are given in Table 7.1.

The only structural difference between perfect competition and monopolistic competition is that perfectly competitive firms produce identical products (also known as homogeneous products), whereas monopolistic competitors produce differentiated products (also known

Table 7.1   Market Structures

Structural Characteristic	Perfect Competition	Monopolistic Competition	Oligopoly	Monopoly
Number of firms	Many	Many	Few	One
Product	Identical	Differentiated	Usually differentiated	Not applicable
Barriers to entry	No	No	Yes	Yes

as heterogeneous products). Under perfect competition, there is one industry price set by the impersonal forces of supply and demand. In contrast, the implication of product differentiation under monopolistic competition is that each firm enjoys some brand loyalty and hence is able to set its own price. The availability of many close substitutes, however, limits the degree of price discretion that can be practiced. The lack of barriers to entry under both these market structures means that entry of new firms will not permit economic profits in the long run.

Oligopoly is an industry dominated by a few large firms that usually produce differentiated products. Barriers to entry permit the possibility that economic profits will be earned in the long run as well as in the short run. Because there are only a few large producers, a change in price, output, or some other competitive action by one company will have an impact on the other companies. This forces oligopolists to practice strategic behavior: Decisions are made only after an assessment of the likely reaction of rivals.

Monopoly involves, by definition, a single seller, so there are no rival firms producing close substitutes. Barriers to entry protect the monopoly position and permit the possibility of economic profits in the long run.

The four industry structures can be regarded as being on a continuum from perfect competition, the most competitive structure, through monopolistic competition and oligopoly, to monopoly, the least competitive structure. Along this continuum, the boundary between monopolistic competition and oligopoly in particular is indistinct. In these cases, the question to ask is whether companies need to consider the reactions of rivals before changing price or making other important decisions. If the answer is yes, the market structure is oligopolistic rather than monopolistic competition.

Albarran (1996, p. 36), in the U.S. context, classifies the market structure of media industries, as shown in Table 7.2.

Table 7.2   Market Structure of U.S. Media Industries

Monopolistic Competition	Oligopoly	Monopoly
Books	Television networks	Cable television
Magazines	Motion pictures	Newspapers (in most markets)
Radio	Music recording	

SOURCE: Albarran (1996, p. 36).

Market structure can change over time, and at least one of Albarran's classifications already looks dated (the table, published in 1996, was no doubt developed at least a year or two earlier). Although cable television for many years enjoyed a monopoly of distant-delivered television signals, and Albarran classifies it as a monopoly, recently cable has faced significant competition from other delivery systems, notably DBS and, to a lesser extent, MMDS (multipoint microwave distribution systems, popularly known as wireless cable). As a consequence it is now better to consider a television signal distribution industry (which includes cable television) rather than a cable television industry. This television signal distribution industry is an oligopoly rather than a monopoly. As well, technological advances have made it possible for cable television operators to offer new elements of service (high speed Internet service and local telephone service) that fall in other industries completely. Competition from local telephone companies means that the industries in which both of these other product elements are sold are oligopolistic rather than monopolistic.

Albarran identifies a television network industry and classifies it as an oligopoly. However, the industry structure has changed from one in which there were three networks (firms) with an audience share of around 92% in 1978 (Vogel, 1998, p. 166) to seven networks in 2003 with an audience share of 48.5% (the original three networks' share has fallen to 37.7%); in the same period, ad-supported cable channels gained a 45.5% share (Cabletelevision Advertising Bureau, 2003). The growing importance of the specialty and other channels delivered by cable and satellite has not removed the need for the networks to consider the competitive reactions of their competitors when making their decisions. Hence, from the networks' perspective, the industry can still be regarded as an oligopoly, but the leading firms (networks) now have less ability to dominate the market.

We will return to the pitfalls associated with identifying industries, the companies competing within an industry, and classifying industries by market structure later in this chapter (section 7.2.5).

7.2 The Industrial Organization Framework

The Theory of the Firm forms the basis of the industrial organization (IO) model that provides an analytical framework for examining

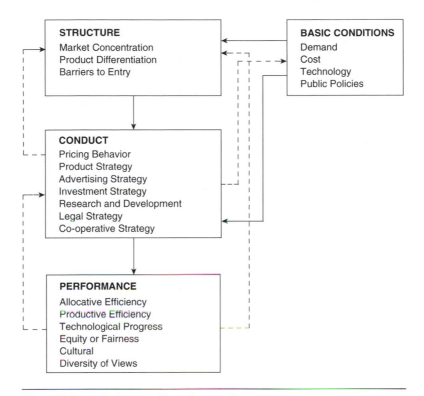

Figure 7.1   Industrial Organization Framework

media and other industries. Most media economics texts, such as that by Albarran (1996), are composed of an exposition of the industrial organization model followed by an analysis of the different media industries, using this framework.

The industrial organization model poses a causal relationship between market structure, conduct, and performance. Market structure determines the conduct of firms, which in turn determines industry performance. The elements of the model are shown in Figure 7.1.

As illustrated in Figure 7.1, and as we shall see from the following discussion, basic conditions relating to demand, cost, technology, and public policy largely explain market structure.

7.2.1 Market Structure

In Figure 7.1, we see that the IO model defines market structure in terms of market concentration, whether the products of the industry are differentiated or homogeneous (identical) and whether or not there are barriers to entry. This is the same as the Theory of the Firm, except a measure of concentration replaces categorizing industries as having many, few, or one firm. The distinction between many and few is imprecise and may not be helpful in classifying a real-world industry we wish to examine. In addition, the likelihood that companies will compete vigorously increases not only with the number of firms but with increasing equality of firm size. Thus industrial organization has developed *measures of concentration* that encapsulate not only the number of firms but their relative size.

7.2.1.1 Concentration

Common measures of concentration are the four-firm concentration ratio (CR4), eight-firm concentration ratio (CR8), and Hirschman-Herfindhal Index (HHI). CR4 measures the percentage of market share (usually of revenue) accounted for by the four largest firms. CR8 measures the percentage of market share accounted for by the eight largest firms. For example, if the largest eight firms had a 10% share each, then CR4 = 40% and CR8 = 80%. The rule of thumb is that the industry is highly concentrated if CR4 ≥ 50% (CR8 ≥ 75%), moderately concentrated if CR4 = 34% to 49% (CR8 = 51% to 74%), and lowly concentrated if CR4 ≤ 33% (CR8 ≤ 50%).

A drawback of CR4 and CR8 is that they do not make allowance for size disparities among the top four or eight largest firms, respectively. Thus CR4 has the same ratio (88%) for an industry in which the largest four firms have a 22% share each and another industry in which the largest four firms have shares of 60%, 10%, 10%, and 8%. Common sense would suggest that there is the possibility of significant competition between the four equal-sized companies in the first industry but little likelihood that another firm would compete vigorously with the dominant company in the second industry. However, there is a measure of concentration, the Hirschman-Herfindhal Index (HHI), that is sensitive to such size disparities.

HHI is the sum of the squared market share, expressed as a percentage, for all firms in the industry. HHI has a maximum value of 10,000 for a monopoly and approaches zero under very competitive conditions. The rule of thumb is that there is high concentration if HHI is greater than 1800, low concentration if HHI is less than

1000, and moderate concentration for the range in between. To be able to calculate HHI, we must know the market share of every firm, not just the largest four or eight firms. If we assume in the examples given that there are two additional firms with a 7% and a 5% market share, then HHI equals 2010 for the first case and 3939 for the second case (in which there is one dominant firm). The calculations are as follows:

$$\text{First industry: HHI} = 22^2 + 22^2 + 22^2 + 22^2 + 7^2 + 5^2 = 2010$$

$$\text{Second industry: HHI} = 60^2 + 10^2 + 10^2 + 8^2 + 7^2 + 5^2 = 3939$$

There is a drawback: HHI requires knowledge of the market shares of all firms, and the calculation can be tedious if there are many firms. Moreover, studies have found a high positive correlation between the various concentration measures (they tend to rank different industries similarly in terms of concentration), so in practice, it is likely to make little difference which measure is chosen.

Table 7.3 shows Albarran and Dimmick's (1996, p. 47) measurement of CR4 and CR8 for 14 U.S. communication-related industries for 1994. These numbers indicate moderate or high concentration largely consistent with oligopoly.

Table 7.3   Concentration Ratios for U.S. Communications
Industries, 1994 (percentages)

	CR4	CR8
TV networks	83	88
TV and radio stations	60	87
Cable systems	55	71
Cable networks	88	98
Film entertainment	72	81
Recorded music	84	99
Newspapers	42	48
Book publishing	48	74
Consumer magazines	49	52
Professional publishing	81	95
Advertising agencies	87	100
Interactive digital media	81	90
Miscellaneous communications	45	66

SOURCE: Adapted from Albarran and Dimmick (1996, p. 47).

But the digital revolution, making the scope of some markets global (or, in the words in the title of a book by Francis Cairncross (1997), causing "the death of distance") and causing convergence of previously distinct industries or industry segments, is resulting in a pronounced decrease in concentration in some sectors. For example, a recent analysis by Chysi and Sylvie (1998) concluded that the structure of the electronic newspaper market constitutes monopolistic competition. We will return to the digital revolution and its implications for market structure and competition in section 7.2.6.

7.2.1.2 Product Differentiation

Product differentiation is worthwhile for a company if the value added by differentiation, reflected by the increase in price customers are prepared to pay for the attributes added, is greater than the cost to the company of supplying these differentiating characteristics.

Product differentiation results in brand loyalty. Some customers will still buy a company's product even if the price is raised above that of rival firms. The consequence is a negatively sloped demand curve. If there is no product differentiation, the product becomes a commodity, like wheat, coal, or iron ore. Customers do not know, or care, which firm supplies the product and will buy purely on the basis of price. Under such circumstances, companies have no control over price, as the price will be determined by industry supply and demand. Note that long distance telephone services are increasingly becoming a commodity, with consumers more and more basing their decisions on price.

Cable companies and telecom ADSL services are able to charge more for Internet access than the standard dial-up modem service provided by telephone companies because of two differentiating attributes: faster transmission of data and leaving the telephone line free for voice calls.

Creative industries such as film, television, book, magazine, newspapers, and audio recording thrive on differentiation. Every new film or book is a differentiated product.

7.2.1.3 Barriers to Entry

Barriers to entry are impediments to entry by new companies. Cost conditions may provide a deterrent. Large economies of scale mean that a new entrant would have a very difficult task quickly achieving the high output and sales necessary to have any chance of competing effectively. As we saw in chapter 5, technological conditions, in the form of technical economies, are an important source of economies of scale.

Economies of scope enjoyed by multiproduct firms may deter entry. Economies of scope sometimes involve vertical integration, with the same company involved in production, distribution, and exhibition (retailing). It is often argued that the Hollywood studios' dominant position in distribution makes it difficult for other film producers to compete.

In extreme cases, economies of scale or scope may lead to a natural monopoly. For a single-product industry, a natural monopoly exists if there are economies of scale throughout the relevant output range so that a single firm can produce a given industry output at a lower total cost than two or more separate firms. For a multiproduct industry, a natural monopoly exists if economies of scope, perhaps augmented by economies of scale, result in a situation where the total cost of producing the multiple outputs is less if they are produced by a single firm than if they were produced by two or more distinct firms.

If incumbents have already achieved large learning curve economies, this would pose a barrier. Control of scarce raw materials or other resources by existing firms would also constitute a barrier. Set-up costs needed to purchase the required capital equipment, develop the product(s), build a brand image, establish the R&D facility necessary to be competitive, and develop a distribution network may be so large that entrants are deterred.

The barrier may be legal, arising from patents or copyrights. New Internet distributors of music (in the case of Napster) and television programming (in the case of iCraveTV.com) both encountered legal actions by copyright holders designed to block entry. In the face of legal action, both Napster and iCraveTV went out of business. But the makers, such as Kazaa and Grokster, of other peer-to-peer (music) share-swapping software have proved harder to deal with because their software does not reside on central computer services.

The barrier may arise from government public policies. Historically, there has been spectrum frequency scarcity, and this has led governments to require a license to broadcast. In most countries, governments consider intervention necessary in cultural industries to further cultural goals. Regulation is thus directly aimed at affecting conduct and performance. Such intervention is most pervasive in television and film but often extends to music recording, book publication, and magazines. Telecommunication carriers have traditionally been viewed as natural monopolies and subject to public utility–type regulation.

7.2.2 Conduct

Conduct covers the behavior of firms. The leeway that firms have over pricing depends on the industry structure. In perfectly competitive industries, the firms have to accept the market price for the homogeneous good. Under monopolistic competition, companies have very limited discretion over price because of the competition from many close substitutes. Pricing by oligopolists is a strategic decision that has to consider how rivals may react. A monopolist has complete discretion over the price it charges and no rivals to consider. However, even a monopolist has to consider the effect of a price increase on consumers' willingness to buy.

Product strategy and advertising is important for industry structures, where products are differentiated and brand image is important. R&D is vital when competition to develop new products is intense. This certainly applies to media industries, where each film, television program, recording, or book is a new product. The extent to which firms cooperate when making decisions is an important aspect of behavior. It is most likely to occur under an oligopolistic structure.

Public policy, in the form of antitrust or competition legislation, makes some forms of cooperation or collusion illegal. The rationale is to prevent collusion aimed at achieving monopoly profits by restricting competition and exploiting customers by raising prices.

Conduct, and how it depends on market structure, will be examined in the next two chapters.

7.2.3 Performance

If firms are attempting to maximize profits, it is to be expected that, from the firm's point of view, the level of profits is a key indicator of company performance. Economics takes a somewhat broader view—assessing performance from society's perspective and in a number of dimensions. The dimensions we identify in Figure 7.1 are allocative efficiency, productive efficiency, technological progress, equity, cultural objectives, and diversity of views. The last two are dimensions we have added to the standard list in recognition that many people (and governments) regard media industries as having unusual responsibilities. We will introduce each dimension in turn.

- *Allocative efficiency* exists if resources are allocated to the production of different goods and services in an optimal manner. This implies that they are allocated to the goods and services that consumers want, up to the point where the price a consumer is willing to pay for an additional unit is equal to the cost of producing it (marginal cost).
- *Productive efficiency* exists if the industry output is being produced at minimum total cost, given the state of technology.
- *Technological progress* involves invention and innovation and is the key to productivity and growth. It can involve a new production process or a new product. Technological progress with respect to the production process occurs when the new process permits an increase in output with the same resources. Technological progress with respect to the product involves introduction of a new product that provides consumers with attributes they value sufficiently to permit the company to sell the product at a profitable price.
- *Equity* is primarily concerned with income distribution effects and tends to involve value judgments. Positive economic profits result, in the long run, from companies with market power charging a price higher than that associated with very competitive conditions. The result is that producers prosper at the expense of consumers.
- *Cultural objectives* are considered important by most governments in broadcasting, film, publishing, and music recording. The reason usually given is that the health of the nation-state requires citizens to be well informed on public issues and events and on citizens being able to "share their stories." Regulation, such as government subsidies and domestic content requirements in broadcasting, are often used to pursue cultural goals. The cultural significance attached by many governments is the reason these industries are sometimes known as "cultural industries." The United States is an exception, viewing them as entertainment industries rather than cultural industries. We note, however, that even the United States has foreign ownership restrictions in broadcasting and newspaper publishing. Indeed, Rupert Murdoch took out U.S. citizenship to evade these restrictions.
- *Diversity of views* is universally recognized by democracies as a desirable objective for media industries. A well-functioning political system requires that its citizens be exposed to a wide range of sources and opinions.

How the various industry structures measure up on these dimensions will be explored in the next two chapters.

7.2.4 Direction of Causality

Although the primary direction of causality flows from structure to conduct to performance, the direction is not entirely one way. This is recognized in Figure 7.1 by the broken lines. Heavy advertising can increase set-up costs for a potential entrant and hence provide a barrier to entry. Technological progress, in the form of a process innovation by one firm, could give that company a significant cost advantage over its rivals and lead it to try and force rivals out of the industry through aggressive price competition. If successful, this would make the market more concentrated. On the other hand, technological progress may permit new forms of competition—for example, DTH satellite and MMDS (or "wireless cable," as it is often called) competition for cable television—and decrease market concentration.

7.2.5 Pitfalls in Measuring
Concentration and Applying the IO Framework

If measures of concentration are to be useful, it is necessary to correctly define the industry and correctly identify the companies that comprise the industry. This sounds trivial, but, as we have already seen in section 7.1, often it is not. As an example, let us consider U.S. newspapers. There are some 1500 daily newspapers produced. At first glance, this suggests low concentration, with many companies producing a differentiated product, a structure consistent with monopolistic competition. Further examination reveals chains, such as Knight-Ridder, Inc., with multiple papers under the same ownership. Even after taking this into account, one might conclude that the newspaper industry in the United States is quite competitive. But all but a handful of these papers are not competing in a national U.S. market at all; Picard (1993) found that 90% of U.S. newspapers were not distributed beyond the place of publication. In most places in the United States, the only newspapers available are one local paper and several nationals, including *USA Today* and the *Wall Street Journal*. It is doubtful whether the local paper is a close substitute for the nationals or vice versa. They are providing very different information and hence not rivals for the readers' attention. Also, the local newspaper carries mainly local advertising, whereas the nationals carry mainly national advertising. It might be concluded that many local newspapers have a monopoly. Our reasoning so far no doubt explains why Albarran (1996) classifies most newspapers as monopolies in his text (see our Table 7.2) but, interestingly enough, is not consistent with the CR4 and CR8 measures of newspaper industry concentration made by Albarran and Dimmock (1996; see our Table 7.3).

Should local newspapers with no in-market newspaper competition be regarded as monopolists? The answer depends on whether the industry is correctly identified. Is there a local newspaper industry or a local media industry, which also includes local television stations, radio stations, and community magazines and newssheets, all competing to sell advertising space? The key to answering this question is to remember that an industry is composed of firms producing close substitutes. A measurement of cross-elasticity would indicate the degree of substitutability, with a high positive cross-elasticity signifying close substitutes, which should be classified as being in the same industry, and a low cross elasticity indicating poor substitutes best regarded as being provided by firms in different industries.

Another pitfall is whether to distinguish between different horizontal activities when defining an industry. For example, is there *a* movie industry, or this really three industries, namely movie production, movie distribution, and movie exhibition? The Hollywood studios are vertically integrated, and different activities may operate under different competitive conditions. Thus, although film distribution is oligopolistic, film production operates more as monopolistic competition.

More fundamentally, digitalization and convergence have blurred industry boundaries, and as a consequence, industry segment distinctions that are crucial to the IO approach are losing their meaning.

Data limitations often cause difficulties in applying the IO framework. Data is usually collected on a national basis, and there is a tendency to view markets as national in scope, but many markets are in fact local or regional or global. Also, government and trade statistics are sometimes based on industry classifications that may have made sense 30 years ago but do not now. Unless the researcher is extremely careful, there is a danger that the availability of statistics drives the definition of the industry and the competitors in that industry. Where this occurs, the resulting measures of concentration and analysis of structure, conduct, and performance may be largely meaningless.

7.2.6 Trends in Structure
and Competition in Media Industries

During the past 25 years, one trend has been to increase company size, with multinational conglomerates growing through acquisition. In chapter 5, we examined horizontal merger activity, which involves mergers between companies that produce the same product, such as the 1998 merger of Alliance and Atlantis, Canada's big two TV and film studios. We also examined vertical merger activity, such as Disney's purchase of Miramax, the independent film distributor, and the ABC television network. We suggested that economies of scale were a motive in the former and economies of scope a motive for the latter. In chapter 6, we also suggested that risk reduction is a motive. Although this is undoubtedly true, one of the concerns with the growth of media conglomerates such as AOL-Time Warner, the News Corporation, and Bertelsmann is market power. Some mergers or growth may be motivated more by increasing profitability through achieving and exploiting market power than by cost reductions. (This behavior is called *rent seeking.*) For this very reason, countries typically have a competition or antitrust agency to judge whether major mergers should be permitted. We will examine public policy with respect to mergers in chapter 9.

In the media industries, another major concern regarding the rise of the media conglomerates has been the effect on diversity of opinion and expression. For example, in the United States in 1994, only 33 cities were served by two or more newspapers operating under separate ownership. This was down from 65 in 1975 (Newspaper Association of America, 1994, Figure 3-11).

During the same 25 years, however, broadcasting became much more competitive as analogue and, later, digital cable and satellite delivery systems increased the number of television and radio signals that could be carried.

Recently we have seen technological innovations associated with digitilization that foster competition. Cable television now has to compete with DTH satellite and wireless cable MMDS delivery of television signals. Cable provided the telecoms with new competition in Internet access and local telephone service, and the telecoms responded with their own high-speed ADSL service and video on demand. The Internet provides competition for long distance telephone calls and traditional mail. Barriers to entry into the music recording industry have dissolved, with studio-quality sound possible from a home basement equipped with $10,000 of computer hardware and software. The Internet is making retailing and distribution more competitive. Virtual book and music stores, such as Amazon.com, receive orders online and ship directly to customers. Amazon.com owns no physical bookstores and, in its early days, although this is changing, had no distribution facility, kept no inventory of books, and employed only a small staff of programmers and others. Newspapers and magazines can be accessed by Internet; some, such as the Canadian business magazine *CanadaOne*, are only available online. It is already possible to download music recordings, both legally and illegally, in MP3 format. Radio signals from around the world can be accessed through the Internet. The first Internet release of a feature-length film distributed by a major studio (*Guinevere*, distributed by Miramax Films, which is owned by Disney) occurred in January 2001. Distribution of movies to cinemas is also changing to digital delivery. The cost is expected to decrease 90% as digital distribution of movies replaces printing and shipping of 35-mm film. Market power based on control of distribution may be undermined.

As Neuman, McKnight, and Solomon (1997) explain:

> Through digital processing, a single medium can offer all the services once provided by a range of media. Packaged and print media services can move to electronic delivery; the telephone company can deliver multichannel television; the cable company can provide telephone service; and each of these formerly distinct services (along with other competitors) can provide electronic shopping, electronic encyclopedias, magazines and newspapers—all delivered to high-speed home printers. What were once noncompeting, parallel, and highly profitable sectors of the economy have all been thrown into the same electronic marketplace. (p. 2)

7.3 Summary

In this chapter, we introduced the Theory of the Firm, the subject matter of chapters 8 and 9. We also examined the industrial organization framework, which is designed to operationalize the Theory of the Firm to analyze real-world industries.

The Theory of the Firm explains and predicts firm and industry behavior and performance on the assumption that firms are motivated by profit maximization. However, because the implications of profit maximization depend on market structure, there are four variants of the Theory of the Firm. Four market structures are distinguished according to the number of firms, product differentiation, and barriers to entry. From most to least competitive, these market structures are perfect competition, monopolistic competition, oligopoly, and monopoly. We saw that Albarran (1996) classifies books, magazines, and radio under monopolistic competition; television networks, motion pictures, and music recording under oligopoly; and cable television and newspapers under monopoly.

The industrial organization framework, laid out in Figure 7.1, assumes a causal relationship whereby market structure determines conduct (behavior), which determines performance. Most media economics texts consist of an explanation of the IO framework followed by the application of this framework to the various media industries.

In the IO framework, market structure is examined in terms of market concentration, product differentiation, and barriers to entry. Measures of concentration take into account the number of firms and, to a greater or lesser extent, their relative sizes. Market structure itself is largely explained by basic conditions with respect to demand, cost, technology, and public policies related to the industry. Conduct includes pricing, product, advertising, investment, R&D, legal, and cooperative strategies. Dimensions of performance are allocative efficiency, productive efficiency, technological progress, equity, cultural objectives, and diversity of views.

There are pitfalls and limitations in applying the IO framework. The direction of causality from market structure to conduct is not all one way. Digitalization and convergence are blurring the boundaries of what used to be distinct industry segments. Data limitations add to the difficulty.

The chapter concluded with an examination of trends in structure and competition in communications industries. We found conflicting trends. On the one hand, there has been the rise of multinational media conglomerates, growing mainly through acquisition. On the other has been the effect of digitalization in reducing barriers to entry.

8

Perfect Competition and Monopoly

I n this chapter, we examine perfect competition and monopoly, the market structures at the opposite ends of the scale in terms of competitiveness. Although, as we mentioned in chapter 7, none of the media industries is perfectly competitive, this industry structure is worth studying because it provides a base of comparison for examining the conduct and performance of media industries that operate under monopoly, monopolistic competition, or oligopoly.

This chapter should give you answers or insights into the following questions. Is local telephone service a natural monopoly? Why have governments traditionally asked regulators to set the rates for telephone calls? Why have some governments used competitive bidding to award cable TV franchises and allocate spectrum frequencies? If monopoly is bad, why is it that governments do not award numerous cable franchises for the same territory? How did monopoly encourage invention and innovation in the distribution of distant television signals? Why did cable lose its monopoly in delivery of distant television signals? How did the U.S. Post Office lose its monopoly in delivery of text communications? Why did Canadian cable television companies not object to a regulatory decision that they provide a money-losing community channel? What is a cross-subsidy and what form has it often taken in telephone services? Would a perfectly competitive industry or a monopoly be more open to regulatory persuasion to provide culturally significant products? Why would perfect competition, which is allocatively efficient and often regarded as ideal from both a consumer and a society viewpoint, not be a desirable structure for media industries?

8.1 Perfect Competition

As we briefly discussed in chapter 7, a perfectly competitive industry is characterized by many small firms producing a homogeneous (identical) product. Small is a relative term here. It signifies that the output of any one firm is an insignificant proportion of industry output. By this definition, the largest wheat producer in the Canadian province of Saskatchewan and the largest corn producer in Nebraska are small firms. One of the implications of this is that a change in output by one firm has no discernible effect on industry supply. Each firm produces an identical product, and consumers are aware of this, so firms make no attempt to brand their product, and consumers are unaware whether their lettuce comes from the Gonzales or the Prothero farm in the Imperial Valley of California, and they could not care less.

Another condition for perfect competition is that there are no barriers to entry. As a consequence, only zero economic profits can be earned in the long run.

8.1.1 Short-Run Equilibrium Under Perfect Competition

In the short run, the interaction of demand for the industry's product and short-run industry supply, with the number of firms and their capacity given, determine the equilibrium price and industry output. These are shown by P_0 and Q_0, respectively, in Figure 8.1.

Firms are price takers. They may or may not like the industry price, but they have no control over it. The demand curve (d_0) and average revenue curve (ar_0) for each firm is thus horizontal at the industry price of P_0, as shown for a typical firm in Figure 8.2. As the firm can sell an additional unit at the given market price, marginal revenue (mr_0) is equal to price.

Firms do decide how many units of output to supply at the industry price. According to marginal analysis, each firm will produce the output for which marginal revenue (mr_0) equals marginal cost (SMC), as this output maximizes profits. This results in an output of q_0 in Figure 8.2. As drawn, ATC = ar_0 at this optimal output, so the firm is earning zero economic profits.

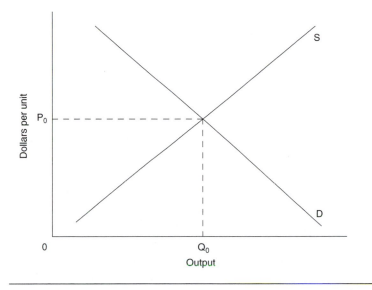

Figure 8.1   Equilibrium Price and Industry Output Under Perfect
Competition

Note: D indicates demand curve; P, price; Q, quantity; S, supply curve.

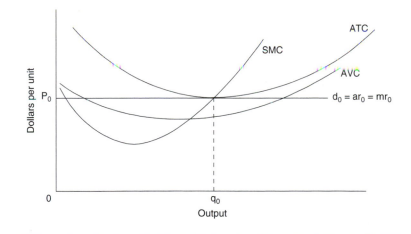

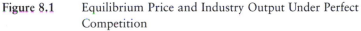

Figure 8.2   Equilibrium Output for a Typical Firm Under Perfect
Competition

Note: ar indicates average revenue curve; ATC, average total cost; AVC, average
variable cost; d, demand curve; mr, marginal revenue; P, price; q, quantity; SMC,
short-run marginal cost.

However, in the short run, the firm may earn positive economic profits or negative economic profits, depending on the level of industry price established. For example, suppose there is an increase in industry demand, perhaps caused by an increase in income. In Figure 8.1, this would be shown by a shift of the demand curve to the right, which would result in a higher industry price. The impact of such a price, P_1, on the typical firm is shown in Figure 8.3. The firm will have a new marginal revenue curve, mr_1, and this will equal SMC at a larger output, q_1. At this output, the firm will earn positive economic profits, as ar_1 is greater than ATC.

A decrease in industry demand will cause the price to fall. If the price falls to P_2, mr_2 = SMC at the lower output of q_2. At this output, ar_2 is less than ATC, so the firm is earning negative profits. Should the firm produce at all under these circumstances? In considering this *shutdown* decision, we should first remember that fixed costs will be borne by the firm irrespective of its level of output. Producing nothing does not avoid fixed costs. Whether the firm should produce output q_2 or shut down—that is, produce zero output—depends on whether the revenue earned from production more than covers the variable costs

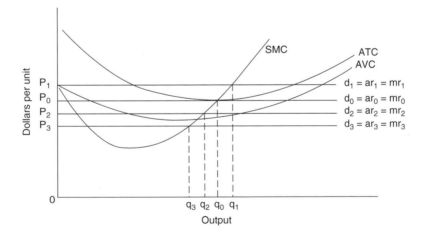

Figure 8.3   Perfectly Competitive Firm Output at Various Industry Prices

Note: ar indicates average revenue curve; ATC, average total cost; AVC, average variable cost; d, demand curve; mr, marginal revenue curve; P, price; q, quantity; SMC, short-run marginal cost.

incurred. At price P_2, the firm should produce q_2 because ar_2 $(= P_2)$ is greater than AVC. Each unit is contributing ar_2 – AVC toward fixed costs. The total contribution is $(ar_2 - AVC) \times q_2$.

If the market price were to fall further, to P_3, where, at output q_3, ar_3 is less than AVC at the output where $mr_3 = SMC$, the firm should shut down in the short run. This is not equivalent to going out of business, as the plant would be mothballed in the short run and could be quickly put back in operation if this were justified by an increased price.

It should be noted that, at prices above the lowest point of the AVC curve, the SMC curve is also the short-run supply curve of the firm. For example, at industry price P_2, the firm will supply q_2; at P_0, it will supply q_0; at P_1, it will supply q_1; and so on. The industry supply curve is the horizontal summation of the supply curves for all the firms in the industry. To take an example, industry supply of Q_0 at price P_0 in Figure 7.1 is made up of the sum of q_0 for our typical firm and similar amounts for all other incumbent firms.

To illustrate the short-run output decision for the firm, in the three parts of Table 8.1, we return to the New Sound Company case. The short-run costs are as reported earlier in Table 5.3. We are now assuming that the New Sound Company operates in a perfectly competitive industry, and we will consider the firm's optimal output at various industry prices.

At a market price of $200, shown in Table 8.1A, mr = SMC at an output of seven units. Producing the seventh unit adds $200 to both total revenue and total cost, so the firm is actually indifferent to whether its output rate is six or seven units. Total profits, TR – TC, at either of these output levels is maximized at $170; as this is greater than zero, the firm earns positive economic profits. The profit per unit (rounded to the nearest dollar) at an output of seven units is ar – ATC = $24.

At a price of $172, as we see in Table 8.1B, economic profits approximate zero (they are actually zero at $171.67) at the optimal output of six units. At six units, mr = $172 and SMC = $120, so the sixth unit adds $172 to total revenue but only $120 to total cost. Hence the sixth unit should be produced. On the other hand, a seventh unit would add $172 to total revenue and $200 to total cost, so a seventh unit should not be produced. At all outputs other than six units, the New Sound Company would take a loss.

The situation at a price of $100 is shown in Table 8.1C. The New Sound Company makes negative economic profits, as ar is less than

Table 8.1A   New Sound Company's Output Decision at a Price of $200

P	200	200	200	200	200	200	200	200	200
Q	0	1	2	3	4	5	6	7	8
TVC	0	90	160	210	280	370	490	690	1010
TFC	540	540	540	540	540	540	540	540	540
TC	540	630	700	750	820	910	1030	1230	1550
TR	0	200	400	600	800	1000	1200	1400	1600
TR – TC	–540	–430	–300	–150	–20	90	170	170	50
TR – TVC	0	110	240	390	520	630	710	710	590
ar		200	200	200	200	200	200	200	200
AVC		90	80	70	70	74	82	99	126
ATC		630	350	250	205	182	172	176	194
mr		200	200	200	200	200	200	200	200
SMC		90	70	50	70	90	120	200	320

Note: ar indicates average revenue; ATC, average total cost; AVC, average variable cost; mr, marginal revenue; P, price; Q, quantity; SMC, short-run marginal cost; TC, total cost; TFC, total fixed cost; TR, total revenue; TVC, total variable cost.

Table 8.1B   New Sound Company's Output Decision at a Price of $172

P	172	172	172	172	172	172	172	172	172
Q	0	1	2	3	4	5	6	7	8
TVC	0	90	160	210	280	370	490	690	1010
TFC	540	540	540	540	540	540	540	540	540
TC	540	630	700	750	820	910	1030	1230	1550
TR	0	172	344	516	688	860	1032	1204	1376
TR – TC	–540	–458	–356	–234	–132	–50	2	–26	–174
TR – TVC	0	82	184	306	408	490	542	514	366
ar		172	172	172	172	172	172	172	172
AVC		90	80	70	70	74	82	99	126
ATC		630	350	250	205	182	172	176	194
mr		172	172	172	172	172	172	172	172
SMC		90	70	50	70	90	120	200	320

Note: ar indicates average revenue; ATC, average total cost; AVC, average variable cost; mr, marginal revenue; P, price; Q, quantity; SMC, short-run marginal cost; TC, total cost; TFC, total fixed cost; TR, total revenue; TVC, total variable cost.

Table 8.1C   New Sound Company's Output Decision at a Price of
$100

P	100	100	100	100	100	100	100	100	100
Q	0	1	2	3	4	5	6	7	8
TVC	0	90	160	210	280	370	490	690	1010
TFC	540	540	540	540	540	540	540	540	540
TC	540	630	700	750	820	910	1030	1230	1550
TR	0	100	200	300	400	500	600	700	800
TR – TC	–540	–530	–500	–450	–420	–410	–430	–530	–750
TR – TVC	0	10	40	90	120	130	110	10	–210
ar		100	100	100	100	100	100	100	100
AVC		90	80	70	70	74	82	99	126
ATC		630	350	250	205	182	172	176	194
mr		100	100	100	100	100	100	100	100
SMC		90	70	50	70	90	120	200	320

Note: ar indicates average revenue; ATC, average total cost; AVC, average variable
cost; mr, marginal revenue; P, price; Q, quantity; SMC, short-run marginal cost;
TC, total cost; TFC, total fixed cost; TR, total revenue; TVC, total variable cost.

ATC at all outputs. Should the firm shut down or operate? If it does
operate, it should produce five units, the highest output for which mr
exceeds MC. A comparison of ar with AVC indicates that this output
should indeed be produced, as the five units contribute, on average,
$26 each to unavoidable fixed costs that total $540. The total contribution is (ar – AVC) × Q, which equals $130, which is also given by
TR – TVC. Another way of viewing the same decision is to note that
economic profits, TR – TC, are –$540 if the firm shuts down (zero
output) but only –$410, $130 less, if five units are produced.

How far can the industry price drop before the New Sound
Company will decide to shut down? Remember that graphically,
this is where the average revenue curve (demand curve) for the firm
falls just below the lowest point of the AVC curve. As we see in
Table 8.1D, if the industry price is $70, equal to the minimum
AVC, the firm will be indifferent to producing an output of three
or four units or shutting down. The economic profit is –$540 in
each case. At any price below $70 the decision is clear: The New
Sound Company should shut down.

Note that the shut-down criterion (i.e., the company should shut
down if production would merely add to losses—average revenue

Table 8.1D   New Sound Company's Output Decision at a Price of $70

P	70	70	70	70	70	70	70	70	70
Q	0	1	2	3	4	5	6	7	8
TVC	0	90	160	210	280	370	490	690	1010
TFC	540	540	540	540	540	540	540	540	540
TC	540	630	700	750	820	910	1030	1230	1550
TR	0	70	140	210	280	350	420	490	560
TR – TC	−540	−560	−560	−540	−540	−560	−610	−740	−990
TR – TVC	0	−20	−20	0	0	−20	−70	−200	−450
ar		70	70	70	70	70	70	70	70
AVC		90	80	70	70	74	82	99	126
ATC		630	350	250	205	182	172	176	194
mr		70	70	70	70	70	70	70	70
SMC		90	70	50	70	90	120	200	320

Note: ar indicates average revenue; ATC, average total cost; AVC, average variable cost; mr, marginal revenue; P, price; Q, quantity; SMC, short-run marginal cost; TC, total cost; TFC, total fixed cost; TR, total revenue; TVC, total variable cost.

is less than average variable cost) also applies to the other industry structures.

8.1.2 Long-Run Equilibrium Under Perfect Competition

In the long run, firms can freely enter or exit a perfectly competitive industry. If, in the short run, firms are earning positive economic profits, then, in the long run, new firms will enter the industry attracted by a return that is superior to that available elsewhere at similar risk. If, in the short run, firms are earning negative economic profits, then firms will exit the industry when capital equipment needs replacing, as such replacement cannot be justified at a return that is less than that available elsewhere at similar risk (the NPV would be negative). If firms are entering or exiting, there is a state of change, and hence the industry is not in long-run equilibrium.

Another form of adjustment possible in the long run is that firms are able to change their plant size so that they produce at the lowest point on their long-run average cost (LAC) curve.

A perfectly competitive industry is in long-run equilibrium when firms in the industry are earning zero economic profits. As shown in Figure 8.4, the price is P_0 such that $ar_0 = LAC$ at the optimal output

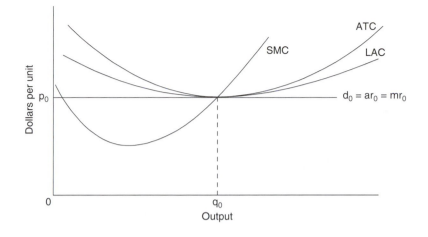

Figure 8.4   Long-Run Equilibrium of the Firm Under Perfect
Competition

Note: ar indicates average revenue curve; ATC, average total cost curve; d, demand
curve; LAC, long-run average cost curve; mr, marginal revenue curve; P, price; q,
quantity; SMC, short-run marginal cost.

q_0 where $mr_0 = SMC$. ATC and SMC are the average total cost and
marginal cost curves associated with the optimal plant size and
hence show how these costs vary with output in the short run when
capacity is fixed at this level.

8.1.3 Effects of a Permanent Change in Demand

Suppose an industry in long-run equilibrium enjoys a permanent
increase in demand. The effect for a *constant-cost industry* is shown
in Figure 8.5. A constant-cost industry is one in which the prices of
inputs are unaffected by changes in the employment of these factors
by this industry. The supply of scripts to the independent production sector appears to be characterized by constant cost. There
appears to be a bottomless supply of aspiring screenwriters willing
to enter the industry under existing terms and conditions.

The original industry price is P_0 and output Q_0 in Figure 8.5(b),
where industry demand D_0 equals industry supply S_0. The typical firm,
in Figure 8.5(a), produces q_0, where $mr_0 = SMC$ and earns zero economic profit, as $ar_0 = ATC = LAC$. Hence this is a long-run equilibrium. Now there is a permanent increase in industry demand to D_1. In

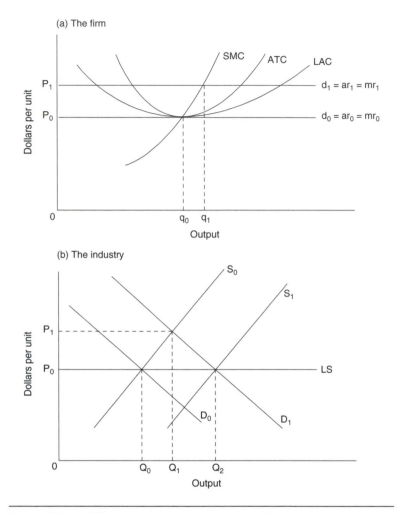

Figure 8.5   Effect of a Permanent Increase in Demand on a Constant-Cost Industry

Note: ar indicates average revenue curve for the firm; ATC, average total cost curve for the firm; d, demand curve for the firm; D, demand curve for the industry; LAC, long-run average cost curve for the firm; LS, long-run supply curve for the industry; mr, marginal revenue curve for the firm; P, price; q, quantity for the firm; Q, quantity for the industry; S, short-run supply curve for the industry; SMC, short-run marginal cost for the firm. Note also that the same scale is not used to measure output in the two parts of the figure.

the short run, this will result in an increase in industry price to P_1 and industry output to Q_1 where $D_1 = S_0$ in Figure 8.5(b). At price P_1, the typical firm will expand output to q_1 in Figure 8.5(a) where $SMC = mr_1$

and make positive economic profits, as $ar_1 >$ ATC. In the long run, the positive economic profits attract entry of new firms into the industry. Entry of new firms shifts the short-run supply curve to the right, increasing industry output and decreasing industry price. This process will continue as long as positive economic profits are available, as they will be at any price above P_0. Thus equilibrium will be reestablished when the short-run supply curve is S_1, price is back to P_0, and industry output has increased to Q_2. Faced by a price back at P_0, the typical firm will return to producing q_0 and earning zero economic profits. Hence the increase in industry output of $Q_2 - Q_0$ is produced entirely by the new firms. A comparison of the long-term equilibrium of the constant-cost industry after the permanent increase in demand with the long-term equilibrium before shows that the larger output is associated with the same price. The long-run supply curve of the industry, LS in Figure 8.5(b), is thus a horizontal line joining the long-run equilibria.

The analysis for a permanent decrease in demand is similar. The decrease in demand would cause the price to fall, resulting in economic losses in the short run. Firms would exit the industry in the long run, and this would continue until decreasing industry supply resulted in the price returning to P_0.

In an *increasing cost industry*, a change in output by the industry causes the price of at least one factor to rise if output and, consequently, employment increase or to decrease if output and employment fall. This occurs if the industry is a significant purchaser of these factors. A permanent increase in demand for the industry product increases the prices of inputs and thus causes the cost curves for firms to shift up. Thus, as new firms enter and product price starts to fall, costs increase. Because of these higher costs, zero economic profits will ensue when some price above P_0 but below P_1 has been established. The long-run supply curve, LS, would be positively sloped. An increasing cost example is provided by film and television program production in the Vancouver area. As the industry expanded rapidly in the 1990s, labor achieved greater bargaining power, unions and union membership increased, and labor costs rose, although the effects for U.S. producers were mitigated by the falling Canadian dollar.

In a *decreasing cost industry*, a change in output, and consequently employment of factors, by the industry causes factor prices to change in the same direction. This usually occurs because of external economies and is due to the growth of specialist support services. For example, the expansion of demand for Hollywood movies in the

1920s led to the creation in the Hollywood area of support services such as agents (who often act as the deal makers), financial and distribution experts, entertainment lawyers, script writers, postproduction specialists, and other providers of infrastructure and expertise. (Even today, Hollywood remains the single physical location in the world where all the necessary ingredients of a commercially successful movie are readily accessible.) What are termed *agglomeration economies* led to lower costs as film production expanded. For a decreasing cost industry, a permanent increase in demand will result in a decrease in per-unit costs; hence price will fall below P_0 before long-run equilibrium is reestablished. LS is thus negatively sloped.

8.2 Monopoly

In our examination in this chapter, we will examine the case of the single-price monopolist; that is, a monopolist that sells all units of its product at the same price. A discussion of price discrimination, in which different prices are charged to different consumers or groups of consumers, will be left to chapter 10.

A monopoly is a "single-seller": By definition, there are no close substitutes for its product. Barriers to entry make positive economic profits possible in the long run as well as the short run. The firm is free to make a price or an output decision but still faces the trade-off that the higher the price chosen, the lower the resulting sales, or the higher the output chosen, the lower the price at which it can be sold. However, demand will not be very sensitive to a price change, as consumers do not have the option of switching to a close substitute produced by a competitor, although demand will still fall somewhat, as some people will decide that the industry product is no longer worth purchasing.

8.2.1 Short-Run Equilibrium Under Monopoly

Referring to Figure 8.6, you can see that the monopolist produces at price P_0 and output Q_0 where MR = SMC. With the average total cost curve shown, the firm makes positive economic profits, as AR > ATC at output Q_0. However, there is no guarantee that even a monopolist will make positive economic profits. Profits will depend on the demand for the product and the cost of making it. The firm might make zero economic profits (in such a case, the ATC curve is tangent to the demand curve) or even negative economic profits.

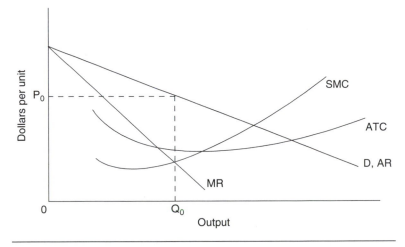

Figure 8.6   Short-Run Equilibrium Under Monopoly

Note: AR indicates average revenue; ATC, average total cost curve; D, demand curve; MR, marginal revenue curve; P, price; Q, quantity; SMC, short-run marginal cost.

There is a tendency to regard the demand for a monopolist's product as being price inelastic. This is in fact untrue at the profit maximizing price. Assuming marginal cost is positive (and it cannot be negative and is rarely zero), to equate marginal revenue with marginal cost, the monopolist must be operating in the section of the demand curve where marginal revenue is positive. As we saw in chapter 6, this implies a price elasticity greater than one. If marginal cost is zero, the elasticity will be unitary at the profit maximizing price.

8.2.2 Long-Run Equilibrium Under Monopoly

In the long run, the monopolist may earn positive economic profits or zero economic profits. It will leave the industry rather than earn negative economic profits. If we consider the monopolist, shown in Figure 8.6, that is earning positive economic profits in the short run, this situation will continue to apply in the long run because of barriers that prevent entry of new firms. The monopolist can adjust plant capacity if necessary to produce the optimal output at lower average total cost, but this is the only adjustment likely.

One form of barrier to entry, identified in chapter 7, is cost conditions that lead to a natural monopoly. For a single-product industry, a natural monopoly exists if there are economies of scale throughout the relevant output range so that a single firm can produce a given industry output at a lower total cost than two or more competing firms. For a multiproduct industry, a natural monopoly exists if economies of scope, possibly augmented by economies of scale, result in a situation where the total cost of producing the multiple outputs is less if they are produced by a single firm than if they were produced by two or more distinct firms.

A single-product natural monopoly is illustrated in Figure 8.7. Economies of scale result in long-run average cost declining throughout the relevant output range; marginal cost is declining too and less than average cost. The monopolist produces Q_1 at a price of P_1. Demand is insufficient to permit another firm to enter the industry, produce a comparable volume of output, and enjoy similar low costs.

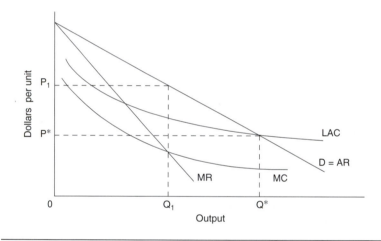

Figure 8.7   Single-Product Natural Monopoly

Note: AR indicates average revenue; D, demand curve; MC, marginal cost; MR, marginal revenue; P, price; Q, quantity.

It has often been suggested that local telephone services constitute a natural monopoly because of the very large fixed costs associated with the cable and switching infrastructure used. Indeed, regulation of this service has been largely based on this belief, with rates set by a regulator to prevent the monopolist exploiting consumers. However, the data available for reaching such a conclusion is poor and the evidence mixed. Albon et al. (1997), after reviewing several empirical studies, concluded:

Recent empirical tests for natural monopoly still rely primarily on data from large incumbent telecommunications carriers, data that display only limited variation over time and contain relatively few observations for the number of parameters being estimated. This makes the results very sensitive to specification and estimation techniques. . . . No conclusive empirical evidence exists which proves or disproves that the local network has cost characteristics conducive to a natural monopoly. (pp. 28-29)

It is important to note that even where the conditions of economies of scale or scope are consistent with a natural monopoly, a natural monopoly ensues only if potential entrants are constrained to use the same technology. Where cable TV companies have been permitted (by industry regulators) to provide a local telephone service, telephone companies no longer enjoy a monopoly.

8.2.3 Monopoly and Competitive Bidding

Even where economies of scale mean that market demand can be met at the lowest cost by one firm producing the entire output, it may be possible to introduce competition to determine which company provides the service. For example, suppose that Hometown, USA is about to award a cable television franchise. Although, assuming cable is a natural monopoly, only one franchise can be awarded, there are many companies capable of providing the service. Competition can be introduced to determine which company should win the franchise.

The authority could stipulate the service level that has to be supplied and ask cable companies to bid in terms of the price households would pay for that service. The winning bid would be that stipulating the lowest price for this service level. With reference to Figure 8.7, obviously the cable companies would like to bid price P_1, the monopoly price, but each company would recognize that such a bid is most unlikely to win. In fact, if competition for the franchise is intense, we would expect the winning bid to be close to the perfectly competitive level of P^*, where zero economic profits would be earned.

A number of jurisdictions in the United States have awarded cable television franchises using a competitive bidding process of this sort. It does entail monitoring by the authority to ensure that the cable company continues to honor the contract by providing the service stipulated at the bid price.

The method used by the United States to allocate electromagnetic spectrum frequencies for personal communication services and for other services (discussed in chapter 3) is an example of an alternative form of competitive bidding. In this type of auction, the winner is the company that bids highest for the rights. The highest bid any company would be willing to make would be the present value of the monopoly profits available from ownership of the rights. The winner would then, after allowing for the bid payment (a form of fixed cost), earn zero economic profits. If competition between companies to obtain exclusive use of a segment of the spectrum is intense, the size of the winning bid could be expected to approach this level.

8.3 Performance: Perfect Competition and Monopoly Compared

As we saw in chapter 7, performance is assessed from a society perspective and has the following dimensions: allocative efficiency, productive efficiency, technological progress, equity, cultural objectives, and diversity of views. We will consider each in turn.

8.3.1 Allocative Efficiency

Allocative efficiency exists if resources are allocated to production of different goods and services in an optimal manner. This implies that they are allocated to the goods and services consumers want, up to the point where the price a consumer is willing to pay for an additional unit is equal to the cost of producing it (marginal cost). In Figure 8.8, we compare the output, and hence the implied allocation of resources, of a perfectly competitive industry with that of a monopolist.

D represents the demand curve and S the supply curve of a perfectly competitive industry. Equilibrium is at price P_C and output Q_C.

If this industry operates not as a perfectly competitive industry but as a monopoly, what was a firm under perfect competition would become a plant of the monopolist. Recall that under perfect competition, each firm's marginal cost curve is also its supply curve, and the industry supply curve is the sum of the marginal cost curves of all firms. The supply curve of the perfectly competitive industry thus

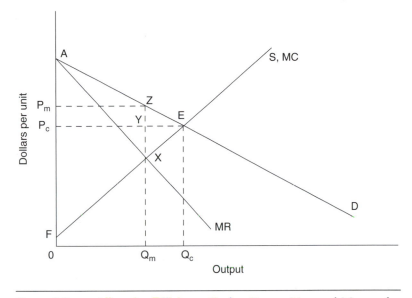

Figure 8.8   Allocative Efficiency: Perfect Competition and Monopoly
Compared

Note: D indicates demand curve for the industry; MC, marginal cost curve for the
monopolist; MR, marginal revenue curve for the monopolist; P, price; Q, quantity;
S, supply curve for the perfectly competitive industry. A, E, F, X, Y, and Z are points
referred to in the text in the explanation comparing perfect competition and
monopoly.

becomes the monopolist's marginal cost curve, MC. With demand
curve D, the monopolist has marginal revenue curve MR. The profit
maximizing price and output are P_M and Q_M, respectively. The
monopolist selects a higher price than that prevailing under perfect
competition and sells a smaller output. (Note that this assumes the
monopoly was *not* awarded through competitive bidding.)

Consider the benefits and costs to society of producing additional
units of output. In the absence of externalities (benefits received by
people who have not bought the product or costs borne by people
or organizations other than the producing firm), perfect competition
will be allocatively efficient. The benefit of an additional unit of output is the maximum price, as indicated by the point on the demand
curve, that a consumer is willing to pay. The cost is the marginal
cost of its production. Under perfect competition, output is Q_C
where the price someone will pay for the last unit is equal to the cost
of producing it. For all prior units, benefit exceeded cost. At the

monopoly output Q_M, price exceeds marginal cost. This output is not allocatively efficient because the excess benefit over cost for each unit between Q_M and Q_C is foregone; the sum of this difference is area ZXE and is known as the *deadweight loss.*

An alternative form of the explanation is that perfect competition is allocatively efficient because it maximizes the total surplus, the sum of consumer surplus, and producer surplus. As we have seen, consumer surplus is the difference between the maximum amount consumers would be willing to pay for the units bought and the amount they actually pay. Under perfect competition, consumer surplus is equal to triangular area $P_C AE$ in Figure 8.8. *Producer surplus* is an analogous concept and is defined as the difference between the price the producer actually gets for the units sold less the opportunity cost of supplying, where the opportunity cost is the marginal cost or minimum price at which the producer would be willing to supply. Under perfect competition, the producer surplus is triangular area $P_C FE$ and total surplus is thus $P_C AE + P_C FE$.

Under monopoly, at the higher price and lower output, consumer surplus shrinks to $P_M AZ$. Producer surplus becomes $P_M FXZ$. The monopolist has captured as producer surplus the area of rectangle $P_C P_M ZY$ that was consumer surplus under perfect competition but has lost area YXE because of the reduction in output to Q_M. Besides the loss of area $P_C P_M ZY$ to producer surplus, consumers have lost triangle ZYE as a result of the reduced output. The area ZXE, equal to the sum of areas YXE and ZYE, the producer surplus and consumer surplus, respectively, is lost due to the monopolist's profitable strategy of restricting output to sell at a higher price, and is thus the deadweight loss.

8.3.2 Productive Efficiency

Productive efficiency exists if the industry output is being produced at minimum total cost, given the state of technology. If there are economies of scale (or scope for multiproduct firms) and these economies of scale are large relative to demand for the industry product (the natural monopoly being the extreme case), perfect competition would not be productively efficient. None of the many firms would obtain a market share and, consequently, output level necessary to achieve minimum efficient scale. The absurdity of imagining many competitive cable TV companies, laying their own trunk cables and cable links to individual households, illustrates the point.

A monopolist would be able to exploit any economies of scale or scope but may not be productively efficient for another reason. The lack of competitive pressure tends to make monopolists lazy, and laziness leads to *X-inefficiency*, where the output produced by the factors employed by the firm is less than these factors are capable of producing.

8.3.3 Technological Progress

Technological progress involves invention and innovation and is the key to productivity and growth. Schumpeter (1950) argued that the positive economic profit that a monopolist may enjoy in the long run motivates outsiders to invent and innovate to obtain access to these profits. Through invention and innovation, a company may be able to bypass product or process patents, a monopolist's control of a raw material, a natural monopoly resulting from cost conditions associated with the existing technology, or other barriers to entry. As an example, cable TV has been established in the United States for more than 25 years and in Canada for even longer. Each cable TV franchise in the mid-1980s had (with a few exceptions) a monopoly in its franchise area for delivery of distant television signals and nonbroadcast television signals. Consequently, cable TV was very profitable. These profits, though, provided the incentive for the development of direct broadcast satellite and wireless cable multichannel, multipoint (MMDS) distribution technologies. Now most households in North America have a choice of delivery between their cable TV company, two or more DTH satellite services, and, in a few places, an MMDS service. Similarly, the development of facsimile transmission and e-mail has destroyed the monopoly enjoyed by government mail or post office services in the delivery of written communications.

Schumpeter (1950) coined the expression "creative destruction" to indicate that the very success monopolists have in generating positive economic profits provides, in the very long run, the seeds for the destruction of that monopoly position.

8.3.4 Equity

Equity is concerned with income distribution effects and tends to involve value judgments. In our discussion of allocative efficiency, we noted that area P_CP_MZY in Figure 8.8 is consumer surplus under perfect competition but producer surplus under monopoly. By using its market power to charge a higher price (P_M rather than P_C), the monopolist is able to capture this consumer surplus and enjoy positive economic profits, even in the long run. The result is that producers prosper at the expense of consumers. Under perfect competition, firms possess no market power, and this form of inequity is not an issue.

Governments often have their own views on what is equitable. For example, some governments, or their regulating agencies, have viewed local telephone service as a necessity and long distance as a luxury. As a consequence, in the past, regulators have set rates for local phone service below cost and rates for long distance above cost. Monopoly is amenable to this form of cross-subsidy. It would be impossible under perfect competition because competition would not permit a higher long distance price that provides the economic profits to compensate for losses in delivering local phone service.

8.3.5 Cultural and Similar Nonprofit Objectives

Cultural objectives are considered important by most governments in broadcasting, film, book publishing, magazine publishing, and music recording. However, most private companies operating in such industries are commercial operations whose main motivation is profits. Typically they are not too impressed if the government, or regulating agency, tells them they should be pursuing cultural goals (at the expense of profits). In fact, firms in a perfectly competitive industry would be unable to comply, as attempting to do so would result in negative economic profits and exit from the industry. Monopolies are more amenable to such pressure because of the slack provided by positive economic profits. A monopoly is able to take a bow in the direction of providing culture because the reduction in the level of positive economic profits may be viewed as a small price to pay, especially if the monopoly position is itself dependent on regulatory rules. An example is cable television in Canada. For a period during the 1980s and 1990s, the regulator (CRTC) protected cable franchises by discouraging entry of Canadian DTH services and made subscriptions by Canadians to U.S. DTH services illegal. It is not surprising that cable did not object too strongly to a requirement to operate a (money-losing) local community channel.

Some organizations actively pursue cultural or similar nonprofit objectives. The organization may be set up specifically as a nonprofit organization. An example is the National Geographic Society, which was formed, in 1888, "for the increase and diffusion of geographic knowledge" (NationalGeographic.com, 1996). This objective has been pursued primarily through its publication of the *National Geographic Magazine*. Even in organizations that are not specifically set up as non-profit, profit sometimes appears to be a secondary motive. Auteurs provide an example. An auteur is a film director, such as the Canadian director Atom Egoyan, who so dominates the filmmaking process that it is appropriate to call the director the author (*auteur* is French for "author") of the motion picture, the person primarily responsible for the creation and distinctive style of the film. For an auteur, film direction is a matter of expression, and profit considerations are secondary. Some family-controlled newspapers, such as the *Washington Post*, also seem to view profits as a secondary consideration.

Such nonprofit goals would be impossible to pursue at the expense of profits under perfect competition (or monopolistic competition). Even under other industry structures, such as monopoly or oligopoly, financial breakeven must be achieved for the organization to survive; hence sources of revenue must be explored and the operations conducted in a cost-efficient manner. Even an auteur needs to eat. In the case of Egoyan, availability of public (government) funding for production and distribution of Canadian films has facilitated the pursuit of nonprofit goals.

8.3.6 Diversity of Views

A major concern with monopoly in the mass media is the effect on diversity of opinion. Democracy works best when many independent voices are heard. It is thus a problem if, for example, the number of newspaper chains dwindles or the growth of media conglomerates results in cross-ownership. For example, a person living where the same company owns the local newspaper, the television station, and one of the radio stations is not likely to be exposed to a wide range of editorial opinion. However, there is no product differentiation under perfect competition, so the same concern applies to this industry structure.

8.4 Summary

In this chapter, we examined perfect competition and monopoly, the market structures at the opposite ends of the scale in terms of competitiveness.

In perfect competition, because there are many small firms producing an identical product, market price is determined by the interaction of industry supply and demand. Firms have to accept this price but can adjust their output to that at which mr = MC. In the short run, firms will produce as long as, at the output where mr = MC, average revenue (equal to price) is greater than average variable cost, and thus units produced at least contribute toward unavoidable fixed costs. Conversely, if average revenue is less than average variable cost, the firm should close its plant. This produce–shut-down criterion also applies to other industry structures.

The lack of barriers to entry means that perfectly competitive firms can only earn zero economic profits in the long run. If positive economic profits are earned in the short run, this is the signal for new firms to enter the industry. The entry of new firms expands industry supply and causes price to decrease until economic profit is reduced to zero. How far price falls depends on cost conditions; that is, whether the industry experiences constant cost, increasing cost, or decreasing cost as output expands.

A monopolist is the only seller of a particular product (a "single-seller") and can thus select the price for its product in the knowledge that there are no close substitutes available to consumers. The monopolist faces negatively sloped demand and marginal revenue curves and, for the single-price case assumed in this chapter, maximizes profits by selling at the price where MR = MC. Because of barriers to entry, the company can earn positive economic profits in the long run as well as in the short run.

A special category of monopoly is the natural monopoly, where economies of scale (or scope) are so great that only a single-seller can produce at lowest total cost.

Even where a natural monopoly exists, it may be possible to use competitive bidding to determine which company provides the product or service. In such cases, the price may approach the competitive price rather than the monopoly price.

Comparing the performance of the two industry structures, perfect competition is allocatively efficient; monopoly is not. Perfect competition will not be productively efficient if there are substantial economies of scale or scope. A monopolist can achieve economies of scale or scope but is likely to suffer from X-inefficiency, as the easy life permitted by the absence of competitive pressure results in inefficient use of inputs. Technological progress is more likely to occur under monopoly, as the positive economic profits provide a motivation for outsiders to invent and innovate to bypass product or process patents, a monopolist's control of raw materials, a natural monopoly associated with existing technology, or other barriers to entry. In terms of equity, a monopolist, by restricting output and setting a high price, prospers at the expense of consumers. However, a monopolist has the slack to be able to cross-subsidize between the services it offers, if the government or industry-regulating agency deems this desirable. Similarly, a monopolist, but not a perfect competitor, has the leeway to pursue cultural and similar goals partially at the expense of profits, but a profit constraint remains. Neither industry structure is consistent with diversity of views, an important objective for media industries.

9

Monopolistic Competition and Oligopoly

W hy were video stores very profitable in the early 1980s but not now? What has caused the fall in profits of commercial television broadcasters and the "crisis" in public broadcasting? Why did the Hollywood majors form the Motion Picture Export Association of America in 1945? What is conscious parallelism, and what judgment on this behavior was made by the U.S. Supreme Court in *Theater Enterprises, Inc. v. Paramount Film Distribution Corp.?* Why has Disney established a reputation for bringing legal actions against any person or company it perceives as encroaching on its brand-name copyrights? Why did Chapters (a large Canadian book-selling chain) follow a policy of having two or more bookstores in each major Canadian market? Why was it a winner takes all situation in the Betamax versus VHS battle of VCR standards? What strategic errors did Sony make in promoting its Betamax format? Why did Sega make its new Dreamcast videogame machine available for rent at 1000 Hollywood Video stores? Why did Sony design its Playstation 2 videogame machine to be backwards compatible with its first Playstation system? Why did Sony and Philips, in the early 1980s, agree on a compact disk standard rather than compete to establish the standard? What happened when competition in delivery of cable television services was introduced in Paragould, Arkansas? Why have there been complaints that television networks provide common denominator programming?

Why did the U.K. government block the bid of Murdoch's BskyB satellite service for Manchester United? What concerns would the U.S. Federal Communications Commission (FCC) weigh when considering AT&T's bid for U.S. cable companies TCI and MediaOne or MCI WorldCom's proposed acquisition of Sprint?

In this chapter, we examine monopolistic competition and oligopoly, the two industry structures located between perfect competition and monopoly on the competitiveness continuum. Most media industries fall under either monopolistic competition or oligopoly. As we saw in chapter 7, Albarran (1996) classifies book publishing, magazine publishing, and radio as monopolistic competition and classifies television networks, motion pictures, and music recording as oligopoly. Owen and Wildman (1992) categorize television program production as monopolistic competition because "entry is easy, [and] the industry is unconcentrated" (pp. 61-62). Vogel (1998, pp. 286-287) argues that most entertainment industries are oligopolistic because, at least beyond the early stages of their development, the amount of capital required and its cost constitute a formidable barrier to entry by new competitors. All these authors were making their market structure classifications in the context of the United States.

9.1 Monopolistic Competition

This market structure is similar to perfect competition, with free entry and exit and many small firms, but in monopolistic competition, the firms produce differentiated products. A monopolistic competitor thus has some control over price because no other firm makes an identical product. This price discretion is very limited, however, because there are many competitors producing close substitutes. A given customer may prefer the XYZ Video Store because of its location, selection, layout, or some other feature. The customer may stay loyal to the store if its nightly rental rate is $0.25 higher than some competitors, but not if it is $0.50 higher. The demand curve for the firm is thus negatively sloped.

In monopolistic competition, as in perfect competition, each of the many small firms has such a small market share that a decrease in price by one company will have no significant effect on the sales of any other firm. Thus each monopolistic competitor will make its price decision in the belief that other firms will leave their prices unchanged. This differs from oligopoly, where other firms feel a need to follow the price decreases of a competitor to protect market share. (If you think that the video stores in the area you live in would react to the price cut of a competitor, then video stores in your market are not an example of monopolistic competition but of oligopoly.)

Free entry and exit means that only zero economic profits can be earned in long-run equilibrium.

9.1.1 Short-Run Equilibrium Under Monopolistic Competition

The short-run equilibrium is the price and output at which $MR = SMC$. P_0 and Q_0 for a typical firm are shown in Figure 9.1. In short-run equilibrium, the firm may make positive, zero, or negative economic profits. To illustrate this, three alternative average total cost curves are drawn under different assumptions about the level of fixed costs. If ATC_1 applies, the typical firm enjoys positive economic profits, as $AR > ATC_1$ at the profit maximizing price and output. If ATC_0 applies, zero economic profits are earned, as $AR = ATC_0$. If ATC_2 applies, negative economic profits are earned, as $AR < ATC_2$. However, the firm will still produce output Q_0 at price P_0, rather than shut down, as long as AR is greater than average variable cost (not shown in Figure 9.1).

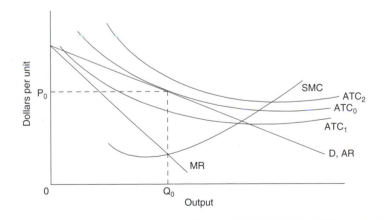

Figure 9.1   Short-Run Equilibrium of a Firm Under Monopolistic Competition

Note: AR indicates average revenue; ATC, average total cost; D, demand; MR, marginal revenue; P, price; Q, quantity; SMC, short-run marginal cost.

9.1.2 Long-Run Equilibrium
Under Monopolistic Competition

Let us suppose that the actual average total cost curve faced by the typical firm is ATC_1 (as shown in Figure 9.1), and the firm is thus earning positive economic profits. This situation cannot endure in the long run because the above-normal profit will attract new firms into the industry. As new firms selling different varieties of the industry product enter the industry, this new competition will begin to erode the market share of the incumbents. The demand curve for our typical firm, which before entry was D, begins to shift to the left. This process continues until the demand curve for the typical firm has shifted to D* (as shown in Figure 9.2). Entry will then cease, as the typical firm can only earn zero economic profits at the optimal price, P*, and output, Q*, where MR* = SMC. Long-run equilibrium has been established at a lower price and firm output, although industry output will have expanded. Notice that the monopolistic competitor, unlike the perfect competitor, does not produce at the minimum point of the ATC curve. Hence there is unused, or excess, plant capacity.

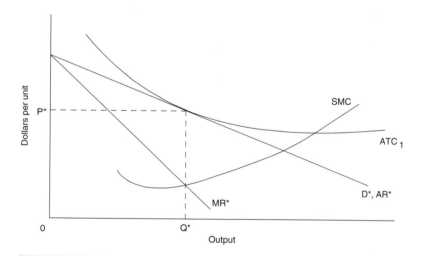

Figure 9.2   Long-Run Equilibrium of a Firm Under Monopolistic
                  Competition

Note: AR indicates average revenue; ATC, average total cost; D, demand; MR, marginal revenue; P, price; Q, quantity; SMC, short-run marginal cost.

This case—positive economic profits in the short run attracting entry in the long run that decreases the market share and profits of incumbents—describes a situation that has occurred in both video stores and television program services. The boom in VCR sales in the late 1970s and early 1980s led to a surge in demand for a complementary good, stores renting prerecorded (movie) videotapes. Video stores were very profitable until the entry of new stores increased competition and brought economic profits down to zero.

Television broadcasting organizations, through to the late 1970s and, in many countries, mid- or late 1980s, were protected from entry by the scarcity or regulation of spectrum frequencies. Commercial television broadcasting was very profitable, "a licence to print your own money" (Oxford Concise Dictionary of Quotations, 1997, p. 332). Public broadcasting organizations enjoyed large market shares and were widely regarded as providing good value for the license fee paid or government grant provided. Then new distribution technologies and less restrictive regulation led to entry by new television program services and reductions in audience share. As private broadcasting organizations lost audience share and faced new competition for the advertising dollar, their profits fell. As public broadcasting organizations lost audience share (e.g., from 1990 to 1992, the audience share of SVT2/TV2 in Sweden fell from 54% to 36% and that of ARD in Germany from 31% to 22%), people began to question whether they were providing value for money. This has led to the "crisis" in public broadcasting.

9.2 Oligopoly

An oligopolistic industry exists if the industry is dominated by a small number of large companies and there are barriers to the entry of new firms. Companies usually, but not always, sell a differentiated product.

Because of barriers to entry, companies under oligopoly may, like the monopolist, enjoy positive economic profits in the long run.

The distinctive feature of oligopoly is the interdependence of demand. Because there are only a small number of companies, the output of the individual firm is significant in the total industry output. Hence the price (or capacity or advertising or other competitive action) selected by one company affects the demand and revenues of its rivals. A change in price (or other competitive action) may cause competitors to change their price (or other competitive action). Firms must therefore practice *strategic behavior* by anticipating the possible reactions and counter moves of competitors and making the best decision accordingly.

The interdependence of demand also has the effect of making the conduct (and hence the performance also) of companies in an oligopolistic industry much less predictable than their conduct under other types of industry structures. Some oligopolistic industries exhibit cutthroat competition, whereas others exhibit, at least at times, cooperative behavior, and the industry operates like a monopoly.

9.2.1 The Kinked Demand Curve

To illustrate strategic behavior, suppose the NBC network is considering an increase in television advertising rates. It must consider whether CBS, ABC, and Fox (and, to a lesser degree, UPN, Warner Bros., and PAX) will follow the increase. If they do follow the price increase, NBC will not lose many customers, as relative prices will remain unchanged. But NBC's sales of advertising spots will drop substantially if its major competitors do not follow the price increase because many of its customers will switch their advertising to a rival network. Similarly, for a price decrease, NBC will gain many new customers if rivals do not follow, but the increase in demand will be smaller if rivals do follow the price decrease. Thus there are two basic demand curves. Assuming a current price P_1 and output Q_1, the demand curve dTd_1 and marginal revenue curve dAr in Figure 9.3(a) are drawn under the assumption that rival firms will follow *neither* a price increase nor a price decrease (this is like the demand curve assumed by the firm under monopolistic competition). The demand curve DTD_1 and marginal revenue curve DBR in Figure 9.3(b) are drawn under the assumption that other companies will follow *both* a price increase and a price decrease.

There is evidence to suggest that companies often assume that rivals' reactions will be the worst possible; that is, rivals will not follow a price increase, and hence the dT and dA segments of the demand curve and marginal revenue curve, respectively, apply for an increase but will follow a price decrease, and hence TD_1 and BR apply for the decrease. This results in the kinked demand curve shown in Figure 9.4. The demand curve is dTD_1 and is kinked at T. The marginal revenue curve is dA . . . BR, with a discontinuity

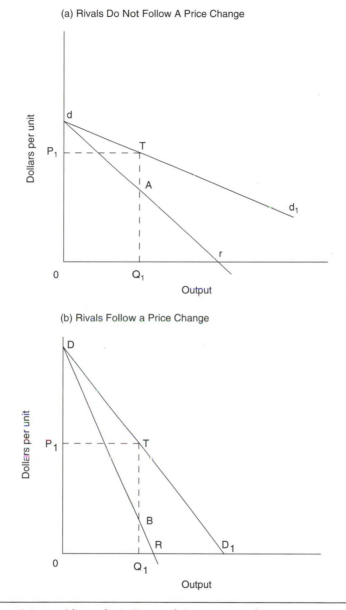

(a) Rivals Do Not Follow A Price Change

(b) Rivals Follow a Price Change

Figure 9.3   Oligopolist's Demand Curve, Depending on Reaction of
Rivals
(a) Rivals Do Not Follow a Price Change
(b) Rivals Follow a Price Change

Note: dAr and DBR indicate alternative marginal revenue curves; DTD_1 and dTd_1,
alternative demand curves; P, price; Q, quantity. T is a point on the demand curve
at the current price and output.

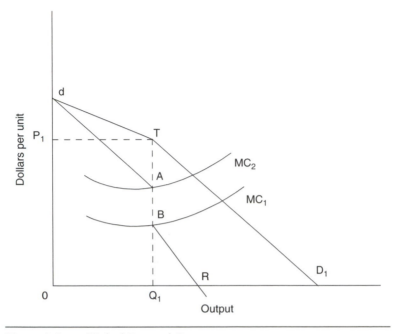

Figure 9.4   Kinked Demand Curve

Note: BR indicates marginal revenue for a price decrease; dA, marginal revenue for a price increase; dTD$_1$, demand curve; MC, marginal cost; P, price; Q, quantity.

between A and B. As long as marginal cost (MC) is A or B or in between at the current output, the firm cannot increase profits by changing price. For example, suppose the marginal cost increases from MC$_1$ to MC$_2$ in Figure 9.4. If the firm believes it faces a kinked demand curve, it will leave the price unchanged.

The kinked demand curve is not desirable for the companies in an oligopolistic industry. Assume the same increase in marginal cost was experienced by all companies in the industry. Although each firm knows that a higher industry price would increase industry profits, each company is afraid to initiate a price increase because they fear rivals will not follow, and consequently many sales will be lost and profit reduced. This situation provides an incentive for the firms to agree on an industry price and output and the division of this output among the companies. Collusion would eliminate the kink and make DTD$_1$ the relevant demand curve and DBR the marginal revenue curve. However, such matters are best examined in a Game Theory context.

9.2.2 Game Theory

Game Theory is the tool most commonly employed to examine and illustrate strategic behavior in business and other facets of life. The competitors are called *players*. Competition between oligopolists is viewed as a game, with the payoff to each player (for convenience, it is usually assumed that there are two competitors, a subset of oligopoly called *duopoly*) depending not only on the strategy that company chooses but also on the strategy chosen by the rival. These payoffs (usually profits in a business game), for each combination of strategies, are shown in a table called the *payoff matrix*.

9.2.3 The Payoff Matrix for a Pricing Game

To illustrate, suppose that two monthly magazines, *West Coast Gardening* and *Growing in Cascadia* (henceforth shortened to *West* and *Growing*, respectively) serve a regional niche market. There are no other competitors in this market niche. Both magazines have two possible price strategies: They can price an issue at $3 or at $2. Consumers will always buy the lower priced magazine if the prices are different, whereas they will split evenly between the two magazines if the prices are the same. The total number of magazines sold per month is 100,000 if both magazines price their issues at $3 and 150,000 otherwise. The magazines cost $1.00 to produce but (to keep the example simple) there is no loss associated with unsold magazines because, as a last resort, a recycling company will buy unsold magazines for $1.00 each.

To examine this game, we will first identify the payoff matrix in terms of sales and then in terms of profits. The sales payoff matrix, with *West's* sales shown before the colon and *Growing's* sales shown after the colon, is presented in Table 9.1.

Table 9.1   Magazine Sales Payoff Matrix

		Growing's strategy	
		Price $2	Price $3
West's strategy	Price $2	75,000 : 75,000	150,000 : 0
	Price $3	0 : 150,000	50,000 : 50,000

Table 9.2   Magazine Profits Payoff Matrix

		Growing's strategy	
		Price $2	Price $3
West's strategy	Price $2	$75,000 : $75,000	$150,000 : $0
	Price $3	$0 : $150,000	$100,000 : $100,000

For both competitors, the profit margin is $1 if the magazine is sold for $2 and $2 if it is sold for $3. Profits are the profit margin multiplied by the number of magazines sold. The profit matrix, with *West's* profit again shown first, is given in Table 9.2.

9.2.4 Dominant Strategy and Nash Equilibrium

The *dominant strategy* is the strategy that is best whatever the strategy selected by the rival. In any given game, a dominant strategy may exist for both, one, or neither of the players. For our magazine game, the dominant strategy for both players is to price at $2. Regardless of the strategy chosen by *West*, *Growing* gets more profit at a price of $2. If *West* selects a price of $2, *Growing* earns $75,000 at $2 but $0 at $3. If *West* chooses a price of $3, *Growing's* profit is $150,000 at $2, compared to $100,000 at $3. Similarly, the dominant strategy for *West* is a price of $2.

If both *Growing* and *West* follow their dominant strategy, both will price at $2 and receive $75,000 profits.

A *Nash Equilibrium* is found if player X is pursuing the best action given the action of player W, and player W is taking the best action given the action of player X. The solution in which *West* chooses a price of $2 and *Growing* selects a price of $2 is a Nash Equilibrium, as it meets these conditions. Given that *Growing* is selecting a price of $2, $2 is the best price strategy for *West*. Given that *West* is choosing a price of $2, $2 is the best price strategy for *Growing*. It is an equilibrium because a change in strategy by either magazine, given the strategy of the other, will reduce its profits.

The solution resulting from both companies adopting their dominant strategy is a noncooperative solution because both players are pursuing their own best interests in isolation.

9.2.5 Cooperative Games, Collusion, and Cheating

The magazine game is a *nonconstant sum game*. A nonconstant sum game is one in which the total prize varies according to the combination of strategies chosen by the players. Total profits, the sum of the profits of *West* and *Growing*, are $150,000 if both price at $2 or one prices at $2 and the other at $3. But if both price at $3, total profits are $200,000.

In a nonconstant sum game (business games are usually of this variety), there is an incentive to cooperate, as cooperation results in an increase in the profits of both companies. The cooperative solution for the magazine game is to agree to price at $3. This would result in $100,000 profits each per month, in both cases, $25,000 more than for the noncooperative Nash equilibrium solution. Note that $3 is the price a monopolist would choose. Colluding oligopolists select the monopoly price.

The cooperative pricing solution is not a Nash Equilibrium. Given that *West* is pricing at $3, *Growing* would do better at $2, as this would result in a profit of $150,000 rather than $100,000. Similarly, given that *Growing* is pricing at $3, *West* would make more profits at a price of $2. There is thus an incentive to cheat. If one magazine cheats by pricing at $2, the other magazine's profit, if it maintains a price of $3, is reduced to zero. The other magazine can thus be expected to reduce its price as well. Cooperation would collapse, and the magazines would return to the noncooperative solution in which both are following their dominant strategy.

9.2.6 Forms of Collusion, Facilitating Practices, and Commitment

The most explicit form of collusion is a formal contract to cooperate in strategic decisions. This is known as a *cartel* agreement. An example of a cartel is the Motion Picture Export Association of America, established in 1945 under the Webb-Pomerene Export Trade Act of 1918. As Guback (1982) explains:

> The Act permitted domestic competitors to cooperate in trade by forming export associations which might otherwise have been held illegal under the Sherman and Clayton antitrust acts. In effect, this exemption allowed American companies to combine and to fix prices and allocate customers in foreign markets. (p. 342)

One of the first actions of the Motion Picture Export Association of America, which comprised the then eight major U.S. film distributors, was to implement a boycott of Great Britain for an 8-month period over 1947 through 1948. The boycott, which involved refusing to supply films to the British market, was implemented in retaliation to imposition by the British government of a 75% ad valorem duty on imported films. The boycott was successful in getting the duty rescinded (see Jarvie, 1992, pp. 213-214).

Such formal agreements, unless the government is a participant or actively condones the arrangement, are illegal in most jurisdictions, as they contravene competition or antitrust laws.

Collusion may occur, however, through *conscious parallelism*. Conscious parallelism arises from similar behavior of oligopolists— oligopolists acting in the same manner as a result of their independent judgment concerning what is best for the industry, and confident that their rivals will also perceive and act in this common interest. The pricing of fuel at gasoline stations is sometimes given as an example. But the understanding certainly breaks down fairly frequently, as "gas wars" do break out.

Conscious parallelism in itself does not indicate conspiracy and is not illegal. For example, in the United States, the judgment on *Theater Enterprises, Inc., v. Paramount Film Distribution Corp.* (1954) declared that "this Court has never held that proof of parallel behavior itself constitutes a Sherman Act offense."

In some industries, historical practice facilitates collusion. For example, there may be a tradition that one of the companies, the *price leader,* initiates price changes, and the other firms follow. This price leadership is only likely to survive as long as the price leader continues to make decisions that are viewed by other companies as being in the industry's interest.

Facilitating practices are practices that aid in creating or sustaining implicit collusion. They usually involve provision of information aimed at reducing uncertainty. For example, a top executive of one of the major companies may make a public speech indicating that current industry prices will have to be raised if costs continue to increase. This may help create a common climate of opinion in the industry.

Advance notice of a price increase can be given. This has the advantage that rival companies are not caught by surprise. They have time to reflect on the desirability of a similar price change and perhaps announce that, given the increasing costs faced by the industry, they will follow suit. Alternatively, if it becomes obvious that other firms are not going to make a similar price increase, the initiating firm can rescind its decision (before it is implemented).

Such facilitating practices involve *signalling;* that is, indicating what the company believes to be the strategy that is in the best interests of the industry, or indicating a change in price or some other action that the company is contemplating.

There are also practices that facilitate maintaining collusion once that collusion has been achieved. These are aimed at removing the incentive to cheat through guaranteeing punishment by making retaliation appear inevitable. This may involve establishing a reputation. In another context, Disney has established a reputation for going after any person or company it perceives as encroaching on its brand-name copyrights. Seen in isolation, many of these legal actions by Disney may seem irrational, as the legal costs obviously outweigh any damage from letting the infringement continue. However, this view ignores the deterrent effect (deterring others from infringing on Disney copyrights) that Disney's reputation in this field has achieved. In terms of collusion, a firm may attain a reputation for rigidly following a "tit-for-tat" strategy. A tit-for-tat strategy involves always retaliating if any cheating is involved but upholding the agreement otherwise. Such a strategy is most useful for frequently repeated games.

Our magazine game can be used to illustrate signalling and a tit-for-tat strategy. Suppose the game starts with a noncooperative Nash equilibrium, with both magazines selling for $2. However, *West* would like to facilitate collusion. *West* could announce that, due to increased newsprint costs, it plans to increase the price to $3 commencing with the July issue. (It is diplomatic to provide a cost-based reason even if the real motive is to encourage collusion that would result in monopoly profits.) If *Growing* also changes its price to $3, then cooperation has been achieved. If *West* is following a tit-for-tat strategy, it will maintain a price of $3 as long as *Growing* does. If *Growing* cheats by lowering the price to $2, *West* will retaliate by adopting a $2 price a month later. When it thinks this retaliation has taught *Growing* a lesson, it may again try a $3 price and see if *Growing* follows. The important characteristic of the tit-for-tat strategy is that the other player is led to realize that punishment for cheating is inevitable. It is an attractive strategy for frequently repeated games. *West* realizes that by trying a $3 price for 1 month, it risks getting $0 profit rather than $75,000 (as it does under the Nash equilibrium, where both magazines are sold for $2) but believes this risk is worth the possibility of establishing a collusive price of $3, which would result in additional profits of $25,000 for each month the tacit agreement holds.

A deterrent to cheating has to be credible. One way to achieve credibility is to make a commitment that guarantees punishment. Suppose we have two consumer electronic stores, Insane and Wild, competing in a given locality. Both are currently selling a well-known brand of television set for $500. However, Wild is considering a price reduction to $400. Insane then announces a policy that if a consumer buying from Insane finds a lower price elsewhere within 3 months, *Insane* will refund double the difference. Wild knows that Insane is committed to this policy because of the public nature of the announcement. (Insane has "burnt its boats," just as Cortes did in a literal sense after landing in Mexico.) Wild figures out that the consequence of going ahead with the proposed price cut on the TV set is likely to be that consumers buy from Insane at $500, and then ask for a $200 rebate, double the difference between the posted prices. Insane's effective price would be $300. Insane has guaranteed that any price cut by Wild will be met by a still lower effective price from Insane. Hence Wild may decide not to proceed with its price cut. The beauty of Insane's strategy is that at face value it appears to be very competitive, but in practice it is likely to forestall price competition.

9.2.7 Conditions That Make Collusion More Difficult

It is never easy to achieve or maintain collusion. A historical analysis of collusion bears this out. This is not widely understood, especially by those who find conspiracy theories attractive. In the mid-1970s, when OPEC appeared omnipotent, economists were in a minority in treating projections of ever-increasing oil prices with skepticism. Collusion is never easy, but depending on the industry conditions, it may be more or less difficult. Here we identify factors that will make collusion more difficult.

A. *The less concentrated the industry.* The greater the number of firms in the industry and the more equal they are in size, the more difficult it will be to establish and sustain cooperation. Unless the government itself plays a role—for example, as it does in some countries in establishing agricultural product marketing boards—collusion is impossible under perfectly competitive or monopolistically competitive conditions.

B. *The more differentiated, complex, and changing the product.* A collusive agreement on price and output becomes increasingly difficult the more differentiated the products are. If Company Y's product is known to be superior to Company X's product, Company X will not be party to any agreement that calls on the two products to be sold at the same price. An agreed-upon price differential would have to be negotiated, but it is difficult to determine the appropriate spread. If the products are complex and differentiated on the basis of several attributes, this becomes even more problematic. If the products are frequently changed, as they tend to be in high-tech industries, a new agreement would need to be reached after each new product or model is introduced. For example, it is easy to imagine the difficulties that consumer electronic producers would have if they ever attempted to collude.

C. *The higher the ratio of fixed to variable cost.* The higher the ratio of fixed to variable cost, the greater the incentive to cheat when business is slow. In the event of a recession, sales will fall, but costs for a company with a high ratio of fixed to variable cost will decrease little. Companies will be tempted to break the collusive agreement by decreasing price to fill the unused capacity.

D. *The less frequently the game is played.* In the extreme case of a nonrepeated game in which the players move simultaneously, any threat of punishment is meaningless, as a player cannot reverse a selected strategy. The incentive to cheat by not implementing an agreed-upon cooperative strategy is overwhelming. Although such an extreme case may be exceptional, the frequency with which games are repeated varies widely. Pricing games, such as the magazine game discussed, are usually repeated frequently. Capacity games and some R&D games are repeated infrequently, if at all.

To illustrate, suppose there are two cinema chains, Multicin and Theaplex, serving a city. Both are considering an expansion involving a new cinema complex. Both Multicin and Theaplex realize that the additional cinema seats such an expansion would entail would put a downward pressure on seat price. The payoff matrix (profits in thousands of dollars per month, with Multicin's profits shown first) might be as given in Table 9.3.

Table 9.3   The Cinema Capacity Game: Profit Payoff Matrix in
Thousands of Dollars

		Theaplex's capacity strategy	
		Do not expand	*Expand*
Multicin's capacity	*Do not expand*	19 : 18	15 : 20
strategy	*Expand*	21 : 14	16 : 15

The dominant strategy for both Theaplex and Multicin is to expand. If Multicin expands, Theaplex obtains profits of 15 (in thousands of dollars per month) if it expands, rather than 14 if it does not expand. If Multicin does not expand, Theaplex earns profits of 20 if it expands, and 18 if it does not expand. Similarly, if Theaplex expands, Multicin receives profits of 16 if it expands, and 15 if does not expand. If Theaplex does not expand, Multicin earns profits of 21 if it expands, and 19 if it does not expand. If both follow their dominant strategy and expand, this will lead to a Nash Equilibrium, with profits of 15 for Theaplex and 16 for Multicin.

Collusion not to expand would look attractive, raising profits to 18 for Theaplex and 19 for Multicin. However, both have an incentive to cheat by expanding, as this would increase the profits of Theaplex to 20 or Multicin to 21. Suppose Multicin decides to cheat, whereas Theaplex has had every intention to comply. Cheating by Multicin would no doubt lead Theaplex to reverse its decision and expand also. However, reversing a capacity decision takes time. Theaplex would have to find a suitable site, find a builder, and so on. The longer the lag or delay in retaliation, the more attractive cheating becomes and, hence, the less likely a cooperative agreement will be attempted in the first place.

Suppose we change the rules of the game by assuming that there is only one suitable site on which to build a new cinema complex. The payoff matrix will be the same as shown in Table 9.3, except it is now impossible for both companies to expand. Although the total prize is still highest in a cooperative solution whereby neither expands, both realize that expansion will increase profits and preempt expansion by the rival. Any threat of punishment would not be credible, as retaliation is not possible. There will be a race to see which company can buy the site and expand first. The game is only played once.

In fact, there is evidence of competitive overexpansion by rival theater chains in North America. Rival chains rapidly built mega-plexes in the mid- and late 1990s, but long-term leases made it difficult to offset this increased capacity by closing down some of the older cinema complexes.

The CEO of Chapters in Canada has given deterring entry by rival bookstores as the reason Chapters has built two or more stores in each major city (Lorinc, 1999).

An R&D game might have a payoff matrix similar to that shown in Table 9.3. Each firm realizes that if both increase expenditure on R&D, this will result in lower profits, as both spend a lot of money developing similar new products that make their current products obsolete. Collusion to constrain R&D expenditure is thus attractive but difficult to sustain because of the high rewards available from cheating and being the only company to develop the new product.

E. *The more difficult it is to detect cheating.* Threats of punishment lose their credibility if cheating is difficult to detect. Some prices are negotiated between buyers and sellers; this is common with industrial goods or services sold to other companies. Both parties to the transaction are likely to regard such prices as confidential. Sometimes the supplier of goods and services is determined through a bidding process. The details of a winning bid are often not made public.

Any cooperation to raise price also involves an agreement to reduce output (price cannot be raised unless output is curtailed) and a decision as to how the decrease in output is to be shared. Cheating often involves selling more than the quota output rather than directly undercutting the agreed price. It may be more difficult for companies to monitor each other's output than each other's price. An example is the OPEC oil cartel, which has been repeatedly undermined by countries exceeding their quotas.

How difficult it is to detect cheating varies with the area of cooperation. For example, detecting cheating with respect to an agreement curtailing R&D expenditures is likely to be more difficult than it would be for an agreement to curtail advertising expenditures. The results of advertising expenditures can be quickly and easily observed, whereas higher than agreed levels of R&D are harder to detect, and the consequences are likely to be delayed.

9.2.8 Case Study: The U.K. Newspaper Game

The quality newspapers in the United Kingdom participated in a noncooperative game for much of the 1990s. As we discussed in chapter 3, in September 1993 the price of Rupert Murdoch's *The Times* was reduced from 45p to 30p. As this is an oligopolistic industry with *The Times, The Telegraph, The Independent,* and *The Guardian* being the close competitors, Rupert Murdoch would have been aware that this price reduction would decrease sales of rival newspapers. (We noted previously that *The Independent*'s daily sales did in fact drop from 360,000 to 240,000.) He would realize that this drop in sales might cause a rival to retaliate by also reducing price. For a while the rivals held off, perhaps in the hope that the price cut in *The Times* was temporary, but in June 1994, Conrad Black, proprietor of *The Telegraph,* reduced the price of his newspaper from 48p to 30p. In making this decision, Black would have had to consider the possible reactions of Murdoch and his other rivals. He did not have long to wait: The price of *The Times* was reduced to 20p the next day. Later in the year, *The Independent* finally reduced its price from 50p to 30p. All the newspapers saw reductions in share value during this price war. The shares of *The Telegraph* fell more than a third in the day following the cut in its own newspaper price (Barnard, 1994-1995). The size of the total prize, the industry's profits, was lower at the reduced price.

9.3 Product Competition

As we have seen, a key characteristic of both monopolistic competition and oligopoly is product differentiation. Firms compete to provide a product with a mix of attributes that consumers find valuable. For it to be profitable to provide a given attribute, however, the value added to the consumer, and, hence, the extra price the consumer must be willing to pay, must be greater than the incremental cost to the producer of providing the attribute. Advertising is a method of informing consumers about the attributes provided.

Many media software products, especially feature films, video-games, and computer programs, are experience goods characterized by a lack of transparency, meaning that it is hard for consumers to become aware of the attributes of the product prior to purchase. Advertising can show a few scenes, but what will the movie really be like? Once the shrinkwrap is removed, will the game work or the program run? Will it have the compatibility and usability features that are desired? Lack of transparency also characterizes new media content delivered over the Internet. As mentioned, advertising can help overcome the problem, but, in general, for experience goods, the lack of transparency hinders product competition because it is not easy for consumers to ascertain the value to them of product improvements; hence it is difficult to decide if the price is justified.

In some circumstances, success in product competition breeds further success, and a winner takes all situation results. This tends to happen in an advertising-based network economy. Popular sites attract advertising revenues, to the detriment of less-popular sites. But these additional advertising revenues make it possible for the more popular websites to improve their content and to become even more popular. Coupled with the corresponding revenue starvation of the less popular sites, this feedback process leads to a winner take all result. AOL and other sites that gained recognition early came to dominate the net because of their ability to create content of a given level of quality at a lower cost per user.

Another example is provided by competition between product systems. Most products provide consumers with attributes when consumed in isolation. For example, the flavor, texture, and appearance of an apple can be appreciated by eating that apple. Many communication products, however, are unusual in that they comprise hardware and software components of a product system. If two or more complementary products have little or no value to a consumer in isolation but have considerable value when combined together, then they belong to a *product system*. For example, a DVD player and a digital video disk comprise a product system. Only in combination do they provide the consumer with value.

In the remainder of this section, we will examine strategic decisions faced by companies making components of a product system. Recall that in chapter 4 we said that demand for hardware, used in conjunction with complementary software, exhibited network externalities. Product systems are sometimes called "virtual networks" because they share this feature with physical networks such as telephone services. Network externalities exist if an additional subscriber to a network provides a benefit to current subscribers to that network. Thus the value of belonging to a network is a positive function of the number of people subscribing to the network. In terms of our DVD example, the Hollywood majors had to be convinced that sales levels of movie disks would be sufficient for it to be profitable for them to supply movies in DVD format. However, sales of DVDs largely depend on the number of people owning a DVD player. Thus, as sales and, hence, the stock of DVD players in the hands of consumers increased, it became more attractive for movie distributors to provide new films and old films in DVD format. For example, Disney, which ignored the DVD format during the first 2 years of the standard's existence, decided to supply DVDs of nine of its animated films in fall 1999. But the more movies that are made available on DVD, the greater the value from owning a DVD player, so more people will buy one. This is known as a *positive feedback* effect. It may be accentuated if there are economies of scale or learning, as the expansion in output then reduces the cost of production and price.

Companies producing the hardware component of a product system have to make important strategic decisions. One option is for the company to go it alone and make a product in the hope that it either becomes the de facto industry standard or can successfully coexist with an incompatible product made by a rival. *Incompatibility* exists if the two hardware components cannot use the same software. An alternative option is for the company to cooperate with its rivals to agree on an industry standard and then compete in making products to that standard. The nature of these decisions and the issues that have to be considered are best examined by looking at some examples.

In chapter 4, we analyzed the Betamax (often known simply as Beta) versus VHS standards battle in terms of the attributes provided by the competing videocassette recorder (VCR) product systems introduced respectively by Sony in 1975 and JVC in 1976. The Betamax system provided a slightly better picture, but the VHS system provided a longer recording time. The first issue to examine in the context of this example is why there was not room for two product systems. We suggested in chapter 4 that a greater number of viewers valued the longer recording time of VHS more than the slightly better picture quality of Betamax, but this does not explain why the market did not stabilize at market shares of, say, 60% and 40%, respectively. In fact, what happened is that Betamax, with its earlier start, had a market share of over 50% in 1977, but this fell to less than half in 1978, one quarter in 1984, and then suffered a rapid decline that resulted in Sony withdrawing the product before the end of the 1980s (see Cusumano et al., 1992).

The triumph of the VHS format illustrates the winner take all nature of competition in many information products. Once one system gained an initial market share advantage, there was a tendency for this advantage to become more pronounced over time. Let us see why this is the case. As the market share of Betamax fell, the Hollywood majors became increasingly reluctant to provide a Betamax as well as a VHS version of their movies. Video stores began to stop carrying cassettes in Betamax format. Consumers, seeing the decline in market share of Betamax VCRs and observing the poorer selection of Betamax cassettes available, began flocking to purchase VHS format VCRs. In the absence of a sizeable group of consumers who valued the better picture provided by Betamax strongly enough that this was the major influence on their purchase decision, the decline in market share became a self-perpetuating trend. Once a *bandwagon effect* of this type was underway, it was unstoppable. Consumers did not wish to purchase hardware for which software would become scarce or unavailable. Particularly in the early stages of a bandwagon effect, it is consumer (and software producer) expectations about market share that are important. By the early 1980s, many consumers observed the trends in market shares and chose VHS because they wanted to be on the side of the winner to protect their investment.

Why did Sony lose the VCR standards battle? Sony had two big advantages. It was first on the market and had an unsurpassed reputation. Being first can be crucial even when the system is inferior to alternatives. An example is the QWERTY keyboard layout, which is inferior to the Dvorak layout. The QWERTY keyboard layout was intentionally designed to slow the typist down to prevent mechanical typewriter mechanisms jamming, but it became the standard (and remained the standard when electric typewriters replaced mechanical ones) because it was first and there was soon a large group of people trained to use it. Sony also had been a pioneer in industrial video recorders and possessed an unrivaled reputation for successfully introducing innovative consumer electronic products. Sony, however, made mistakes that dissipated these advantages. Sony was slow to approach other manufacturers about producing the Betamax standard under license and would not sell VCRs to other manufacturers to resell under their own labels. In contrast, JVC, and its parent Matsushita, moved quickly and had lined up Hitachi, Mitsubishi, and Sharp by the end of 1976 and RCA in early 1977. JVC and its allies were able to deliver more units to market and at a lower price. In addition, Sony did not permit other manufacturers to improve the Betamax standard, whereas JVC encouraged others to make refinements, such as increasing recording time. Matsushita, unlike Sony, facilitated the production of prerecorded VHS cassettes by developing and making available equipment for high-speed duplication in this format.

At the time of the VCR standards battle, Sony was not in a position to supply its own prerecorded movies in Beta format. If it had been, by quickly providing such software it might have prevented the market from tipping in the direction of the VHS format. Sony's experience with Betamax was no doubt a factor in its decision to purchase Columbia Pictures, a Hollywood major, in 1989.

Similar standards wars have been fought in computer operating systems and videogames. The IBM PC-Windows combination has largely won out over Apple-MacOS. The PC got a lead, and this turned into a bandwagon effect. As the market share of the Macintosh fell, software providers either stopped developing software for the Macintosh or only produced a Mac version after a considerable delay. Poorer availability of Mac software led to consumers selecting PCs. In addition, people who exchanged files with others found this process easier if they were using the dominant operating system. Apple, with the Mac, made some of the same mistakes as Sony with Betamax, as well as some of its own. Sony was slow to license manufacture by others; Apple refused to license its hardware and software. This is in contrast to IBM, which made its platform available to "clones" and encouraged independent software developers to write IBM-compatible software. Whereas Sony's low-end prices were somewhat higher because costs were higher, Apple charged high prices for the early Macs to boost short-term profits. Of course, despite these errors in strategy, the Macintosh still survives, albeit with a market share of less than 5%. The reason is that, unlike the case of Betamax, there is a core of loyal Macintosh users who, despite software and exchange disadvantages and a premium price, value Mac attributes such as ease of use and superior graphic capabilities sufficiently highly that they keep replacing their old Macs with new ones.

Atari, Nintendo, Sega, and Sony have fought a continuing battle with incompatible videogame systems. In this industry, the product systems have been replaced by a new standard every 5 years or so. The winner in one round may be the loser in the next. Atari was dominant in 8-bit systems, Nintendo with 16-bit systems. Sega was first with a 32-bit system and achieved a 60% market share. Nintendo and Sony, with its PlayStation machine, then contested the market with their 64-bit systems. By summer 1999, Sony was dominant, with a market share of about 60%. Nintendo followed with over 30%, and Sega had less than 5%.

In fall 1999, Sega introduced its 128-bit Dreamcast video system. This had a modem that permitted owners to browse the Web, send and receive e-mail, and play games online as well as from game cartridges.

Shortly before the introduction of the Dreamcast, Sony announced that it would introduce its own 128-bit PlayStation 2 system in 2000. It said this would have capabilities similar to those of Dreamcast, plus two additional attributes. The PlayStation 2 system would be able to play CDs and DVD movies. The product preannouncement is a well-established strategy for discouraging consumers from buying a rival's product prior to the introduction of one's own. To be effective, the company making the preannouncement must have established a good reputation so that the promise to supply certain attributes is widely believed. Sony has such a reputation.

A ploy used by Sega with its Dreamcast videogame machine has been to make the machine available for rent at 1000 Hollywood Video stores. This strategy has two advantages. First, it permits consumers to try the product system and overcome the lack of transparency problem without committing to the product. The availability of a low-cost trial is important for an experience good of this type. (We return to this in the discussion of penetration pricing in the next chapter.) If the trial is successful, the consumer may decide to purchase. Second, the consumer may regard renting as an attractive alternative to buying because renting negates the risk of having invested in an obsolete system.

However, sales of Dreamcast proved disappointing, and Sega ceased production of videogame machines early in 2001 to concentrate on developing new games for Sony, Nintendo, and others (as well as for the stock of Dreamcast machines held by consumers). But new competitors for PlayStation 2 were on the horizon, each claiming superior attributes. In November 2001, Microsoft entered the videogame machine market with its X-box and Nintendo launched its GameCube.

Some of the videogame machine manufacturers have promoted a wide availability of games by actively seeking independent software suppliers to develop games. Nintendo is an example. Consumers find the wide availability of games attractive, and Nintendo earns a royalty on each game sold. Furthermore, Nintendo has insisted on a 2-year exclusive contract; the games are denied to rivals during this period.

Where a new standard replaces an existing one, the hardware producer has to decide whether to make the new system backward compatible. It is backward compatible if the new hardware will operate the software designed for the previous system. For example, Sony designed PlayStation 2 to be able to play games designed for its original PlayStation system. Backwards compatibility is, obviously, a worthwhile feature for owners of current software. If it can be provided at low cost and without sacrificing performance unduly, then it makes sense for the company to supply this attribute. This is not always the case, however. For example, a high-definition standard (HDTV) called HD-MAC, adopted by Europe in the early 1990s, failed because, by making the signal decipherable by existing conventional television sets, the picture quality was so compromised that it was little better than the existing PAL and SECAM standards.

An alternative to battling with incompatible standards is for the companies in the industry to agree on a common standard and then compete in producing to that standard. Agreement involves the willing participation of all the companies involved. This is more likely if no one company has a clear advantage that leads it to believe it would win a standards war.

In the early 1980s, Sony and Philips agreed on a compact disk standard. Other producers were drawn into supporting the standard through licensing agreements.

One problem with cooperation to reach a standard is that, in retrospect, the standard chosen may prove to be the wrong one. This was true of the HDTV standards selected by both Europe (the HD-MAC standard already discussed) and the Japanese "Muse" standard. Both were analog systems and, although the Muse system is still in use, it is now clear that digital systems are far superior and will prevail.

In a case like HDTV, where the television signal is system specific, it is obvious that only one new system can be adopted for a given territory. In such cases, it is probably inevitable that the government will be involved in determining which standard is chosen. This was the case in Europe and in Japan and is the case also in the United States. Initially, the U.S. government sponsored a competition to determine the standard. Most of the original submissions were for an analog system, but when it became obvious that a digital standard would be adopted, the remaining competitors cooperated by agreeing to merge technologies and share licensing fees. The regulator, the FCC, side-stepped the backward compatibility problem by awarding each broadcaster additional bandwidth to permit the simultaneous transmission of digital HDTV and NTSC, the existing North American standard, signals for about 10 years.

This section has drawn on Besen and Farrell (1994), Katz and Shapiro (1994), and Shapiro and Varian (1999). For more information, see these readings.

9.4 Performance

In this section, we examine the performance, in various dimensions, of monopolistic competitive industries and oligopolistic industries. Comparisons of performance will be made not only between these industry structures but with perfect competition and monopoly.

9.4.1 Allocative Efficiency

In Figure 9.5, we compare the long-run equilibrium price and output of a firm under monopolistic competition with that of a firm under perfect competition. The perfect competitor, facing a horizontal demand curve, d, at P_C, the market price determined by industry supply and demand, produces output Q_C, where marginal revenue equals marginal cost (mr = MC). Because of product differentiation, the firm under monopolistic competition faces a negatively sloped demand curve, D, and associated marginal revenue curve, MR. This results in a smaller profit maximizing output of Q_{MC} (where MR = MC), higher price of P_{MC}, and excess capacity of $Q_C - Q_{MC}$. As in monopoly, the monopolistic competitor thus sells at a price greater than marginal cost and restricts output below the allocatively efficient perfect competition level. The consequence, again, is a deadweight loss. However, this deadweight loss would be considerably less than that associated with monopoly because the competitive pressure present in monopolistic competition will result in a lower price.

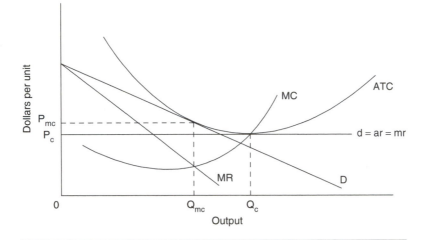

Figure 9.5   Allocative Efficiency: Perfect Competition and
Monopolistic Competition Compared

Note: ar indicates average revenue for the firm under perfect competition; ATC, average total cost; D, demand curve for the firm under monopolistic competition; d, demand curve for the firm under perfect competition; MC, marginal cost; MR, marginal revenue curve for the firm under monopolistic competition; mr, marginal revenue curve for the firm under perfect competition; P, price; Q, quantity.

Oligopolists also face a negatively sloped demand curve and hence sell at a price greater than marginal cost and restrict output below the allocatively efficient perfectly competitive level. Because oligopolists have greater market power than monopolistic competitors, reflected by the fact that they may earn positive economic profits in the long run, the oligopoly price may be higher than that for monopolistic competition and the deadweight loss may be greater. As we indicated earlier, however, the level of competition and, hence, price varies considerably among oligopolistic industries. However, unless there is very effective collusion, competition between oligopolists should provide lower prices than monopoly.

Confirmation of this is provided by Barrett's (1995) case study of cable television service in Paragould, Arkansas. The 1991 entry of City Cable into a market where Paragould Cablevision, Inc. previously had a monopoly resulted in lower prices, increased program choice, improved customer service, and technological upgrades. For example, before the threat of entry, Paragould Cablevision was charging $14.50 per month for a basic cable service of 40 channels and $10 for each additional premium channel such as HBO. After City Cable announced its rates, Paragould Cablevision reduced its basic cable rate to $9.50 per month, with additional premium channels charged at $3 to $5 per month. Prices then remained unchanged during a period when the average U.S. cable rates (largely comprising rates set by monopoly franchise holders) increased by 16.9%.

9.4.2 Productive Efficiency

If there are substantial economies of scale or scope, the monopolistic competitor is likely to be too small to exploit these economies. Oligopolistic companies, on the other hand, are usually large enough to exploit any such economies available and be productively efficient. Depending on how competitive the oligopoly is, X-inefficiency may or may not be exhibited.

Sometimes an industry is not productively efficient because some resources are diverted from production to *rent seeking*. Rent seeking denotes an attempt to decrease the level of competition in an industry to divert consumer surplus to producer surplus and increase profitability. (Note that economists use the term *rent* or *economic rent* to mean a surplus, rather than its common usage.) Rent seeking may involve buying out competitors or suppliers or lobbying to influence the political process to obtain monopoly rights. Rent seeking is most prevalent under oligopoly. For example, in Canada, the traditional private broadcasters have continually lobbied the industry regulator (the CRTC) and the Canadian government to prevent, or at least slow down, entry of new competitors. The television program production community has expended large quantities of resources to ensure that domestic content requirements and subsidy programs continue.

In addition, if rent seeking is successful, further negative implications ensue for performance with respect to allocative efficiency, equity, cultural, and diversity dimensions.

9.4.3 Technological Progress

The prospect of positive economic profits in the short run will induce firms in monopolistic competition, unlike perfect competition, to seek a temporary advantage through product innovation.

Many economists consider that Schumpeter's concept of creative destruction, discussed with respect to monopoly in chapter 8, applies with even more force to oligopoly. Oligopolists are large enough to afford substantial, organized, R&D activities. Competition is usually strong enough to force them to be innovative to survive and flourish. The barriers to entry permit the companies to enjoy the fruits of successful innovation in terms of economic profits in the long run (an incentive for innovation not present under monopolistic competition). Certainly many oligopolistic companies and industries are extraordinarily innovative. Consider, for example, producers of consumer electronic goods such as Sony, Matsushita, and Philips.

9.4.4 Equity

As price under monopolistic competition is typically less than under oligopoly, and the oligopolistic firm may enjoy economic profits in the long run, monopolistic competition is generally more equitable for the consumer. However, if a government considers that a cross-subsidy, such as between long distance and local telephone services, is desirable in the name of equity, an oligopolistic industry could sustain such a cross-subsidy, although a monopolistic competitive industry could not. The reason is the same as that discussed in the last chapter in the comparison of perfect competition and monopoly. Long-run economic profits are necessary to make cross-subsidy feasible.

9.4.5 Cultural and Other Nonprofit Goals

As we argued in chapter 8, economic profits in the long run are necessary if firms are to be persuaded, or required, by a regulatory agency to further cultural goals at the expense of profit. Similarly, the opportunity to earn economic profits in the long run permits other goals to be pursued willingly. In the context of this chapter, oligopolies may permit other goals to be pursued, but monopolistic competitors will not unless compensated by government or other subsidies.

9.4.6 Diversity

Both monopolistic competition and oligopoly, unlike perfect competition and monopoly, provide the consumer with product choice. Monopolistic competition is ideal from this perspective: Witness the wide choice of magazines available and the almost infinite selection of books.

Hotelling (1929) has argued that an oligopolistic industry is likely to provide less variety of product than might be expected. Steiner (1952) used the Hotelling approach to demonstrate that a small number of competing, advertising-financed broadcasting services have an incentive to provide similar programs because each gets a higher rating from sharing the large audience for a popular program type than from gaining all the audience for a minority-interest program. We explore this further in chapter 11.

9.4.7 Public Policy and Competition

Mergers have the potential to reduce competition and even change market structure. For example, a merger of duopolists changes the structure from an oligopoly to a monopoly. Given the trade-off of advantages and disadvantages associated with the various industry structures, public policy with respect to mergers requires a weighing of factors. Most countries have a competition or antitrust agency that evaluates each major merger and judges whether it is in the public interest. The authority of the agency and the criteria it applies vary from country to country, but typically such an agency will assess whether a given merger would reduce competition unduly and whether it would reduce operating costs.

An example is provided by the October 1998 $1 million bid for Manchester United, the most popular soccer team (and, arguably, sports team) worldwide, made by Rupert Murdoch through his satellite television service, BskyB. This followed a well-established pattern of buying professional sports franchises. Earlier in 1998, Murdoch had bought the Los Angeles Dodgers (baseball) to add to his 40% interest in the New York Knicks (basketball) and New York Rangers (ice hockey) and Madison Square Gardens, where the two New York franchises play. BskyB already had exclusive rights to televise English Premier League games live (some of the games are shown live by Murdoch's Fox Sports in the United States), and this could be interpreted as an attempt by Murdoch to tighten his control of this source of valuable live television programming. The bid was accepted by the Board of Directors (Manchester United operates as a public company), but the U.K. government referred it to the Monopolies and Mergers Commission. When blocking the bid in April 1999, Stephen Byers, the Trade and Industry Secretary, was quoted by Pye (1999) as saying that the commission had concluded that "the merger would adversely affect competition between broadcasters" (p. A32). It would also give BskyB "additional influence over Premier League decisions about the organisation of football leading to some decisions which would not reflect the game's long-term interests" (p. A32).

AT&T's purchases of U.S. cable companies TCI and the MediaOne group drew the attention of the FCC. The mergers were made possible by the 1996 Telecommunications Act, which gave the telephone companies the option of offering services via cable and permitted cable to offer local telephone services. With respect to TCI, America Online and others argued that the merger should only be approved if AT&T opened up its prospective high-speed Internet facilities to all ISPs. But the FCC approved the merger, with no conditions attached, ruling that conditions were unnecessary because cable telephony and cable Internet services are still in their infancy. Interestingly, AOL has been accused of backing off its support of open access since its merger with Time-Warner, a company with large cable interests, was announced. Not only does public policy affect industrial competition, it appears that corporate activities in the public policy sphere can become, themselves, elements of interfirm competition.

It took a year for the FCC to approve the AOL merger with Time Warner, and this approval was made conditional on AOL Time Warner allowing competing Internet companies open access to its cable customers and agreeing to support rival high-speed Internet access technology.

The proposed acquisition of Sprint by WorldCom (now MCI) raised questions with respect to the effect on the level of competition in long distance telephone services. Are WorldCom and Sprint currently at a cost disadvantage relative to AT&T, and would a merger reduce their costs? Would WorldCom and Sprint provide more effective competition for AT&T if they were merged, or would the reduction in the number of players reduce competition? The U.S. Justice Department and the European Union (EU) competition commissioner thought the latter. Joel Klein, an assistant attorney general who heads the Department of Justice's antitrust division, considered the merger would lead to "higher prices, lower service quality and less innovation for millions of American consumers and businesses," and the U.S. Department of Justice announced that it was suing to block the deal. Meanwhile, the EU competition commissioner said the merger would sharply reduce competition for Internet services. In the face of such opposition, the principals called the merger off in July 2000 (Tribune Wire Services, 2000).

An associated concern of many governments has been to ensure that oligopolistic industries behave competitively. Most nations have laws prohibiting various forms of collusion, such as price fixing.

9.5 Summary

In this chapter, we examined monopolistic competition and oligopoly, the market structures in which most media industries are found.

A monopolistic competitor produces a differentiated product and thus faces a negatively sloped D curve. Its price discretion is very limited, however, because of the many competitors selling close substitutes. The lack of barriers to entry means that zero economic profits will be earned in the long run.

Under oligopoly, a small number of firms each produce a significant proportion of industry output. As a consequence, there is an interdependence of demand, and companies must practice strategic behavior by anticipating the reactions and countermoves of competitors and make the best decision accordingly. This makes the conduct and performance of oligopolistic industries much less predictable than those of other industry structures. Conduct can vary from cut-throat competition to explicit collusion.

In pricing decisions, an oligopolist has to anticipate whether rivals will follow a price increase or a price decrease. There is some evidence that oligopolists assume the worst; that is, rivals will not follow a price increase but will follow a price decrease. This results in a kinked demand curve and a reluctance to change price.

Game theory is the tool most commonly employed to examine and illustrate strategic behavior. A payoff matrix shows the rewards (usually profits in business games) that each duopolist will get, depending on the strategy it chooses and the strategy chosen by the rival. A dominant strategy is the strategy that is best no matter what strategy is chosen by a rival. A Nash Equilibrium exists if both players are pursuing the best action given the action of the other player. In any particular game, there may or may not exist a dominant strategy for one or both players or a Nash Equilibrium.

Many business games are nonconstant sum games where the total prize (usually profits) varies according to the combination of strategies chosen by the players. There is then an incentive for oligopolists to cooperate to ensure joint actions that maximize total industry profits. The form of cooperation may be explicit collusion, which is usually illegal, or conscious parallelism, in which companies act in the same manner as a result of their independent judgment concerning what is best for the industry. Conscious parallelism may be facilitated by price leadership or signalling.

However, a cooperative solution is unstable, as it is not a Nash Equilibrium. Given that one firm is following a cooperative strategy, the other makes more profits by cheating. Collusion is more difficult to achieve and harder to maintain, if it is achieved in the first place: (a) the less concentrated the industry; (b) the more differentiated, complex, and changing the product; (c) the higher the ratio of fixed to variable cost; (d) the less frequently the game is played; and (e) the more difficult it is to detect cheating. A tit for tat strategy may deter cheating.

Product systems comprise complementary hardware and software. Typically, the software of one system cannot be used with the hardware of another; for example, a Sega game cannot be played on a Nintendo videogame machine. Often, markets for product systems are characterized by winner takes all outcomes, because once one system gains an initial market share advantage, there is a tendency for this advantage to become more pronounced over time. Strategies for fighting a standards battle include licensing other manufacturers to produce and even help develop the hardware and software. A company may be advised to try to cooperate with a rival to establish a common standard rather than enter a standards battle.

With respect to performance, neither monopolistic competition nor oligopoly is allocatively efficient. Typically, the output under monopolistic competition will be closer to the optimal level.

Substantial economies of scale or scope, where they exist, would prevent monopolistic competition from being productively efficient. But oligopolistic industries are particularly prone to diverting resources from production to rent-seeking activities aimed at reducing competition and diverting consumer surplus to producer surplus.

Technological progress often flourishes under oligopoly. The possibility of economic profit in the long run is the carrot, and competition is often strong enough to provide the stick.

Government-mandated notions of equity and culture are more easily accommodated by oligopolistic industries than by monopolistic industries, as only the former can enjoy the positive economic profits that make noneconomic goals possible in the absence of a subsidy.

From the viewpoint of diversity, monopolistic competition is ideal, with many close substitutes made available. Oligopolistic industries also provide choice, although sometimes less than might be expected.

Given the trade-off of advantages and disadvantages associated with the various industry structures, most nations have a competition or antitrust bureau or commission that evaluates major mergers and assesses whether they are in the public interest. Typically, the bureau is concerned with the impact of any given merger on the level of competition and operating costs. Most nations also have laws prohibiting various forms of collusion, such as price fixing.

10

Pricing and
Market Segmentation

Why are the prices for foreign sales of U.S. television programs and movies so low? Are these prices unfair, and do they constitute dumping? Why do publishers of academic journals have different subscription prices for institutions (libraries), students, and other individuals? Why did the first video stores in the late 1970s have a membership fee, and why is that no longer the case? Why has block booking of movies (i.e., selling them only in packages or bundles) been prevalent? Why are books first introduced in hardback form, with a lower priced paperback only becoming available later? Why do magazine publishers offer first-time subscribers a special low price? Why is the mark-up (above cost) lower for videogame machines than for the videogame software? Why do telephone companies have peak and nonpeak prices for long distance calls? An understanding of pricing strategies, the subject of this chapter, provides the knowledge base needed to answer these and similar questions.

We begin by examining the role of cost and the role of demand in pricing. Cost-based pricing formulae were once prevalent, but do they make sense? Price discrimination, bundling, and two-part tariffs are demand-based pricing techniques that can increase the profits of oligopolists and monopolists. Pricing of product systems involves pricing complementary goods. The demand for the software depends on the price of the hardware and vice versa. Predatory pricing is a strategy whereby a low price is used temporarily to eliminate competition or deter new entry. New product pricing considers the price strategy for introducing a new product. This is a particularly important subject for media industries, where new products are being developed continuously: Every movie, television program, and music recording can be viewed as a new product. Another set of pricing issues arises as a result of short-run capacity constraints. Congestion costs and peak-load pricing are discussed in this context. Throughout, examples and applications, including answers to the questions posed in the first paragraph, will be drawn from media industries.

10.1 The Role of Costs in Pricing

Survey research was used in the 1950s and 1960s to identify the pricing practices companies actually use. *Full-cost pricing* (also known as *cost-plus pricing*) was found to be most prevalent. This method calculates price on the basis of the following formula:

$$\text{Full-cost price} = \text{Direct costs (per unit)} + \text{Indirect cost}$$
$$\text{(per unit)} + \text{Fair profit margin}$$

Direct costs are expenditures on factors of production, such as raw materials and labor, that are made in the period in which the factors are employed. We referred to these costs as explicit costs in chapter 6. Indirect costs are an allocation of overhead (what economists refer to as fixed costs). The basis for allocating might be the number of hours of labor needed to produce a unit of the product or the number of machine-hours necessary. The "fair" profit margin, expressed as a percentage of total costs, is usually the historical norm for the industry.

Superficially, the full-cost pricing method looks attractive. Summing all costs and adding a mark-up would seem to guarantee a profit. This is not the case, however.

The greatest drawback with the full-cost method is that it completely ignores demand. Note first that the full-cost price can only be calculated if an output is initially assumed. The indirect costs per unit will, obviously, vary inversely with the number of units over which the fixed overhead is to be allocated. (Over some output ranges, direct costs per unit can also be expected to vary.) But it is the demand for the good that will determine whether this quantity can be sold at the price derived from the full-cost formula. If demand is insufficient, less will be sold, and the company may indeed make a loss at the full-cost price. The optimal price depends on a consideration of demand as well as cost.

The other drawback is the inclusion of costs that are irrelevant to the price and output decision. Recall that, in the Theory of the Firm, the profit maximizing price is explained as the price that results in sales or output where MR = MC. This may sound very abstract, but what it means is that only that element of total cost that varies with output is relevant to the price or output decision. Thus direct (explicit) costs are relevant. Also relevant, but not represented in the full-cost formula, are the implicit or opportunity costs discussed in chapter 6. On the other hand, indirect (or fixed) costs, which are included in the full-cost formula, are not affected by the current output level and hence are not germane to pricing decisions.

Variable costs can be thought of as providing a floor for possible prices. Under no circumstances should a company price below this level. As we saw in chapter 8, the firm should shut down rather than produce at a price less than the average variable cost.

10.2 The Role of Demand

How much above the floor the price should be depends on demand or, to be more specific, the price elasticity of demand (η). It can be shown (see, for example, Douglas, 1992, pp. 424-427) that the optimal price is given by

$$P = AVC + [1/(\eta - 1)] \times AVC$$

where AVC is average variable cost and η is the price elasticity of demand.

The term $[1/(\eta - 1)]$ represents the optimal mark-up over variable costs, and this is a function of the price elasticity of demand. Expressed in percentage terms, if, for example, $\eta = 6$, the optimal mark-up is 20% (= $[1/(6 - 1)] \times 100$); if $\eta = 3$, it is 50%; if $\eta = 2$, it is 100%; and so on. The less sensitive (elastic) quantity demanded is to price, the higher the profit maximizing price. Thus, if AVC = \$30 and $\eta = 6$, the optimal price is \$36 (= $30 + [1/(6 - 1) \times 30$). If $\eta = 3$, the optimal price is \$45; if $\eta = 2$, the optimal price is \$60; and so on.

It is not easy for firms to determine the price elasticity of demand for their product. Often, a more practical demand-based approach is the *economic value* approach. In chapter 4, we saw that consumers attempt to allocate a limited budget in such a way that they maximize the total utility (or value or benefit) from consumption. We also saw that this involves equating the ratio of marginal utility to price for each product purchased. Thus, in setting a price, it is important to give target consumers "value for money" relative to substitute products to persuade them to buy the company's product. We suggested in chapter 4 that products can be viewed as a set of attributes. The closest substitute will be the product with the most similar mix of attributes. The price of this substitute product then provides a base or reference for consideration of the company's own price. Even the closest substitute will not have identical attributes, however, so it is important to identify aspects where the company's product differs and assess the positive or negative value that target consumers are likely to attach to these differences. This suggests the following steps (based on Nagle & Holden, 1995, pp. 72-77) in setting a price:

- Identify the closest substitute product and the price for which it is selling. The price of this substitute is known as the *reference value*.
- Identify how the attributes of your product differ from those of the closest substitute.
- Assess the value, both positive and negative, to a target customer of these differences. This value is the *differentiation value*.
- Sum the reference value and the differentiation value to obtain the total economic value on which to base price. The price selected might be just below this to provide superior value for money.

The company may wish to go through this exercise for several competing products before settling on a price. Bringing in the cost side, a further step would be to check that the price does, indeed, cover variable costs.

There are several demand-based pricing methods that attempt to increase profits by charging some customers more than others based on their differing demand characteristics, such as price elasticity. This is known as *price discrimination*, which can take three forms. These are personalized pricing, declining block pricing, and group pricing. Another pricing strategy, a *two-part tariff*, attempts to capture consumer surplus by charging a flat access fee in addition to a price per unit consumed. Finally, *bundling*, or packaging products together, can also increase profits under some conditions. As we examine these strategies, we will assume that marginal cost is constant throughout the relevant output range and is the same for each consumer or group of consumers supplied. This enables us to identify optimal price differentials that are solely demand related.

10.2.1 Personalized Pricing

Up to now, we have assumed that companies sell all units of their product at a single price. The price is posted, and consumers buy or do not buy the product depending on whether their reservation price (the maximum price the consumer is willing to pay) is greater than the posted price. All people buying the product, except for the one whose reservation price equals the posted price, thus enjoy a consumer surplus.

The other extreme to a single-price policy is to charge every consumer a different price. If a company is successful in selling to each consumer separately at the consumer's reservation price, then the company is practicing *personalized pricing*. Personalized pricing has been traditionally known in the economics literature as *first-degree price discrimination*.

Figure 10.1 shows the equilibrium for a company achieving personalized pricing. Each point on the demand curve for the firm's product indicates a consumer's reservation price (the maximum price he or she is willing to pay), and the company succeeds in selling to each consumer at this price. For example, one consumer has a reservation price X and pays this price, another has a reservation price Y and pays that price. Because each unit of the product is sold separately, offering a low price to one customer (with a low reservation price, such as G) to make an additional sale does not entail decreasing the price for everyone else. As a consequence, for each sale, the marginal revenue from making that sale is equal to the price paid for that unit. Marginal revenue is equal to price and not, as is the case for a single-price monopolist, less than price. Assuming that each unit is sold at a consumer's reservation price, as these different reservation prices are traced by the demand curve, the marginal revenue is represented by the same curve as the demand curve. Profits are maximized by selling Q*, where MR = MC. As in perfect competition, for the last unit sold, P = MC, and hence the output is the same as for a perfectly competitive industry. Unlike perfect competition, however, all sales other than the last unit will be at prices, traced

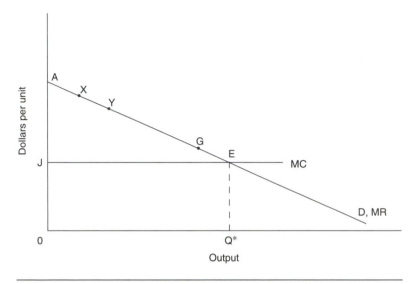

Figure 10.1   Personalized Pricing

Note: D indicates demand; MC, marginal cost; MR, marginal revenue; Q, quantity. G, X, and Y indicate the prices paid by different consumers. Area AEJ represents profits.

along the demand curve from A to E, above marginal cost. Profits under personalized pricing equal the area of triangle AEJ; this area would be consumer surplus under perfect competition.

If it can be achieved, personalized pricing is ideal from the company's standpoint. It results in the maximum possible profit, as it satisfies three conditions:

- *Complete extraction:* No individual realizes a consumer surplus on purchases.
- *Exclusion:* No individual with a reservation price less than marginal cost consumes the good.
- *Inclusion:* Every individual with a reservation price greater than marginal cost does consume the good.

Complete extraction is satisfied by personalized pricing because each individual is charged his or her reservation price. Exclusion is satisfied because those individuals consuming have a reservation price greater than or, in one case, equal to marginal cost. Inclusion is satisfied because violating this condition would follow from supplying less than Q*.

In contrast, a single-price policy would violate two of the three conditions. Referring to Figure 10.2, where the demand curve and marginal cost curve are the same as for Figure 10.1, the optimal single-price equilibrium for the same company would involve selling Q_1 at a price of P_1 where MR (now drawn in the usual way, with twice the slope of the demand curve) equals MC. Complete extraction is not satisfied because individuals with reservation prices above P_1 (represented by points on the demand curve above B) enjoy a consumer surplus equal, in aggregate, to the area of triangle ABP_1. Exclusion is satisfied; everyone consuming has a reservation price greater than MC. Inclusion is violated, as output is only Q_1, and individuals with reservation prices along segment BE of the demand curve do not consume the good even though their reservation prices are greater than MC. Because the single-price monopolist does not produce this output ($Q^* - Q_1$), the area of triangle BEF, which would be consumer surplus under perfect competition but is captured by the first-degree price discriminator, is deadweight loss. Thus the profit under first-degree price discrimination, relative to single-price monopoly, is greater by the sum of areas ABP_1 and BEF.

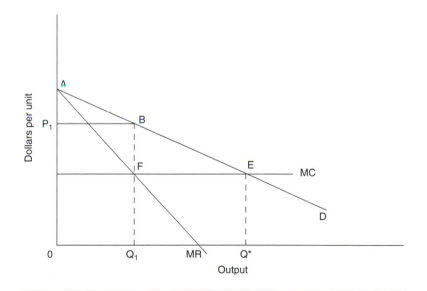

Figure 10.2   Single-Price Strategy Compared to Personalized Pricing

Note: D indicates demand; MC, marginal cost; MR, marginal revenue; P, price; Q, quantity. Points A, B, E, and F are used for explanatory purposes in the text.

In the real world, personalized pricing would never work perfectly. Through negotiation, a car dealership will try to determine each consumer's reservation price and sell at that price, although consumers are often likely to be successful in retaining some consumer surplus. (We would expect dealers, typically, to enjoy the best of the bargain, as they are more experienced negotiators.) Attempting first-degree price discrimination also results in additional costs. The car dealer who negotiates the price of each sale obviously incurs transaction costs not borne by a dealer who uses a single posted price for all customers. As a consequence, personalized pricing is only worth attempting for expensive goods where the additional revenue generated is likely to exceed these additional costs.

Producers of U.S. television programs approximate personalized pricing in their sales of programs to broadcasters and other exhibitors. The price charged differs according to the country and often by broadcasting organization within a country. For example, in 1995, for a top U.S. drama, a U.S. network paid as much as $2,000,000 per commercial hour (50 minutes); the BBC or ITV in the United Kingdom paid $100,000; Germany, $80,000; France, $60,000; Spain, $30,000; Mexico, $10,000; Belgium, $5000; Egypt, $1200; Zimbabwe, $250; and Aruba, $100. For some nations, there are separate language markets. For example, in Canada, the CBC English Network paid $60,000, but the CBC French Network paid $25,000. With the rise of cable and satellite channels, the price will vary by the type of exhibitor. In the United States, a program sale to a basic cable channel went for no more than $250,000. (The source of this data is the *Television Business International Yearbook 95*, 1995, p. 182.)

To practice personalized pricing, it must be possible for producers to separate buyers and prevent them from reselling. In the case of television programs, this is achieved by not selling the program as such but selling each broadcasting organization a license to exhibit a program in a prescribed geographic area for a given number of occasions during a certain time period. Reselling has not been a major problem, although bootlegged copies are found in some parts of the world and on the Internet (this is a greater problem for feature films and video).

The number of copies of a given program a producer will wish to sell is explored in Figure 10.3. The U.S. producer would like to sell to an exhibitor in each country, at the exhibitor's reservation price, as long as that reservation price is greater than or equal to marginal cost. If the producer is successful at selling at these reservation prices, then the demand curve in Figure 10.3 is traced by the prices paid by the broadcasters in the various countries. For a top U.S. drama in 1995, points on this demand curve would include a sale to the United States for $2 million; to the United Kingdom at $100,000; to Germany (location on the demand curve shown as G) at $80,000; to Italy (I) at $55,000; to Spain (S) at $30,000; to Mexico (M) at $10,000; and to Aruba at $100. Some of these points are shown on Figure 10.3. Once a decision has been made to go ahead and produce a program (this includes script writing, shooting, and postproduction), the only incremental costs are those associated with making and distributing another copy of the program. (Note that TV performers do not receive a royalty per viewer, unlike music performers or authors, who receive a royalty per CD or book sold, respectively.) This is the marginal cost shown in Figure 10.3. These costs are low. The lowest price paid for a U.S. program in 1995, by Aruba, was $100, so it would be safe to assume that this is around the level of marginal cost. (For more on the pricing of television programs, see Hoskins, Mirus, & Rozeboom, 1989, and Hoskins et al., 1997, pp. 68-80.)

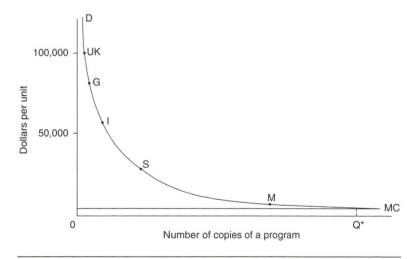

Figure 10.3   Personalized Pricing of a TV Program

Note: D indicates demand curve; G, price paid for the program by a broadcaster in Germany; I, price paid in Italy; M, price paid in Mexico; MC, marginal cost; Q, quantity; S, price paid in Spain; UK, price paid in the United Kingdom.

10.2.2 Declining Block Pricing

Declining block pricing involves a decreasing price for additional blocks of units consumed during a specific time period. It is also known as *second-degree price discrimination*. This is an option for a company that sells a product for which the typical consumer will buy multiple units in a specific time period. For example, most homeowners consume at least a thousand kilowatt hours (kWh) of electricity per month. The electrical supply company employs declining block pricing if it charges $0.07 per kWh for the first 500 kWh, $0.06 per kWh for the next 500 kWh, and $0.05 per kWh for any additional consumption in the month. Some mail-order companies practice this pricing strategy by selling the first X number of CDs in an order at the regular price and additional CDs at a greatly discounted price.

The basis for declining block pricing is the Law of Diminishing Marginal Utility and the consequent negative slope of the demand curve for an individual consumer. The high price for the first block takes advantage of the high reservation price the consumer has for the first units consumed. Price is decreased for subsequent blocks to persuade the consumer to buy additional units. To illustrate, suppose d in Figure 10.4 represents the demand curve of a typical consumer. Assuming that all consumers have the same demand curve, a single-price policy would entail a price of P_2 and sales to this consumer of Q_2, where mr = MC. The consumer would enjoy a consumer surplus equal to the area of triangle ABP_2 and the company a profit (or contribution) equal to the area of rectangle P_2BKJ. An alternative declining block pricing strategy might involve selling the first Q_1 units at P_1, the next $Q_2 - Q_1$ units at P_2, and additional units at P_3. This strategy would increase company profits as the area of rectangle P_1EFP_2, consumer surplus under a single-price policy, is captured as a result of selling the first Q_1 units at a higher price, and a profit equal to the area of rectangle HGLK is made on the additional $Q_3 - Q_2$ units sold. The consumer may or may not enjoy a greater consumer surplus depending on whether the sum of the areas of triangles AEP_1, EBF, and BGH, the consumer surplus under second-degree price discrimination, is greater or less than the area of triangle ABP_2. The output under declining block pricing is more efficient than that associated with a single price, as Q_3 is closer to the allocatively efficient output of Q_4, which would be associated with a price of J, equal to marginal cost.

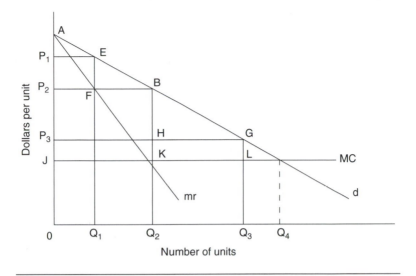

Figure 10.4   Declining Block Pricing and a Typical Consumer

Note: d indicates demand; MC, marginal cost; mr, marginal revenue; Q, quantity; P, price. Points A, B, E, F, G, H, J, K, and L are used for explanatory purposes in the text.

The choice of the number of blocks involves a trade-off. The more blocks, the greater the profit potential, as more consumer surplus is captured (note that in the extreme, where each unit is a block, this form of pricing merges with personalized pricing). However, more blocks also means greater billing complexity and, perhaps, less consumer acceptance.

In the real world, all consumers will not have the same demand curve, and points E, B, and G will not be on many consumers' demand curves. The profits from supplying such consumers will be less than those shown in Figure 10.4. However, even for the consumer represented in Figure 10.4, declining block pricing violates both complete extraction of consumer surplus and, unless the price of the last block is equal to MC, the condition of inclusion.

A variant of declining block pricing is widely practiced in the consumer electronics hardware and media industries. We will examine this variant and provide examples of its application when discussing the "cream skimming" strategy for introducing new products.

10.2.3 Group Pricing

Group pricing, also known as *third-degree price discrimination,* involves dividing consumers into two or more groups or markets having different price elasticities and charging a different price to each group. The group with the least elastic demand is charged the highest price. To successfully practice group pricing, it is necessary not only to be able to separate consumers into markets with different price elasticities but to keep these markets separate. Otherwise, either everyone will buy in the cheaper market or people in the cheaper market will buy more than they desire for their own consumption and will resell the excess, at some intermediate price, to people in the higher price market.

In Figure 10.5, we examine group pricing for a company that separates consumers into two markets, A and B. The price elasticity of demand is less in Market B than in Market A. The demand curve D, for the firm as a whole, is the horizontal sum of the demand curve d_A in Market A and the demand curve d_B in Market B. That is, at any given price, if the same price is charged in both markets, the quantity demanded shown by D is equal to the quantity demanded in Market A plus the quantity demanded in Market B. The marginal revenue curve, MR, for the company is, similarly, the horizontal sum of the marginal revenue curve mr_A in Market A and mr_B in Market B. The optimal output for the company is, as usual, Q^*, where MR = MC for the firm as a whole. Under a single-price policy, this would entail selling all Q^* units at price P^*. However, greater profits can be earned by selling separately in the two markets at a price and output found by equating the marginal cost of the last unit produced, MC^*, with marginal revenue in each market; remember, the cost of supplying each market is the same. This involves setting a price of P_A and selling Q_A in Market A and setting a higher price, P_B, and selling Q_B in Market B. Note that the price in Market A is less than P^*, whereas the price in Market B is higher than P^*. This discriminatory pricing is more profitable than a single-price policy. If P^* were charged in both markets, then at the quantities that would be bought at this price, $mr_A > mr_B$; also, $mr_A > MC^*$ and $mr_B < MC^*$. The company could increase profits by reallocating units of the product from Market B to Market A until $mr_A = mr_B = MC^*$. But the way to reallocate is to charge a lower price, P_A, in Market A and a higher price, P_B, in Market B.

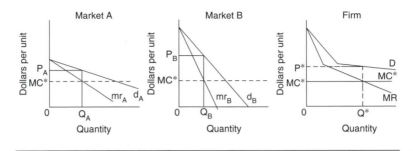

Figure 10.5   Group Pricing

Note: D indicates demand curve for the firm as a whole and d for a market served by the firm; MC, marginal cost; MR, marginal revenue for the firm; MR, marginal revenue for a market served by the firm; P, price; Q, quantity.

A company that knows the price elasticity of demand for its good or service in different markets is able to determine the optimal price ratio. It can be shown that the following relationship holds between marginal revenue and price elasticity of demand:

$$MR = P \, (1 - 1/\eta)$$

(See Douglas, 1992, p. 425, for a proof.)

As profit maximization involves $mr_A = mr_B$, substituting for mr_A and mr_B gives

$$P_A \, (1 - 1/\eta_A) = P_B \, (1 - 1/\eta_B)$$

Rearranging shows that the optimal price ratio depends on relative price elasticities:

$$P_A/P_B = (1 - 1/\eta_B)/(1 - 1/\eta_A)$$

The U.S. Post Office has used this relationship in determining the optimal ratio between the prices for first-class and second-class mail.

Group pricing is the most common form of price discrimination. Most academic journals charge libraries a higher price than individuals. There is often a special price for students. For example, Wilfred Laurier University Press has the following schedule for sales of the *Canadian Journal of Communications* in Canada: individuals are charged C$60; students, C$35; and institutions, C$80. As it is almost mandatory for the library of a Canadian university with a school of communication to subscribe to this journal, the library demand is price inelastic, so the highest price is charged. Individuals have a more elastic demand. They can make do with reading the library's copy, but it is more convenient to have their own subscription. Students, with their lower incomes, have the most elastic demand and are unlikely to take out a subscription unless an attractive price is offered. The subscription pricing of the *Journal of Media Economics* provides another example. For this journal there is no special student rate, but the annual U.S. subscription price is $35 for individuals and $180 for institutions. Note that ratio of institution price to individual price is much higher for this journal than for the *Canadian Journal of Communication*. Either the ratio of price elasticities for the two groups of subscribers is very different for the two journals or one of the publishers is making an error. To keep the groups separate, some publishers require proof, such as a letter from the university department, confirming student status.

Cinemas in North America often have "cheap Tuesdays," when ticket prices are about two thirds their normal rate. Matinees are sometimes priced low. Unlike students or libraries buying journals, moviegoers themselves self-select the group or market to which they belong. Those going to the movie on a cheap Tuesday pay a lower price but have to endure lines and crowded cinemas, unlike moviegoers who attend on a Monday or Wednesday evening. In this example, there is no difficulty keeping the markets separate; the movie ticket bought on a Tuesday is dated and is only valid for that evening.

Other examples of group pricing include the practice of telephone companies that charge different rates for business and residential customers, those video rental stores that have special rates for students or seniors, and computer software companies that have a special educational price for some of their programs.

10.2.4 The Two-Part Tariff

With a two-part tariff, the company charges the customer a flat or lump-sum fee for the right to buy a product, in addition to a price per unit consumed. For example, an amusement park might charge an entrance fee as well as a price for each ride or attraction. This strategy is not viable if resale of the good or service is possible at a low transaction cost. When this is possible, a customer can pay the flat fee and purchase large quantities of the good for resale to others. This would undermine the strategy.

Suppose that demand curve d, in Figure 10.6, is for a typical consumer. If a single price is charged for units consumed, the consumer will enjoy a consumer surplus. But if a fee for the right to buy is added, some or all of this surplus can be captured by the company. The maximum fee that the consumer would be willing to pay is equal to the consumer surplus. If we initially assume either that this is the only potential consumer or that all other consumers have an identical demand curve, the company will maximize profits by charging the marginal cost price of P_1 per unit consumed plus a flat fee equal to area BEP_1, the consumer surplus on the units consumed, Q_1. A higher price per unit consumed would decrease the flat fee that could be charged more than the increase in revenue, if any, from selling units. A lower price per unit would result in a loss of revenue on sales greater than the increase in flat fee possible. Under the circumstances described, a two-part tariff satisfies the condition of complete extraction, as no consumer surplus remains; satisfies inclusion, because units are consumed as long as the reservation price is greater than marginal cost; and satisfies exclusion, as no unit whose reservation price is less than marginal cost is consumed. A two-part tariff strategy is as profitable as personalized pricing (first-degree price discrimination).

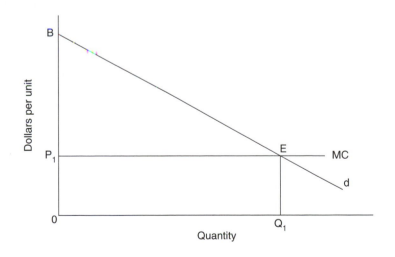

Figure 10.6   Two-Part Tariff for a Typical Customer

Note: d indicates demand; MC, marginal cost; P, price; Q, quantity. Points B and E are used for explanatory purposes in the text.

A real-world market, however, is usually made up of many customers with different incomes and tastes and, hence, different demand curves. If a different flat fee, corresponding to different levels of consumer surplus, could be charged each customer, in effect this would be personalized pricing with respect to the flat fee. Our three conditions would still be satisfied, but this is not likely to be practical, although group pricing, such as a tennis club offering a lower annual membership fee for students, is a possibility. In such a real-world market, customers with demand curves to the right of d in Figure 10.6 will enjoy a consumer surplus, so complete extraction is violated. Potential customers with a demand curve to the left of d will not buy the product at all because the flat fee is in excess of the consumer surplus they would obtain from purchase at P_1. Hence, these people do not purchase units for which their reservation price is greater than marginal cost, and the condition of inclusion is violated. In such circumstances, a price above marginal cost in conjunction with a lower flat fee may be more profitable. (For more on this, see Oi, 1971.)

When video stores first made their appearance in the late 1970s, it was usual for a store to charge an annual membership fee, as well as a price for each night's rental of a videocassette. This profitable two-part tariff strategy was abandoned after several years as video stores dropped their membership fees. Why was the strategy abandoned? The reason is that video stores lost their market power as competition increased. The early stores were local monopolies or oligopolies. However, the positive economic profits earned in the absence of barriers to entry resulted in the entry of new stores, and the market structure changed to monopolistic competition.

A telephone company that charges a fixed service fee per month as well as a price for each minute of call (local and long distance) is employing a two-part tariff.

Cable companies that charge a substantial hook-up fee, a fee that is obviously well in excess of the incremental cost to the company of implementing the hook-up (which may involve no more than throwing a switch in a central location), are practicing a two-part tariff. The one-time hook-up charge is the flat fee.

10.2.5 Bundling

Bundling, or *commodity bundling*, as it is sometimes known, involves selling goods or services together in packages. Pure bundling involves selling the goods or services only in a package; they are not made available for purchase separately. Mixed bundling is practiced if one or more goods are made available separately as well as sold in a package. If no package is made available and goods are only sold individually, it is known in this context as a pure components strategy. Note that, by definition, a pure components strategy is not a bundling strategy.

Under certain conditions, pure bundling or mixed bundling will be more profitable than a pure components strategy. The alternative strategies can be examined in terms of the extent to which they violate the conditions of complete extraction, inclusion, and exclusion.

Pure bundling was, interestingly enough, first analyzed by George Stigler (1963) in the context of block booking of movies. Stigler set out to explain why block booking of films to cinemas and broadcast organizations (i.e., only selling movies together in blocks or packages) continued to be widespread despite being the subject of several antitrust cases (the Paramount cases and the Loew case). He concluded that block booking was more profitable than selling the films separately if buyer valuation of films differed significantly but the package was valued similarly. The illustrative example he provided was for two buyers, A and B, and two movies, X and Y:

A would pay up to $8000 for film X and up to $2500 for film Y.
B would pay up to $7000 for film X and up to $3000 for film Y.

Pricing the block of movies at $10,000 would yield receipts of $20,000. Selling the films separately at a price of $7000 for X and $2500 for Y would result in lower receipts of $19,000.

Mixed bundling is sometimes used in sales of prerecorded videocassettes and books. For example, the "Star Wars" films are sold in a package as well as separately. Similarly, C. S. Lewis's "Narnia" series of books is sold in a bundle, and the books are also available individually. Computer programs are sometimes combined in a suite. Microsoft sells Word and Excel separately as well as bundled together in an Office package that also includes PowerPoint and, in some versions, Access.

Bundling is commonly practiced by cable TV companies. Channels are packaged together into cable tiers. In some cases, channels are only made available in tiers (a pure bundling strategy); in other cases, a channel will be offered separately as well as part of a package (mixed bundling). These contrast with the nonbundling strategy for some channels that are only offered separately. We will use numerical illustrative examples for a cable operation to consider

Table 10.1   Viewers' Reservation Prices for Cable Channels

| | | Viewers | |
		Jock	Maria
Channels	Sports Galore	$9	$2
	Cultural Medley	$2	$9

Note: Pure bundling is optimal if MC = $0; pure components is optimal if MC = $3.

the circumstances under which each strategy is likely to be most profitable. (These numerical examples are similar to those provided by Owen & Wildman, 1992, pp. 133-134.)

Suppose a cable operator offers two channels, Sports Galore and Cultural Medley. There are two viewers subscribing to cable, Jock and Maria. Table 10.1 shows the reservation prices (the maximum they would be willing to pay) of both viewers for access to each channel for 1 month.

We will initially assume it costs the cable operator nothing to deliver these channels to viewers; that is, the marginal cost is zero. If a pure components strategy were adopted, the best price would be $9 for each channel. Jock would subscribe only to Sports Galore and Maria only to Cultural Medley. Profits (or more accurately, the contribution toward fixed costs) would be $18. The pure components strategy would violate the inclusion condition, as Jock would not subscribe to Cultural Medley nor Maria to Sports Galore, although in each case, their reservation price is greater than marginal cost.

If a pure bundling strategy were chosen, the cable operator would offer both channels in a package or tier for $11. Both Jock and Maria would subscribe to the tier, and the cable operator's profits would be $22. In this particular example, pure bundling satisfies the three conditions for appraising pricing schemes. This is not generally the case, however. For example, if Jock's reservation price for Cultural Medley had been $1, then the bundle would have to be priced at $10, and Maria would enjoy a $1 consumer surplus. Thus the condition of complete extraction would have been violated.

Changing the marginal cost to $3 (suppose the cable operator has to pay the specialty channels $3 per subscriber per month) results in a pure components strategy being more profitable. If the channels are offered separately for $9 each, Jock will subscribe to Sports

Galore and Maria to Cultural Medley. Profit would thus be $12 (revenue of $18 less cost of $6) for the pure components strategy. Pure bundling at a tier price of $11 would only result in profits of $10 (revenue of $22 less cost of $12). The profit is lower because pure bundling has violated the exclusion condition: Jock consumes Cultural Medley and Maria consumes Sports Galore even though, in both cases, their reservation price for the respective channels is less than the marginal cost of supplying them.

In the situation shown in Table 10.1, mixed bundling (offering a channel separately as well as part of a tier) would not be a suitable strategy, and we chose not to complicate the example by considering it. However, if we return to assuming that marginal cost is zero but suppose that Jock has lost his job and as a consequence his reservation prices are reduced to $5 for Sports Galore and $1 for Cultural Medley (this situation is shown in Table 10.2), we find that mixed bundling is now the most profitable strategy for the cable operator. A pure components strategy would involve selling Sports Galore for $5 and Cultural Medley for $9. Jock would subscribe to Sports Galore and Maria to Cultural Medley. Profits would be $14. If a pure bundling strategy were followed, the best bundle price would be $6, and profits would be $12. The best prices under a mixed bundling strategy would be to offer Sports Galore for $5 and the tier or bundle for $11. Jock would subscribe to Sports Galore and Maria to the tier. Profits would be $16. Unlike our first example, mixed bundling is the most profitable strategy because the reservation prices that Jock and Maria attach to the package, as well as the individual channels, are appreciably different. Mixed bundling permits the cable operator to persuade Maria to subscribe to the bundle at a high price of $11 and still get $5 from Jock for Sports Galore.

Table 10.2   Viewers Reservation Prices for Cable Channels

		Viewers	
		Jock	Maria
Channels	Sports Galore	$5	$2
	Cultural Medley	$1	$9

Note: Mixed bundling is optimal if MC = 0; pure components is optimal if MC = $3.

Again, changing the assumed marginal cost to $3 affects the optimal strategy. With a marginal cost of $3, profits would be $8 (revenue of $14 less costs of $6) for a pure components strategy. For pure bundling, profit would be $0 (revenue of $12 less costs of $12) if $6 is charged for the bundle or $5 (revenue of $11 less costs of $6) if $11 is charged for the bundle. For mixed bundling, profit would be $7 (revenue of $16 less costs of $9). Pure components is now the best strategy. Mixed bundling is less profitable because the condition of exclusion is violated; Maria is supplied with Sports Galore even though her reservation price is less than marginal cost.

To generalize, a pure components strategy looks better the higher the marginal cost of the product (because this strategy, unlike bundling, does not violate exclusion) and the more similar people's reservation prices are for individual goods.

Pure bundling is a good strategy to consider if marginal cost is low and the reservation price that consumers attach to the package is similar but the reservation prices they attach to the components of the package are negatively correlated. (Jock has a higher reservation price for Sports Galore and a lower reservation price for Cultural Medley than Maria.)

Mixed bundling is most attractive where marginal cost is low and buyers differ significantly in their reservation prices for the package as well as for the individual components. (For more detail, see Adams & Yellen, 1976.)

Note that many media goods and services are produced and distributed at low marginal cost, which means that bundling will often be an attractive strategy to use in their sale.

10.3 New Product Pricing

Two contrasting pricing strategies for new products are cream skimming and penetration pricing. Cream skimming involves a high price initially; the price is reduced in steps over time. With a penetration strategy, a low price is charged initially and then increased. These strategies will be considered in turn. However, it should be emphasized that they are a departure from the usual neutral strategy where the product is introduced at a price consistent with profit maximization (the price shown by the demand curve at the output where MR = MC) during the period of introduction, with the price in subsequent periods only going up or down if demand or cost conditions change.

10.3.1 Cream Skimming

Cream skimming can be thought of as akin to declining block pricing. However, unlike the case examined in section 10.2.2, the product must be a consumer durable, and any given consumer will typically buy only one unit of the product over an extended period of time.

The price of the durable good is reduced, in steps, over time. The idea is to get those people who want the product most (that is, those with the highest reservation price) to buy at the high price. The price is later reduced, one or more times, to persuade additional consumers to purchase the product.

In Figure 10.7, D represents the market demand curve for the consumer durable for a length of time over which the product will not wear out or become obsolete. The product is introduced in period 1 at a high price of P_1. Q_1 is the quantity demanded during this period. In the second period, the market for the product is expanded by reducing the price to P_2. The quantity demanded in period 2 is $Q_2 - Q_1$, as the people who bought the product in period 1 do not repurchase because they already own a unit in working order. Note that no sales would be made in period 2 if the price were maintained at P_1. In period 3, the price is reduced further to P_3, and additional sales of $Q_3 - Q_2$ are made.

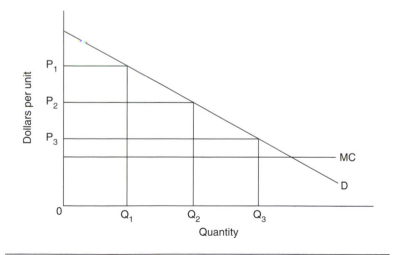

Figure 10.7   Cream Skimming

Note: D indicates demand; MC, marginal cost; P, price; Q, quantity.

A type of cream skimming that involves introducing different versions of a product over time is commonly practiced for books and movies. Books first come out in hardcover and then in a paperback version. For example, *The Tailor of Panama,* by John Le Carre, was first published in the United States in hardcover by Knopf in October 1996 at a list price of $25. A paperback version was introduced in September 1997 at a list price of $6.99. The book publishing example does differ from our general case in the previous paragraph in that the lower price is attached to the new paperback version of the product, and, for a while at least, the hardback version continues to be sold at its original price. The continued sale of the hardback version reflects the fact that not everyone considers the paperback a perfect substitute for the hardback. People with poor eyesight would prefer the larger print of the hardback, and institutions such as libraries are often prepared to pay the premium for the sturdier, longer lasting version. It is true also that the paperback version would cost less to produce. However, the difference in cost of producing another unit of the paperback version versus the hardback version would be $2 at most.

The first opportunity for the average person to view a movie is at a first-run cinema for $10 or so. Large cities often have second-run cinemas, where the movie may be seen a few months later for, say, $6. After 6 months or so, the video version is available for rent at around $4, and soon after, the movie may be shown on a pay movie channel. Eventually the movie is likely to be shown (edited, and with commercials inserted) on "free" TV. These different opportunities to view a movie are called windows, and the alternative methods available to the producer and distributor to supply the market are known as distribution channels. When Internet distribution of movies becomes well established, the studios will have to decide where this window fits into the sequence.

The decision the film distributor faces in determining the optimal sequencing and length of the various windows and even whether a potential window should be included or excluded is a complex one. Owen and Wildman (1992) identify six factors that must be considered in designing a windowing strategy that will maximize profits from all distribution channels.

(1) differences in the per viewer price earned in the different distribution channels; (2) differences in channels' incremental audiences . . . (3) the interest rate as a measure of the opportunity cost of money;

(4) the extent to which viewers exposed to a program through one channel are eliminated from its potential audience in other channels; (5) differences among channels in their vulnerability to unauthorized copying, and (6) the rate at which viewer interest in a program declines following its initial release. (p. 30)

Owen and Wildman (1992) seem to consider the different windows as competing for audience, however they may also in some cases be complementary. The video window for feature films is now bigger than the cinema release window and it may well be that a successful cinema release boosts the audience in the video window and perhaps other later windows; in effect, it is advertising or promotion for the later windows. This phenomenon undoubtedly applies also to the market for music recordings: The television video is an advertising feature for the audio CD.

The profitability of cream skimming will be undermined if consumers with a high reservation price anticipate (correctly) that price will be reduced and sufficient numbers of them are willing to postpone purchase until the lower price materializes. The problem is confounded if an active market for used durable goods develops. For example, publishers of university textbooks find that in new sales they are competing against used copies of their own text. To limit this competition, publishers usually bring out a new edition every 3 years.

Where a company has no intention of cream skimming, it sometimes makes a commitment to this effect. For example, in November 1991, *Fantasia* videocassettes and laser disks went on sale with the commitment from Disney that they would be sold for only 50 days (only rental units would be available thereafter). Such a commitment is particularly important for collector items (see Schnol, 1991).

10.3.2 Penetration Pricing

In penetration pricing, a product is introduced at a low price, and the price is subsequently raised. The rationale for penetration pricing is that the low price encourages more potential customers to try the product. After they have sampled the product, assuming their experience was positive, they are more inclined to repeat buy. When a market of loyal buyers has been established, the price is increased.

A penetration pricing strategy should be considered when introducing experience goods that are purchased frequently. As we explained in chapter 4, an experience good contains attributes that consumers can only evaluate after use. Before purchasing such a good, consumers are uncertain about the utility they will enjoy from consuming the good, uncertain whether the product will "work" for them. This uncertainty is often resolved after the first purchase and experience with the good. It follows that a consumer who has not yet tried the product will be willing to pay less for the good than the same consumer who has bought the product previously and found the experience with the good to be positive. The low initial penetration price recognizes this and is aimed at persuading consumers to give the product a trial. After many consumers have given the product a trial, found that it works, and become loyal repeat buyers, the company can increase the price without losing their customer.

Penetration pricing is more likely to be the optimal policy the more frequently the product is purchased. First, the initial price reduction necessary to induce a trial is less because, from the consumer's viewpoint, purchase of the first unit is less important relative to the entire stream of purchases. Second, the profit contribution from repeat sales at the higher price is greater. (For a more rigorous treatment of this, and other aspects of penetration pricing, see Schmalensee, 1982.)

Variations of penetration pricing are used to induce a trial. Sometimes a product is sold from the start at the regular price but introductory "money off" coupons are widely distributed. This may have the advantage that some consumers may not feel exploited when the coupons are not renewed but would with a more explicit form of price increase. The ultimate penetration price is the provision of free samples, usually in smaller quantities than the regular-size package of detergent or candies or whatever the product is.

Newspapers are an example of a product that satisfies the criteria that make penetration pricing attractive. Newspapers are an experience good. Only by reading a newspaper does the consumer learn its attributes. Newspapers are purchased frequently. In the early 1980s, the *Globe and Mail* transformed itself from a Toronto newspaper into a national Canadian newspaper by, in stages, using a satellite feed to print in Montreal and Calgary, and then in Moncton, Brandon, and Vancouver. When reach was extended to each new market, a low introductory price was offered. Several months later the price was raised to the level prevailing in mature markets.

The *Wall Street Journal* encourages university economics and business students to subscribe by offering them very attractive introductory prices. Professors who encourage their students to subscribe get a free subscription.

A penetration pricing strategy is often used to launch a new magazine. Magazine publishers also frequently employ a related strategy. Even for a well-established magazine, a special low price is often available for first-time subscribers.

Software producers sometimes allow free use of downloaded software for a limited time only. For example, Intuit, in a special offer to customers of TD Web banking in Canada in summer 1999, made available a version of their Quicken personal finance program that could be used for 60 days.

Sometimes a basic version of a program is provided free in the hope that experience with this persuades the consumer that purchase of an enhanced version is worthwhile. For example, the basic e-mail program Eudora Lite is offered free by Qualcomm in the hope that the trial with Eudora Lite will persuade users to switch to the enhanced version, Eudora Pro. Eudora Pro can either be purchased at full price or, alternatively, can be downloaded at no charge provided the user is willing to allow advertisements to appear in a small box in the Eudora window. Another example involves computer games preinstalled on a new computer. These are often a simplified version of the regular game or only include the first couple of levels of the game. Again, the company selling the game hopes that a trial with the simplified version will persuade the consumer to purchase the regular game.

It should be noted that, although not penetration pricing as such, cost conditions, in the form of substantial economies of scale or learning, may also induce a firm to introduce a product at a low price. The low price increases the quantity demanded and the resulting larger output reduces costs. In this case, unlike true penetration pricing, there is no intention to raise the price later.

10.4 Pricing Product Systems

In chapter 9, we examined competition between product systems. Here we examine further the implications for pricing.

The demand for the software depends on the price of the hardware and vice versa. It is more profitable to sell the hardware at a lower price and the software at a higher price than would be the case if the goods were not demand related. The low price for the hardware (called the *tying good* in this pricing context) leads to greater sales of the hardware and, hence, a larger consumer base and bigger sales of the software (called the *tied good*). In other words, the lower the price chosen for the tying good, the further to the right the location of the demand curve for the tied good (remember from chapter 2 that a price decrease in a complementary good causes an increase in demand). Many consumers attracted by the low price of the tying good are not even that aware of the price of the tied good. Once they have bought the hardware, the sunk investment in this good results in a relatively inelastic demand for the software that is used with it (again, see chapter 2).

An example in the entertainment industry is videogame machines and the game software to play on them. When Nintendo introduced its first 8-bit video game machine in the mid-1980s, it sold the machine at close to cost, with the profits being made on the game software.

As documented in chapter 9, Apple did not follow this strategy when pricing the Macintosh. Instead, it instituted a high price for the Mac in pursuit of short-term profits. This proved particularly shortsighted in the winner take all market that developed. Similarly, for low-end models, Betamax VCRs were higher priced than VHS models. This played a part in the VHS victory.

Perhaps the best documented case (see Blackstone, 1975) involved Electrofax. The Electrofax copying process, a rival to Xerox in the early 1960s, used a special coated paper supplied only by Electrofax. Electrofax sold its copying machine at a price about 25% above cost, whereas for the special coated paper, the markup was around 200%. Of course such a practice is most profitable if the company has a monopoly in supplying the tied good. Nevertheless, despite the absence of such a monopoly, manufacturers of inkjet printers sell the printers at a price entailing a smaller markup over cost than the price they ask for their ink cartridges. In such circumstances, consumers are encouraged to buy the company's cartridges by warnings that the warranty on the printer may be void if nonapproved cartridges or refills are used.

10.5 Predatory Pricing

Predatory pricing involves selling a product at an "unfair" low price to eliminate a competitor or deter others from entering the industry. Once the competitor has been eliminated or the potential rival deterred from entering, the company increases price to exploit its monopoly position.

Predatory pricing is illegal in most jurisdictions, but in practice, it is often very difficult to distinguish predatory pricing from low prices resulting from healthy competition. In section 9.1, we argued that a company should shut down rather than produce and sell at a price less than average variable cost. If the firm continues to produce under these circumstances and thus incurs greater losses during the period as a consequence, it is safe to assume that predatory pricing is being practiced, as the only motive can be that this will lead to higher prices and profits in the future due to an enhanced monopoly position. Even here, a proviso is in order. Once a product has actually been produced, product costs are a sunk cost and hence no longer relevant. Thus a one-time sale of an inventory of previously produced goods, especially perishables, may be sold at below the average variable cost of production without this constituting predatory pricing.

The newspaper wars in the United Kingdom provide an example. News International, owner of *The Times* newspaper, was accused by three of its rivals, *The Daily Telegraph, The Guardian,* and *The Independent,* of predatory pricing. The case was referred to the Office of Fair Trading (OFT). In May 1999, the director general of the OFT concluded that "NI [News International] deliberately made a loss on *The Times* during the period between June 1996 and January 1998 when the Monday edition was sold for 10p, and that this affected competition in the national newspaper market. . . . The company is now on notice. The UK has one of the most competitive newspaper markets in the world and we intend to keep it that way." Although the price of *The Times* has been increased several times since January 1998, News International agreed to submit a detailed business plan to the OFT within 10 days of any future price cutting of *The Times* newspaper.

When practiced in export markets, predatory pricing is usually referred to as dumping. We will examine an alleged case of this, with respect to U.S. exports of TV programs, in chapter 14.

10.6 Congestion Costs and Pricing

When telecommunications networks are running at full capacity, extra use of shared resources by one subscriber imposes costs, a negative externality, on other subscribers in the form of delays and deterioration in service quality. This was the problem faced by

Sprint Canada customers after Sprint's change in pricing structure led to an increase in quantity demanded that could not be handled readily by the capacity available (see chapter 2). These costs, borne by consumers, are called *congestion costs.* Note that they are not a function of the number of subscribers per se but of incremental usage in the face of a capacity constraint.

Although congestion costs fall on consumers, they have implications for network providers, as customers complain about the level of service and threaten to cancel their connection. Possible remedies include expansion of capacity or a change in pricing strategy to ration demand.

In Figure 10.8, SMC represents the short-run marginal cost, including, where relevant, congestion costs. With a given capacity, network costs of supplying another unit are typically very low, virtually zero, until congestion costs become a factor as the capacity limit of K_0 is approached. It is because more than K_0 cannot be supplied in the short run that SMC becomes vertical at this output level.

For telecommunication services, the demand varies with the time period. There are predictable peak periods (during the day, Mondays to Fridays) and off-peak periods (weekends, as well as

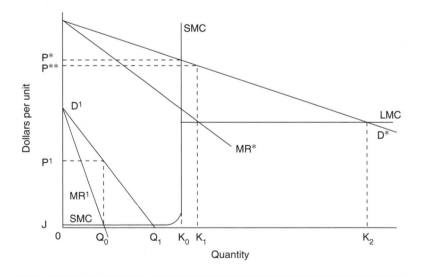

Figure 10.8   Peak-Load Pricing

Note: D indicates demand; J, off-peak price equal to short-run marginal cost; K, output capacity; LMC, long-run marginal cost; MR, marginal revenue; P, price; Q, quantity; SMC, short-run marginal cost.

weekday evenings and nights). Under these circumstances, peak-load pricing makes sense. In Figure 10.8, the off-peak demand in a 24-hour period is D^1 and the peak-period demand is D^* (for convenience, we will assume that both the off-peak and peak periods are 12 hours in duration). The associated marginal revenue curves are MR^1 and MR^*, respectively. For a profit maximizing telephone company, peak-load pricing entails setting a price of P^1 in the off-peak period and selling the quantity Q_0 where $MR^1 = SMC$. In the peak period, the profit maximizing price is P^*, which allocates the full capacity output of K_0.

In the long run, the telephone company may wish to expand capacity to meet the peak period demand. The cost of expanding capacity, expressed on a per unit of output basis, plus the operating costs comprise the long-run marginal cost, LMC. In the long run, the company will wish to expand capacity to K_1, at which output $MR^* = LMC$, and sell at a peak period price of P^{**}. (Note that capacity would not be expanded if $K_1 < K_0$.) The off-peak price would remain at P_1, as the expansion of capacity is in no way attributable to this period.

If the telephone company is government owned or rates are regulated, the allocatively efficient marginal cost price may be preferred to the profit maximizing price. Referring again to Figure 10.8, in this context, peak-load pricing would involve a price of J, equal to SMC at the quantity demanded of Q_1, in the off-peak period. In the peak period, price would remain at P^* in the short run. In the long run, capacity would be expanded to K_2 to supply the quantity demanded at a price set equal to LMC.

Peak-load pricing bears obvious similarities to group pricing. However, as the telephone case illustrates, they are not identical. The difference between peak and off-peak price reflects differences in costs (including congestion costs) of supplying calls to the same group during different periods. In contrast, the different prices charged to home and business users during the same period (group pricing) is based on exploiting the different price elasticities of demand for these groups (the cost of supplying in the period being the same).

Telephone companies practice peak-load pricing in sales of long distance telephone services. However, they face a more complex task than that represented in Figure 10.8, as the demand for peak and off-peak calls are not, as we have implicitly assumed in Figure 10.8, completely independent. If a higher price is charged in the peak period and a lower price in the off-peak period, people will switch some calls they would have made in the peak period to the off-peak time. The greater the price differential, the more calls are likely to be switched. Thus the location of the peak and off-peak demand curves will depend on the differential prices chosen.

In North America, the norm has been not to charge local telephone calls on a per minute basis. As price is not playing a role in rationing calls, this increases congestion costs and adds pressure to expand capacity (see Globerman & Stanbury, 1986).

In some networks, there are not regular, predictable, peak and off-peak periods. For example, with respect to the Internet, MacKie-Mason and Varian (1994) report that "Network statistics reveal very irregular time-of-day usage patterns" (p. 89). Nevertheless, although much of the time the network is uncongested, when it is operating near capacity, "a user's incremental packet imposes costs on other users in the form of delay or dropped packets" (p. 89). MacKie-Mason and Varian's proposed solution is that each user assign his or her packets a bid equal to the value attached to immediate servicing. However, the amount a person pays, if anything, would not be equal to his or her bid but to the lowest bid for a packet admitted to the network. Any user could avoid payment by always bidding $0; in uncongested times, the packets would nevertheless be handled immediately; during congested times, there would inevitably be some delay. Of course, such pricing has not been introduced as yet; most pricing in North America is of the flat fee or per hour of usage variety.

10.7 Summary

In this chapter, we examined pricing decisions. The role of cost and demand was explained. Variable costs can be thought of as providing a floor for possible prices. Traditional, formula-based, full-cost pricing is deficient because it ignores demand and includes a mark-up on fixed costs that are irrelevant to the optimal price.

Demand, or more precisely the price elasticity of demand, determines the optimal mark-up over variable costs. The economic value approach, which uses the price of the closest substitute as a reference value and then examines how the value to the customer will be affected by attributes that differentiate the product from this substitute, provides a practical method of determining price.

Demand-based pricing strategies include the three types of price discrimination, where different consumers (or groups of consumers) pay different prices for the same good; a two-part tariff, in which a flat fee is charged for access in addition to a per-unit price for usage; and bundling, where packages of products are sold. Examples of applications of price discrimination examined include U.S. television producers' sales of programs, publishers charging institutions and individuals different subscription prices for academic journals, and telephone companies having different business and residential rates. Cable tiering was used to illustrate bundling. A prime motivation was found to be the desire to capture consumer surplus. The methods were evaluated in terms of how closely they satisfied three conditions: complete extraction, exclusion, and inclusion.

Among the strategies available for introducing new products, the contrasting cream skimming and penetration pricing methods were examined. Cream skimming is a possible strategy for consumer durables and involves decreasing the price in steps over time. The idea is to extract a high price from those who value the product most and then expand the market by reducing the price. Penetration pricing implies offering a low introductory price to induce consumers to give the product a trial and find out whether it "works"; later, the price is increased. Penetration pricing should be considered for frequently bought experience goods. Sales of books and movies were given as examples of cream skimming; newspapers and magazines were examples of penetration pricing.

The pricing of product systems was considered. These involve hardware and the software that goes with usage. Recognizing that a lower price for the hardware increases the demand for the software, analysis suggests that the optimal policy is a lower price for the hardware and a higher price for the software than would be the case if the products were not demand related. The pricing of videogame machines and the videogames used with them appears consistent with this.

Predatory pricing entails selling a product at an unfairly low price (below cost) to eliminate a competitor or deter others from entering the industry. Once the rival has been driven out or the entrant deterred, the price is raised to exploit the monopoly position achieved. *The Times* was found guilty of selling below cost during the U.K. newspaper war.

In regard to telecommunications, when networks are running at full capacity, extra use of shared resources by one subscriber imposes costs on other subscribers in the form of delays and deterioration in service quality. In times of congestion, a higher price is an efficient method of allocating the maximum output or service that can be provided given capacity constraints. If there are predictable cycles of high and low demand, this entails peak-load pricing, a method adopted by telecommunications companies for long distance calls.

11

Advertising

After studying this chapter, you should be able to answer the following questions: What are the three different views on the role of advertising in a market economy? How important is advertising to the economy? How did a decrease in the subscriber price for *The Times* affect the price the newspaper charged for advertising space, and why? How do demographics and consumer interests affect the price of advertising? Why is the last question relevant to any leading U.S. consumer magazine contemplating a decrease in subscription price? How does a reliance on advertising revenue influence media firms' choices with respect to the information and entertainment content offered to consumers?

Advertising shares many of the characteristics of mass media communication—harnessing creativity to create messages that will achieve a business purpose. As you are probably aware, advertising is a subject worthy of study in its own right. There is an extensive literature on advertising as a managerial function, as an industry, and as a societal force. The managerial work addresses such issues as choice of advertising strategy, target segment selection, message development, media vehicle selection, and assessment of ad effectiveness (see Wells, Burnett, & Moriarty, 2002). Some of these have economic aspects; however, it is not our mandate to address such issues in this book.

What we do consider here is the significance of advertising to media industries. Advertising is an important source of revenue in many segments. We will explore the implications of this for both the quantity and nature of the content produced. We begin, though, by providing context, with a brief introduction to the role of advertising in a market economy.

11.1 The Role of Advertising in a Market Economy

Advertising is both attacked as a monopolistic and wasteful practice and defended as promoting competition and lowering the cost that consumers pay for goods. But there are many different types of advertising—all the way from ads for jobs in the classifieds, to ads that identify this week's supermarket specials, to ads that announce the arrival of the next generation of computers (with all the technical details), to 30-second dramas that out-entertain the regular programming. Economists have explored three views of the role of advertising in society: the persuasive view, the informative view, and the complementary view.

The persuasive view of company advertising is that it primarily affects demand for the firm's product by changing tastes and encouraging brand loyalty. The advertised product then faces a less elastic demand curve so that advertising is said to enable the firm to sell the same quantity at higher prices.

The informative view of company advertising is that it primarily affects demand for the firm's product by conveying information. The advertised product then faces a more elastic demand curve so that advertising is said to enable the firm to lower prices. An extension of this view says that even seemingly uninformative firm advertising acts as a signal of higher quality products, so it plays a useful economic role.

The complementary view of company advertising is that it affects demand by exerting a complementary influence in the consumer's utility function with the consumption of the firm's advertised product. For example, the consumer may value social prestige, and advertising thus positions the product so that its consumption provides social prestige as well as satisfying more obvious needs.

Today, most economists side with the informative view, viewing advertising as a form of promotion comparable with direct selling by sales representatives or other promotional activities.

11.2 Significance of Advertising for Media Industries

Advertising comprises roughly 2% of the GNP in the United States. In 2002, total U.S. advertising spending was $237 billion (Crain Communications, Inc., 2004a) out of a total U.S. GDP of $10,481 billion (Bureau of Economic Analysis, 2004). Table 11.1 reports examples of advertising expenditures (outlays) as a percent of sales (net of discounts and allowances) by different media industries and compares them with some other industries. This data is for the United States, but similar patterns are found for most developed countries. The percentages vary markedly by industry. Media industries with the greatest intensity of advertising are miscellaneous publishing (12.9%) and television broadcast stations (9.3%). However, these pale in significance with such outliers as loan brokers (38.4%), health services (32.5%), and even distilled and blended liquor (14.9%). Media industries with a low advertising percentage include radio broadcasting stations (1.2%) and newspaper publishing (including printing) (1.3%).

Table 11.2 reports the share of advertising revenue obtained by the various media. More than 60% of the total is national, as opposed to local, advertising. In 2002, newspapers accounted for 18.6% of total advertising expenditures, magazines for 4.6%, broadcast television for 17.8%, cable television for 6.9%, radio for 7.9%, and others such as the Yellow Pages, direct mail, billboards, and the Internet for the remaining 44.2%.

Some forms of media rely on revenue from sales of content, some on sale of audience exposures to advertising messages, and some to a mix of both. Figure 11.1 gives the breakdown. Traditionally, book publishers and movie producers have obtained 100% of their revenue from sales (although fees from product placement in the movies, such as Nokia paying Paramount Pictures close to $1 million for Tom Cruise to talk about a Nokia phone in *Mission Impossible*, are really advertising). Some other media, notably commercial broadcast television and radio stations and publishers of free newspapers and newssheets, obtain 100% of their revenue from advertisers. Even some public broadcasting organizations, such as the CBC, have relied on advertising revenues as a source of nongovernment funding. Technological progress has sometimes resulted in changes to this mix, as in the case of migration of some sports from

Table 11.1   Advertising Expenditures as a Percentage of Sales for
Various U.S. Industries

Industry	Advertising Expenditures as a Percentage of Sales
Media related	
Miscellaneous publishing	12.9
Television broadcast stations	9.3
Motion picture and video production	8.4
Cable and other pay TV	7.7
Household audio and video equipment	6.9
Periodicals publishing and printing	6.7
Book publishing and printing	4.5
Communications services	3.7
Video rental	3.5
Record and tape stores	1.7
Motion picture theaters	1.5
Newspaper publishing and printing	1.3
Radio broadcast stations	1.2
Broadcast and communication equipment	0.9
Other	
Loan brokers	38.4
Health services	32.5
Distilled and blended liquor	14.9
Amusement parks	10.7
Food and kindred products	10.2
Beverages	9.2
Perfume, cosmetic, and toilet preparations	7.4
Furniture stores	5.9
Prepackaged software	3.5
Radio, TV, and consumer electronics retailers	3.2
Radiotelephone communication	2.9
Telephone other than radiotelephone	2.5
Motor vehicles and car bodies	2.4
Grocery stores	1.0
Auto dealers, gas stations	0.9
Drug and proprietary stores	0.8
Hospital and medical service plans	0.4

SOURCE: Crain Communications, Inc. (2004a).

advertising-supported broadcasts to pay TV. On occasion, new technology has created the opportunity for consumers to choose between
paying a higher price for content without advertisements or paying a

Table 11.2   Share of U.S. Advertising Revenue by Media Industry for 2002

	Advertising Revenue (In billions of dollars)	% of Total U.S. Advertising Revenue
Newspapers		
National	6.81	2.9
Local	37.23	15.7
Total newspapers	44.03	18.6
Magazines	11.00	4.6
Broadcast TV		
Four TV networks	15.00	6.3
Syndication[a]	3.03	1.3
Spot (national)	10.92	4.6
Spot (local)	13.11	5.6
Total broadcasting	42.07	17.8
Cable TV		
Cable networks	12.07	5.1
Spot (local)	4.23	1.8
Cable total	16.30	6.9
Radio		
Network	0.78	0.3
Spot (national)	3.34	1.4
Spot (local)	14.76	6.2
Total radio	18.88	7.9
Yellow Pages		
National	2.09	0.9
Local	11.69	4.9
Total Yellow Pages	13.78	5.8
Direct mail	46.07	19.4
Business publications	3.98	1.7
Out of home		
National	2.06	0.9
Local	3.11	1.3
Total out of home	5.18	2.2
Internet	4.88	2.1
Miscellaneous		
National	23.41	9.9
Local	7.32	3.1
Total miscellaneous	30.73	13.00
National total	145.43	61.4
Local total	91.45	38.6
Total	236.88	100.00

a. Includes UPN, the WB, and Pax.

SOURCE: Crain Communications, Inc. (2004b).

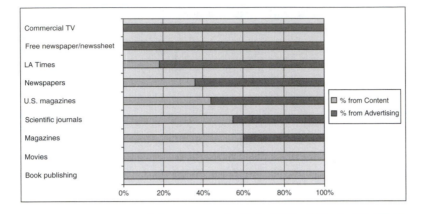

Figure 11.1   Proportion of Revenue From Sale of Content and Sale of Advertising

SOURCE: Ludwig (2000).

lower price and accepting advertisements (see Prasad, Mahajan, & Bronnenberg, 2003).

Several media, notably newspapers, magazines, cable television services, and some subscription Web services, sell joint products to dual markets. They sell information and entertainment content to subscribers (for convenience, we will define *subscribers* to include newsstand sales for media where this is applicable). They also sell space or time to advertisers to enable them to access their audiences (readers and viewers).

11.2.1 The Effect of Selling Advertising Space or Time on Price and Output of Content

The amount an advertiser is willing to pay for access to a media audience depends on the audience size. The key importance of the size of the audience is reflected in the fact that advertising rates are commonly quoted in terms of "CPM" (cost per thousand).

Information and entertainment content and advertising space and time are complementary goods. The number of exposures to advertising messages depends on the number of subscriptions sold, which itself depends on the price charged for subscription. The lower the subscription price, the higher the price that can be charged for advertising. A decrease in the subscription price shifts the demand

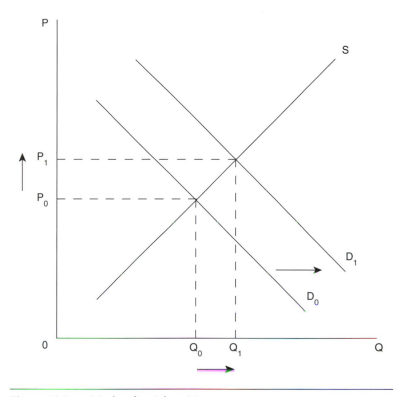

Figure 11.2   Market for Advertising

Note: D indicates demand; P, price; Q, quantity; S, supply.

curve for advertising to the right. This is illustrated in Figure 11.2, with demand increasing from D_0 to D_1. This increase in demand causes an increase in the price for advertising space and time from P_0 to P_1 and an increase in quantity supplied from Q_0 to Q_1.

In Figure 11.3, we examine the effect of selling to dual markets from the firm's perspective. To simplify, we will assume the firm publishes one newspaper. D_E is the demand curve for information and entertainment content, and MR_E is the associated marginal revenue curve for content. Note that only the positive section of MR_E is shown in Figure 11.3, but the negative MR_E above circulation level Q_2 can be found by extending the straight line. MC is the marginal cost of producing the newspaper. If the newspaper sold only content to subscribers, the profit maximizing price of the newspaper would be P^* and quantity (newspaper circulation) would be Q^*, where $MR_E = MC$.

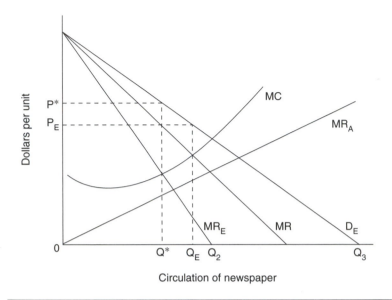

Figure 11.3   Effect of Advertising on Newspaper Circulation and Price

Note: D_E indicates demand curve for content; MC, marginal cost; MR_E, marginal revenue for content; MR_A, marginal revenue for advertising; MR, total marginal revenue; P, price, Q, quantity.

But the newspaper also sells advertising space to companies, government and nonprofit organizations, and individuals (the classifieds). MR_A represents the marginal revenue that the newspaper earns from sale of advertising space as a result of selling additional copies of the newspaper. MR_A is drawn positively sloped because the price the newspaper can charge advertisers for space increases with additional sales of the newspaper and, hence, exposures to that advertising space.

The total marginal revenue for the newspaper is MR, where $MR = MR_E + MR_A$. Graphically, we sum MR_E, including the negative values found by extending the MR_E line at circulation levels above Q_2, and MR_A vertically to find MR at any given circulation level. The optimal circulation is Q_E, where MR = MC. This implies a profit maximization subscription price to consumers of information and entertainment content of P_E. As a consequence of selling advertising space, the subscription price for content is lower ($P_E < P^*$), and more newspaper copies are produced and sold ($Q_E > Q^*$).

The Times case, introduced in chapter 2, provides an application. *The Times* sells in dual markets with subscribers (including newsstand sales) comprising around 40% of revenue and advertising around 60%. A decrease in the circulation price of *The Times* from 45p to 30p in the early 1990s resulted in an increase in circulation from 360,000 to 515,000. Revenue from subscribers decreased by £7500 (from £162,000 to £154,500), but the increase in readership enabled *The Times* to increase the price for advertising space by 10% (Hewitt, 1994). The revenue from advertising hence increased, although we do not have the information to determine whether this offset the fall in revenue from subscribers. What we can say is that, because circulation revenue decreased, *The Times* was operating in the circulation range above Q_2, where MR_E is negative and demand is inelastic. It is feasible, although not the case illustrated in Figure 11.3, that MR = MC in this range.

The increasing number of free, usually weekly, newspapers and newssheets, in which advertising is the sole source of revenue, implies that for these publications the optimal circulation price is zero: MR = MC at circulation level Q_3. Implementing any subscription price would reduce revenue from advertising more than the revenue gained from subscribers (this is a slight simplification because initiating a subscriber fee would also entail some additional costs). The same rationale explains free commercial television and radio broadcasting.

But the size of the audience (number of exposures) is not the only determinant of the value of space or time to advertisers. The price advertisers are willing to pay to access an audience also depends on the audience's demographic characteristics and its level of interest in the advertiser's offerings. To take banner ads on websites as an example, the CPM rates for exposure vary from $7.52 to $27.40, as shown in Table 11.3. The audiences with interests in areas such as computing and technology, travel, and health and fitness are worth more than double those with interests in comics and humor and games. In categories relevant to the media industries, entertainment has a CPM of $15.33, whereas music and streaming media is only $8.28. A media vehicle that attracts a high-income, free-spending audience can charge a higher CPM than a vehicle that attracts a lower income audience.

The importance of the demographics and interests of the audience is underlined by Kalita and Ducoffe (1995). For leading U.S. consumer magazines, they find that a lower circulation price attracts lower income subscribers, who are less appealing to advertisers. If this is the case, the effect of a decrease in circulation price on advertising rates and revenue is not clear.

Table 11.3   Average Full Banner Ad Cost Per Thousand for the
United States by Genre

Genre	CPM($)
Computing and technology	27.40
Travel	23.32
Health and fitness	21.14
Business to business	18.38
Women's interests	18.12
Business and finance	17.31
Local and regional	17.24
Entertainment	15.33
General and national news	14.80
Automotive	13.84
Sports and recreation	12.39
Learning and reference	11.87
Employment	11.49
Yellow and white pages	11.35
Children and family	11.11
Portals and search engines	10.59
Shopping and auction	9.71
Incentive	9.59
Community	9.20
Home and garden	9.01
Games	8.97
Music and streaming media	8.28
Comics and humor	7.52

SOURCE: Ad Resource (2004).

Note: Data is for the United States, both home and work, but excludes all online house ads that are advertisements run on an advertiser's own Web property. Also, due to methodological changes in how rate card value is collected and reported, there are significant decreases between data collected before and after October 1, 2003. Costs shown reflect an average of third- and fourth-quarter data from 2003.

11.2.2 The Effect of Advertising on Media Content

Partial or total reliance on advertising as a source of revenue can be expected to affect the actual information and entertainment content provided.

First, advertising content is often a substantial part of the total content and can affect its value. In the case of most television services in North America, for example, commercial messages take up

10 to 15 minutes of the hour. The interruption of the program is likely to detract from a viewer's enjoyment of the entertainment or information content of the program. This is typically less of a problem for newspapers or magazines because readers can easily ignore advertisements that are of no interest.

Also, editors are likely to consider the impact of information and entertainment content decisions on the size and value of their audience to advertisers. Content that turns off the audience, particularly those segments of the audience with demographics and interests that advertisers value highly, is likely to get less space.

The distinction between advertising and editorial content can be called into question when media firms develop new revenue-generating services that allow advertisers to better target consumers by providing content closely aligned with the advertiser's commercial message. If things go too far, this can undermine the integrity of the editorial product.

Advertisers can exert pressure on the media by threatening to take their business elsewhere. A survey by Soley and Craig (1992) of editors at U.S. daily newspapers found that nearly 90% had experienced pressure from advertisers to change their reporting or editorial content. Some 37% reported capitulating to advertiser pressure. As circulation rose, the number of editors who reported that advertisers had influenced their newspaper's content dropped. However, 85% of the editors reported that their papers nevertheless carry some stories that advertisers find critical or harmful.

As we mentioned in chapter 9, where the number of competing firms is small, reliance on revenue from advertising reduces the diversity of content. Steiner (1952) demonstrated that a small number of competing, advertising-financed broadcasting services have an incentive to provide similar programs because each gets a higher rating from sharing the large audience for a popular program type than from gaining all the audience for a minority-interest program.

To illustrate, consider the example given in Table 11.4. There are ten viewers A to J, and ten program types 1 to 10. The table shows the program type each viewer ranks first, second, and third. For example, viewer D ranks program type 10 first, program type 9 second, and program type 1 third. Thirty percent of viewers rank program 10 highest, 30% rank 7 highest, and 30% rank 4 highest. Nevertheless, if there are three competing, advertising-financed, private broadcasting organizations, and we assume that people are prepared to watch television as long as they get at least

Table 11.4   Viewers' Program Preferences

	Viewers									
	_A_	_B_	_C_	_D_	_E_	_F_	_G_	_H_	_I_	_J_
Program preferences										
First	10	7	4	10	7	4	10	7	4	2
Second	9	8	3	9	6	5	2	6	3	5
Third	1	1	1	1	1	1	1	1	1	1

SOURCE: Hoskins and Mirus (1998, p. 507).

their third preference, none of these programs would be shown. The reason is that each channel maximizes its audience (a 33% share, assuming the audience is equally split), and hence its advertising revenue, by showing program 1. This is despite the fact that program 1 is neither the first nor the second choice of any of the viewers.

This illustration assumes that differences in the demographics attracted by different programs do not result in advertisers preferring a lower rated program. It is also somewhat contrived because the addition of one more broadcasting organization would substantially increase the choice offered. However, it does illustrate the tendency toward common denominator programming in an oligopolistic broadcast system. With the increase in the number of television channels in the last 20 years, however, television broadcasting in many countries is better described today as monopolistic competition rather than oligopoly; viewer choice has expanded greatly.

The relative lack of choice is now better illustrated by film distribution, an industry with high barriers to entry that is dominated by a small number of major Hollywood studios. The major studios concentrate their production on action dramas aimed at the same target audience of 13- to 24-year-old males.

11.3 Summary

In this chapter, we examined the significance of advertising to media industries. "Off-air" (non–cable or satellite) private television and radio broadcasting organizations and free, usually weekly, newspapers rely solely on advertising. Daily newspapers, magazines, cable television services, and some subscription Web services rely on both advertising and subscription revenue. These media sell to dual markets, an advertising market and a consumer market for information and entertainment content. Traditionally, only book publishing and movies have sold exclusively to consumers.

Where media sell to dual markets, the subscription price affects the price that can be charged for advertising space or time. A reduction in the subscription price will cause an increase in the number of subscribers. With more subscribers, there will be more exposures to advertising messages, and the value of the space or time to the advertiser will increase. This represents an increase in demand for advertising space or time (a shift of the demand curve to the right) and results in an increase in price and quantity of that space or time. From the perspective of the individual firm, a decrease in subscription price enables it to charge a higher advertising price for space or time. *The Times* is an example: A decrease in subscriber price from 45p to 30p led to a 10% increase in the price of advertising space.

The number of subscribers or size of audience is not the only factor determining the price of advertising space or time. Some consumers are worth more to advertisers than others. The demographic breakdown and the interests of the consumers exposed to the advertising message are also important.

For media that rely in part or in whole on advertising revenue, these factors are likely to influence the nature of the information and entertainment content provided. Editors can be expected to consider the impact that choices about content will have on the size and composition of the audience. Editorial content may be influenced either through self-censorship or as a result of overt pressure from advertisers. Where the number of firms is small, competition for the mass audience may result in common denominator content and a lack of diversity.

12

Labor Markets

What would be the effect of an increase in demand for videogames on the salaries and employment level of software engineers? What would be the effect of a fall in the price of computer software used for computer-generated special effects on the demand for stuntmen, their wages and employment? Why do many pop stars work relatively few hours? What has been the effect of the depreciation of the Canadian dollar on the wages and employment of Canadian film crews and on the wages and employment of American film crews? What would be the effect of the formation of a union on the wages and employment of film crews? Why have movie projectionists suffered big reductions in wages? Why do superstars, whether a top movie actor, movie director, TV talk show host, author, or pop star, earn such vast salaries? Why do so many top British, Canadian, and Australian movie actors and directors move to Hollywood?

After studying this chapter, you should be able to answer these questions. As labor is not homogeneous—people have different aptitudes, skills, training, and education—we will focus on markets for particular occupations. Within an occupation, people will generally be assumed to have similar aptitudes, skills, training, and education. We will confine our examination to labor markets that are competitive. A labor market is competitive if there are many firms that demand this type of labor and many people willing to supply this type of labor. Most labor markets satisfy these conditions.

12.1 Determination of Wage Rate

Labor and other factor markets are similar in many ways to product markets. Just as the price of a product is determined by supply and demand for the product, the wage rate and employment level for an occupation are determined by the supply and demand for that type of labor.

In Figure 12.1, D is the demand curve for labor for a given occupation, S is the supply curve for labor for the same occupation. The equilibrium wage rate is W^* and employment level L^* where D = S. If the labor market is perfectly competitive, firms will be price takers in the labor market and pay W^* for any units of this type of labor employed.

Before going any further, we should explain what we mean by the wage rate and the employment level. In common usage, the wage rate is the hourly remuneration for work. But many people are paid a monthly salary. We will use wage rate in a broad sense to indicate the price for hiring labor, whether this is expressed per hour, per month, or per year. The employment level, or number of units of labor used, may be expressed as the total number of hours worked (by all employees) per period (typically a week or month) or as the number of workers used (assuming a typical work week of, for example, 40 hours).

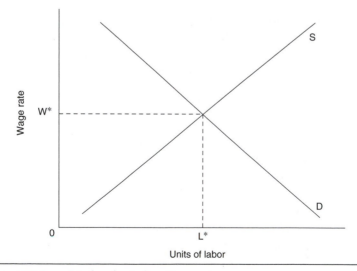

Figure 12.1   Market for Labor Occupation

Note: D indicates demand for labor; L, units of labor; S, supply of labor; W, wage rate.

12.2 Firm's Demand for Labor

The demand for labor (and for the other factors, land and capital) is a derived demand. Firms do not demand labor for its own sake but as a means to produce goods and services. Given a profit maximization objective, firms will demand labor as long as employing that labor will add more to total revenue than to total cost. More precisely, a firm will wish to employ additional units of labor up to the level where the last unit employed adds the same to total revenue as to total cost.

The increase in revenue from employing an extra unit of labor will depend on how productive the worker is; that is, how many additional units of output result, and the marginal revenue resulting from sale of these units. More formally:

$$MRP = MP \times MR$$

where the marginal revenue product (MRP) is the increase in total revenue resulting from employment of one more unit of labor, the marginal product (MP) is the increase in output from employing an additional unit of labor, and the marginal revenue (MR) is the increase in total revenue resulting from selling an additional unit of the firm's product. If the product market is perfectly competitive, then marginal revenue is equal to the price at which the good is sold.

To illustrate, suppose Nicole owns a video store and is deciding how many store clerks to employ. The duties of store clerks include manning the cash register, putting returned videos back on the shelves, and advising customers. Videos can be rented out at a price of $4. As it is assumed that any number of videos can be rented out at this price, marginal revenue is also $4. The wage rate for store clerks is $12 an hour.

In Table 12.1, Q in row 2 indicates the number of videos that can be rented out per hour, depending on the number of store clerks employed, L, in row 1. Marginal product, MP in row 3, is the change in output; that is, the number of videos that can be rented out, when an additional store clerk is employed. Because of the Law of Diminishing Returns, MP declines as more and more store clerks are employed in conjunction with other factors, which are fixed; these factors include the number of cash registers, shelving available, store size, and so on.

Marginal revenue product, MRP in row 4, is found by multiplying MP, in row 3, by the marginal revenue of $4. Nicole is a price taker in the labor market and can hire any number of store clerks at the wage, W in row 5, of $12 an hour. She maximizes profits by employing four

Table 12.1   Profit Maximizing Employment Level at Nicole's Video
Store

1.	L	1	2	3	4	5
2.	Q	20	32	38	41	42
3.	MP	20	12	6	3	1
4.	MRP	80	48	24	12	4
5.	W	12	12	12	12	12
6.	TR	80	128	152	164	168
7.	TVC	12	24	36	48	60
8.	TR – TVC	68	104	116	116	108
9.	MR	4.00	4.00	4.00	4.00	4.00
10.	MC	0.60	1.00	2.00	4.00	12.00

Note: L indicates units of labor input; MC, marginal cost (in dollars); MP, marginal product; MR, marginal revenue (in dollars); MRP, marginal revenue product (in dollars); Q, quantity of product (output); TR, total revenue (in dollars); TVC, total variable cost (in dollars); W, wage rate (in dollars).

or three clerks. The first three clerks add more to total revenue than to total cost; that is, MRP > W. A fourth clerk would add $12 to both total revenue and total cost, MRP = W, so Nicole is indifferent to whether a fourth is hired. She will not hire a fifth clerk because the addition to total revenue of $4 is less than the wage.

A comparison of total revenue and total variable cost confirms that hiring three or four clerks is optimal. Total revenue, TR, is shown in row 6 and is equal to Q multiplied by the video rental price of $4. Total variable cost, TVC in row 7, is L multiplied by the wage rate of $12. TR – TVC, as shown in row 8, is maximized at $116 when four or three clerks are employed.

The profit maximizing equilibrium, in terms of employment in the factor market, is consistent with the profit maximizing equilibrium in terms of output in the product market. They are, in fact, equivalent. As noted in chapter 5, marginal cost (MC) is equal to the wage rate divided by the marginal product; that is, MC = W/MP, and is shown in row 10. For example, a fifth clerk would result in one additional video rental, for an extra cost equal to the wage of $12. The marginal cost of this 42nd video rental unit is $12/1, or $12. If the clerk had added sales of two units, the marginal cost would have been $6 for each of these units. Comparing MR and MC, in rows 9 and 10, respectively, we find that MR = MC at a video rental level, Q, of 41 units. This is the output level associated with employing four clerks. In fact, Nicole is indifferent between an output of 41and an output of 38, the ouput from employing three clerks, as jumping from a video rental level of 38 to 41 adds $4 per unit to both total revenue and total cost.

Note that if the wage rate jumped to $24 an hour or fell to $4 an hour, Nicole would change the number of clerks she employs. At a wage rate of $24, MRP = W when three clerks are employed (and Nicole would be indifferent about employing either three or two clerks). At a wage rate of $4, MRP = W when five clerks are employed (and Nicole would be indifferent as to whether she employed five or four clerks). Thus the quantity demanded of labor at any given wage is the labor input level where MRP equals that wage, and Nicole's demand curve for labor is the same as her marginal revenue product curve.

For a company such as Nicole's Video Store, the equilibrium employment level is shown in Figure 12.2. Because of the Law of Diminishing Returns, the MRP curve and, hence, the firm's Demand for Labor curve is negatively sloped. Assuming the firm hires labor in a perfectly competitive labor market, the Supply of Labor curve for the firm is horizontal at the wage rate W* established by the market demand and supply for this occupation in Figure 12.1. The equilibrium employment level L_1 is where the firm's demand for labor equals the supply of labor to the firm.

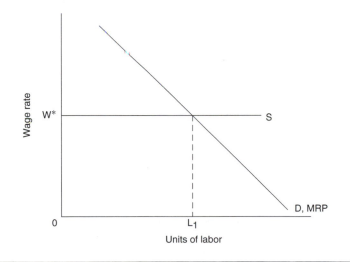

Figure 12.2   Market for Labor Occupation

Note: D indicates demand curve for labor; L, units of labor; MRP, marginal revenue product; S, supply curve for labor; W, wage rate.

12.3 Market Demand for Labor

The market demand curve for a given labor occupation is found by adding the units of labor that all the firms using this type of labor would demand at various prices. In a figure, it would be the horizontal summation (addition) of the demand curves for the firms. For example, if there are 100 firms who will each employ four store clerks at a wage of $12 an hour, then the market demand at this wage rate is 400 clerks.

12.3.1 Elasticity of Demand for Labor

The sensitivity of the demand for labor to changes in wages is measured by the elasticity of the demand for labor. This is calculated as the ratio

% change in the quantity of labor demanded /
% change in the wage rate

The elasticity of demand for labor will depend on how rapidly marginal product diminishes, the labor intensity of the production process, the price elasticity of demand for the product, and the ease with which capital can be substituted for labor.

The more rapidly the marginal product decreases, the less elastic the demand for labor. For example, adding a second film director to a movie project may contribute very little to assisting the production of a film (the two directors may spend much of their time in conflict), but adding another scriptwriter might be very helpful. If this is the case, a given percentage decrease in wage may result in another scriptwriter being hired but not another director.

The more labor intensive the firm's production process, the more elastic is the demand for labor. Let's see why. The higher the labor/capital ratio, the higher the proportion of total cost made up by payments to labor. For example, for a firm where wages comprise 50% of total cost, a 10% increase in the wage rate increases total cost (before any adjustment in employment level) by 5%, but for another firm, where payments to labor comprise 10% of total cost, the increase in total cost is only 1%. Thus, for a given percentage change in wages, the higher the labor intensity, the more total cost will change and the more the firm will adjust employment (and product output). For example, putting out a newspaper can be thought of as comprising two different production processes, one labor intensive and one capital intensive. Making up the content of the newspaper is labor intensive; printing the newspaper is capital intensive. The firm's demand for reporters will thus be more elastic than its demand for print workers.

The greater the price elasticity of demand for the product, the greater the elasticity of demand for labor. An increase in wages increases marginal cost, which causes a decrease in output of the product and an increase in its price. When the price of the product increases, the greater the price elasticity of demand for the product, the greater the reduction in quantity demanded and hence output; consequently, the greater the reduction in labor employed to produce this output.

In the short run, the quantity of capital is fixed, but in the long run, capital is variable. The easier it is to substitute capital for labor, the greater will be the long-run elasticity of demand for labor. Stunts in movies can be done the traditional way on the set with stuntmen or created digitally on the computer. The elasticity of demand for stuntmen, other things being equal, will be elastic in the long run. On the other hand, screen writers cannot be replaced by capital, and demand for them will be inelastic.

12.3.2 Changes in the Demand for Labor

A change in the demand for labor (as distinct from a change in quantity demanded of labor) for a given occupation is caused by a change in a determinant other than the wage rate and will be reflected in a shift in the demand curve. Other determinants are the demand for the final product, the productivity of labor, and the price of a related factor of production.

As the demand curve for labor is also the MRP curve, and MRP = MP × MR, then a change in demand for the product, which will affect marginal revenue, also changes the demand for the labor that makes the product. For example, if there is an increase in the demand for videogames, companies such as Electronic Arts that develop videogames will wish to increase output. To increase output, they will demand more labor in occupations such as software engineering. The market demand curve for software engineers will shift to the right. To summarize, a change in demand for a product will cause a change, in the same direction, in the demand for the type of labor employed to make that product.

Similarly, a change in the productivity of labor, MP, changes MRP and, hence, the demand for labor. An increase in labor productivity can arise because of an increase in the quality of labor (for example, through education or training), providing labor with more capital or land to work with, or through improvements in technology. One instance of this is the improvement in the training of film crews in Australia resulting from the establishment of the Australian Film Television and Radio School. More productive film crews attract more "runaway" productions to Australia. Thus the demand for Australian film crews increases.

Related factors of production can be substitutes or complements for a given type of labor. Other things being equal, a change in the price of a substitute factor will change the demand for labor in the same direction. For example, a fall in the price of the computer software used for computer-generated special effects will decrease the demand for stuntmen. Other things being equal, a change in the price of a complementary factor will cause a change in demand for labor in the opposite direction. For example, a fall in the price of the computer software used for computer-generated special effects will increase the demand for the people who use this software—graphic artists and postproduction effects editors.

In Figure 12.3, we show the effects of an increase in demand for labor, which, as we have seen, could be caused by an increase in demand for the product (made by this labor), an increase in labor productivity, an increase in the price of a substitute input, or a decrease in the price of a complementary input. The increase in the market demand for labor shifts the demand curve for labor to the right from D_1 to D_2. Given the supply curve for labor of S, the effect is to increase the equilibrium wage rate from W_1 to W_2 and the equilibrium number of units employed from L_1 to L_2.

The effects of a decrease in the demand for labor are shown in Figure 12.4. The decrease in the demand for labor could be caused by a decrease in demand for the product (made by this labor), a decrease in labor productivity (for example, due to a restrictive union agreement that reduces the flexibility of labor), a decrease in the price of a substitute input, or an increase in the price of a complementary input. A decrease in the demand for labor causes the market demand curve for labor to shift to the left from D_1 to D_3. Given the supply curve for labor of S, the effect is to decrease the equilibrium wage rate from W_1 to W_3 and decrease the equilibrium number of units employed from L_1 to L_3.

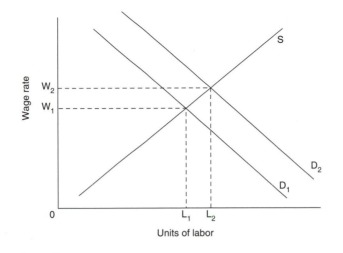

Figure 12.3   Effects of an Increase in the Demand for Labor in an
Occupation

Note: D indicates demand curve for labor; L, units of labor; S, supply curve for
labor; W, wage rate.

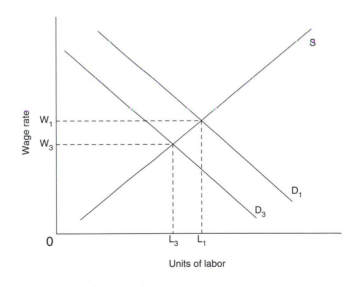

Figure 12.4   Effects of a Decrease in the Demand for Labor in an
Occupation

Note: D indicates demand curve for labor; L, units of labor; S, supply curve for
labor, W, wage rate.

In summary, a change in the market demand for labor causes a change in the same direction in both the equilibrium wage rate and employment. Thus an increase in the demand for videogames increases the demand for software engineers and increases their salary and employment level. An improvement in the training of Canadian film crews increases demand for their labor and increases their wages and employment level. A fall in the price of computer software used for computer-generated special effects decreases the demand for stuntmen and decreases their wage rate and level of employment.

12.4 Supply of Labor by an Individual

As we saw in chapter 4, an individual or household's objective is assumed to be utility maximization. Some people really enjoy their jobs and would choose to work even if they were independently wealthy, but for others, working is a means to an end. That end is to earn income to buy goods, the consumption of which provides utility.

However, time is scarce, so working more hours means less time can be spent in other ways that provide utility. For many people, leisure has intrinsic value, but in any case, leisure is necessary to consume many of the goods and services that provide utility. For example, going to a movie may require a time commitment of 3 or 4 hours, once travel time is included.

Time allocated to furthering one's education is valuable not only for its intrinsic benefit but because it often leads to a better, higher paying job. A better job would permit greater utility from consumption in the future.

Time is also allocated to nonmarket activities that nevertheless have a return equal to the opportunity cost of employing someone else to do the task, such as shopping, cooking, and do-it-yourself–type activities around the home. For example, suppose Scott, a handyman, wants his house decorated. He can do the decorating himself on weekends or accept the weekend overtime he has been offered by his employer and then pay Natalie to do the decorating. He will choose to do his own decorating if he would have to pay Natalie, who is quite as good at decorating, a wage greater than his after-tax wage rate for weekend work.

At low and moderate income levels, an individual will wish to work more hours as wages rise. Working becomes more valuable in terms of the goods and services it enables the person to consume and is substituted for the other demands on the person's time. For example, a sufficient increase in his wage will persuade Scott to accept the overtime he has been offered and pay Natalie to decorate his home.

However, at very high levels of income, this substitution effect may be outweighed by the income effect. An increase in wage and therefore income increases the demand for most goods, and leisure is a "good." If Deb is already enjoying a very high income and is able to purchase nearly all the goods and services she wishes, she may look upon a further increase in wage rate as an opportunity to increase her number of leisure hours. Deb thus cuts back on the number of hours she works, although, with the increase in wage, she still earns more income than she did before. This explains why so many pop stars work relatively few hours.

The resulting individual supply of labor curve is shown in Figure 12.5. It is positively sloped at low and moderate wage levels and backward bending at very high wage rates. An increase in wage from W_0 to W_1 increases the individual's hours of work supplied (say in a week) from L_0 to L_1, but a further increase in wage to W_2 decreases the hours of work supplied from L_1 to L_2.

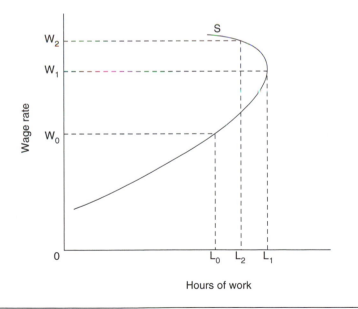

Figure 12.5   Supply of Labor by an Individual

Note: L indicates hours of work; S, supply of labor ; W, wage rate.

12.5 Market Supply of Labor

The market supply curve for a particular type of labor is the sum, or horizontal addition, of the supply curves for the individuals in this occupation. For example, suppose Travis and Bria are the only people in this occupation (in reality, of course, there would typically be thousands of people). If, at a wage of $10 an hour, Travis would want to work 40 hours a week and Bria 45 hours, then the market supply at a wage of $10 would be 85 hours per week, and so on for all other wage rates.

Even at very high wages, however, the market supply curve for an occupation is likely to be positively sloped (not backward bending like that for an individual) because the higher wage persuades some people to switch to this occupation. If writing software manuals pays well enough, Alan, who teaches computing at a community college, may decide to change careers. Also, the higher wage is likely to attract some people not yet in the job market to courses and programs that provide them with the skills needed to obtain employment writing software manuals. The addition of hours worked by people who enter the occupation at very high wage rates will likely outweigh the effect of others reducing the number of hours they work. This is the reason we drew the market supply curves in Figures 12.1, 12.3, and 12.4 positively sloped at all wage rates.

Anything other than the wage rate for the occupation itself that changes the attractiveness of this occupation relative to others requiring similar skills will cause a change in supply. Thus an increase in the wage rate or improvement in the working conditions of an alternative occupation will, other things being equal, decrease supply. On the other hand, a technological innovation that improves working conditions in the occupation in question will increase the supply of labor to that occupation.

In Figure 12.6, an increase in the supply of labor to an occupation is shown by the shift in the supply curve to the right from S_1 to S_2. This causes a decrease in the equilibrium wage rate from W_1 to W_2 and an increase in employment of the factor from L_1 to L_2.

In Figure 12.7, a decrease in the supply of labor to an occupation is shown by the shift in the supply curve to the left from S_1 to S_3. This causes an increase in the equilibrium wage rate from W_1 to W_3 and a decrease in employment of the factor from L_1 to L_3.

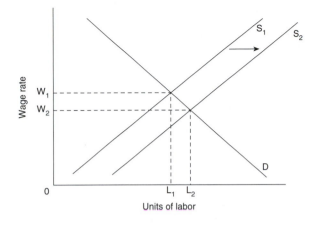

Figure 12.6   Effects of an Increase in the Supply of Labor to an Occupation

Note: D indicates demand curve for labor; L, units of labor; S, supply curve for labor; W, wage rate.

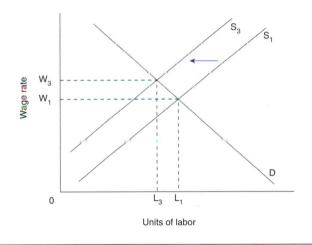

Figure 12.7   Effects of an Decrease in the Demand for Labor in an Occupation

Note: D indicates demand curve for labor; L, units of labor; S, supply curve for labor; W, wage rate.

Thus a change in the supply of labor to an occupation causes the employment level to change in the same direction but the wage rate to change in the opposite direction.

12.6 Labor Market Applications

In this section, we will examine applications in media industries.

12.6.1 The Effect of the Increase in the Number of TV Channels

In most countries, there has been a huge increase in the number of TV channels in recent years as cable and direct satellite distribution systems have expanded. This has led to an increased demand for television programs. Consequently, there has been a substantial increase in the demand for talented performers. This is shown as a rightward shift in the demand curve for talent from D_0 to D_1 in Figure 12.8. But the supply of talent is in short supply, shown by a supply curve S that increases in slope and eventually becomes vertical. The increase in the number of TV channels thus results in a large increase in wages, from W_0 to W_1, and a modest increase in employment of talent, from L_0 to L_1. For example, in the period from 1990 through 1995, the salaries of the top 100 contributors to television in the United Kingdom enjoyed a more than 50% increase in real (adjusted for inflation) income (Graham, 1998, p. 4).

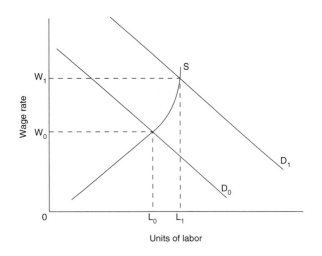

Figure 12.8   Effect of Increase in TV Channels on Talent

Note: D indicates demand curve for labor (talent); L, units of labor (talent); S, supply curve for labor (talent); W, wage rate.

12.6.2 The Effect of the Depreciation of the Canadian Dollar on Movie Crews

Between November 1996 and August 1998, the value of the Canadian dollar fell from US$0.74 to US$0.64. It then traded in a narrow range until the end of 2002, when it was worth US$0.63. The decrease in the value of the Canadian dollar relative to the U.S. dollar had implications for the markets for film crews in both Canada and the United States.

For an American movie studio, which faces a market-determined wage for Canadian film crews, the depreciation of the Canadian dollar would be seen as a decrease in the U.S. dollar wage rate for Canadian crews (and other factors involved in shooting in Canada). For example, for a crew member paid 30 Canadian dollars (C$30) per hour, the wage in U.S. dollars fell from $21.90 to $19.11, a decrease of 13.6% when calculated on the average of the before and after wage rate. This is shown in Figure 12.9 as a decrease in the supply of labor curve for the U.S. studio from S_1 to S_2 and wage from W_1 to W_2. This decrease in wage rate causes a typical U.S. movie studio to increase employment of Canadian crews from L_1 to L_2.

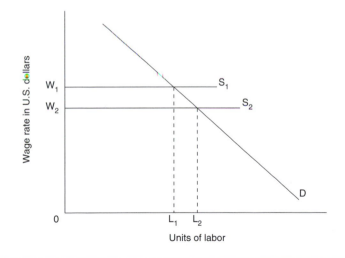

Figure 12.9   Effects of Depreciation of Canadian Dollar on a U.S. Movie Studio's Demand for Canadian Film Crews

Note: D indicates a U.S. studio's demand for Canadian film crews; L, units of labor; S, supply curve of Canadian film crews to a U.S. studio; W, wage rate.

Figure 12.10 shows the effect on the market for Canadian film crews: The wage rate is given in Canadian dollars, the currency in which the crews are actually paid. The currency depreciation has no direct impact on the Canadian dollar wage rate of W* (C$30 in our example) in Figure 12.10; the wage rates of W_1 and W_2 in Figure 12.9 are, in fact, respectively, the U.S. dollar equivalents of W* before and after the depreciation of the Canadian dollar. The market demand is composed of demand by Canadian film producers plus demand by U.S. movie studios. The effect of the depreciation is to shift this market demand curve for Canadian crews to the right; from D_1 to D_2 in Figure 12.10, as U.S. studios demand more at a given Canadian wage rate. The increase in demand from L* to L*** at wage rate W* is equal to the addition of L_1L_2 (in Figure 12.9) for all U.S. movie studios. But, at a wage rate of W*, employment level L*** is not an equilibrium because the quantity demanded of labor exceeds the quantity supplied. This causes an upward pressure on the wage rate until a new equilibrium is established at wage rate W** and employment level L**. Comparing the equilibria before and after the depreciation of the Canadian dollar, we find that the effect is to increase the Canadian dollar wage rate of Canadian film crews and increase their employment level.

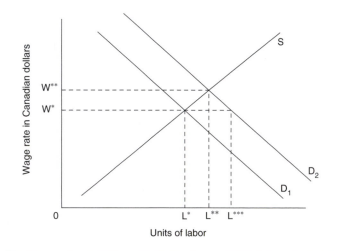

Figure 12.10   Effect of Depreciation of Canadian Dollar on the Market Demand for Canadian Film Crews

Note: D indicates market demand curve for Canadian film crews; L, units of labor; S, market supply curve for Canadian film crews; W, wage rate.

The depreciation of the Canadian dollar also had an impact on the wages and employment of U.S. film crews. The depreciation led to a decrease in the U.S. price of a substitute input, Canadian film crews. The effect of this is to decrease demand for U.S. film crews. This is shown in Figure 12.11 as a shift in the demand curve for U.S. film crews from D_0 to D_1. The consequence is a fall in the wage rate of American film crews from W_0 to W_1 and a decrease in the units of labor employed from L_0 to L_1. This is one of the reasons that Hollywood unions demonstrated in 1999 against Canadians "stealing" their jobs. (They also complained about tax credits provided by Canadian governments to U.S. movie studios that shoot in Canada; see http://www.ftac.net for many articles on this and similar subjects.)

There is a postscript to this case. In 2003, the value of the Canadian dollar rose rapidly from US$0.63 in January to US$0.76 by October. If this appreciation is sustained, what would you predict will be the effect on Canadian movie crews and on American movie crews?

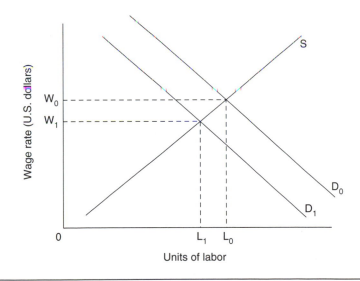

Figure 12.11   Effect of Depreciation of Canadian Dollar on U.S. Film Crews

Note: D indicates demand curve for U.S. film crews; L, units of labor; S, supply curve for U.S film crews; W, wage rate.

12.6.3 Effects of a Trade Union

In the absence of a union, the market supply curve for film crews is S_0, the market demand curve for film crews is D, and the equilibrium wage rate and employment level are W_0 and L_0, respectively, in Figure 12.12.

Suppose a union is now formed and negotiates a wage rate, W_1, that is above W_0. Included in the contract is an agreement by firms not to hire nonunion workers (who would be willing to accept a wage below W_1). The effect of the union contract is that the supply curve becomes W_1FS_0. The supply curve is horizontal from W_1 to F because firms can hire as many units of labor at wage rate W_1 as they wish, up to employment level L_2. Beyond that employment level, higher wages are needed to induce more workers into the occupation.

With the new supply curve of W_1FS_0 and an unchanged demand curve, D, there is disequilibrium. The number of people who wish to work in film crews at wage rate W_1 is L_2, but the number demanded is only L_1. People who retain their jobs are better off as a result of the formation of the union, but those workers who lose their jobs (note that employment has fallen from L_0 to L_1 units of labor) are worse off to the extent that they fail to find alternative employment at a wage rate of W_0 or above.

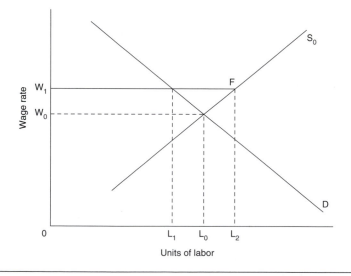

Figure 12.12   Effects of a Union in a Competitive Labor Market

Note: D indicates demand curve for labor; L, units of labor; S, supply curve for labor in the absence of a union; W, wage rate. Point F is used for explanatory purposes in the text.

Thus the introduction of unions could be expected to raise the wages of film crews but decrease the number of film crews or film crew members employed.

12.6.4 Movie Projectionists and Technological Change

Technological change often changes the type and level of skills required by labor. An example concerns movie projection. Operating movie projection equipment used to be a highly skilled occupation, and this was reflected in the high wages that were paid to projectionists. However, improvements in equipment mean that little skill is now required. In terms of labor markets, this can be thought of as an increase in the supply of projectionists, as many people can now handle the equipment, whereas a few years ago it was a skilled few. In Figure 12.13, this is shown as a shift of the supply curve from S_0 to S_1. The result is a decrease in wage rate, from W_0 to W_1 and an increase in employment, from L_0 to L_1. In British Columbia, where projectionists were earning C$31 to C$38 an hour, there was a lockout in 1999-2000 over an attempt by the major cinema chains to reduce this to the range C$14.50 to C$15.50, the rate already agreed to in Ontario.

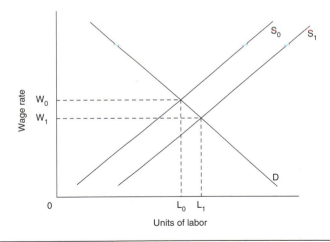

Figure 12.13   Technological Change and the Market for Movie Projectionists

Note: D indicates demand curve for movie projectionists; L, units of labor; S, supply curve for movie projectionists; W, wage rate.

12.7 Economic Rent, Superstars, and the Pull of Hollywood

The wage rate required to induce the supply of a factor is called *transfer earnings*. If a person were not offered at least this wage, he or she would transfer to the best alternative opportunity. Any earnings over and above the transfer earnings are known as *economic rent*. The economic rent can thus be regarded as surplus, an amount above that available in the best alternative occupation. Figure 12.14 shows the usual case for a competitive market for labor where there is a positively sloped supply curve, S; a negatively sloped demand curve, D; an equilibrium wage rate of W*; and an employment level of L*. Transfer earnings for all the people in this occupation is shown by the area 0AEL*, below the supply curve. The economic rent is the area AW*E, above the supply curve.

Top movie actors can earn $50 million or so per year (see Table 12.2, which gives Harrison Ford's earnings in 1998 as $58 million). A huge proportion of this is, typically, economic rent. One top movie star might be able to earn $50,000 in his best alternative occupation, another $100,000 in hers. Their economic rents would be $49,950,000 and $49,900,000, respectively. The reason their economic rent is so

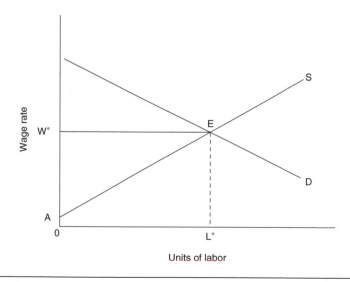

Figure 12.14   Economic Rent and Transfer Earnings

Note: D indicates demand curve for labor; L, units of labor; S, supply curve for labor; W, wage rate. Points A and E are used for explanatory purposes in the text.

high is that there is a large demand but only a limited number of top movie actors available. This is illustrated in Figure 12.15. The number of top movie actors is fixed at L_0, and the supply curve is vertical at that input level. Up to employment level L_0, the supply curve is positively sloped, indicating that more people choose to be movie actors as the annual income paid rises. For example, if Rodney can earn an annual income of $50,000 from his best alternative occupation, he will choose that alternative occupation if he would earn $49,000 as a movie actor, but he will wish to be a movie actor instead if he can earn $51,000 as an actor. With the demand curve at D, the annual income of top movie stars is $50 million, and the economic rent received by all the top movie stars is given by the shaded area above the supply curve and below $50 million.

The huge salaries earned by top movie actors are part of the superstar phenomenon. Table 12.2 identifies the annual salaries earned by some top people in the entertainment industries. Notice that Jerry Seinfeld tops the list. He and his costars earned $600,000 per episode for the last season of *Seinfeld*. This has now been topped by the stars of *Friends*. The six costars signed a 2-year contract in May 2000 for $750,000 each per episode.

Why are these salaries so huge? Part of the reason, which we have already identified, is the very limited supply of such talent. But even given the limited supply, there has to be a very strong

Table 12.2   Top Ten Superstar Salaries for 1998

Name	Occupation	Earnings in millions of dollars
Jerry Seinfeld	TV actor and comedian	225
Larry David	TV producer	200
Steven Spielberg	Movie producer and director	175
Oprah Winfrey	TV talk show host	125
James Cameron	Movie director	115
Tim Allen	TV actor and comedian	77
Michael Crichton	Author	65
Harrison Ford	Movie actor	58
Rolling Stones	Rock band	57
Master P	Rap star	57

SOURCE: La Franco (1998).

Note: Income is the estimated pretax gross income earned (but not necessarily received) in 1998.

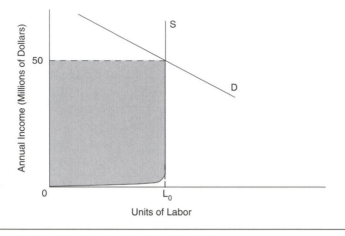

Figure 12.15   The Market for Top Movie Stars

Note: D indicates demand curve for movie stars; L, units of labor; S, supply curve for movie stars. Shaded area indicates economic rent received by all top movie stars.

demand for such superstars. There are many competent actors, directors, authors, and rock bands who only earn a fraction of what these superstars earn.

One key to the strong demand for superstars is the very uncertain market for new movies, television shows, books, and pop recordings. It is difficult to know how the public will react to, for example, a new movie. Using a superstar enables the producer to appeal to that superstar's fans (a form of brand loyalty), thus reducing risk and boosting the expected box office (Ryan, 1999).

Another key is the huge economies of scale, identified in chapter 5, associated with such goods or services. The incremental cost of supplying one more consumer is very low or, in some cases, even zero. For example, if using a superstar TV talk show host, rather than a competent host, results in an additional 2 rating points (a rating point being the percentage of the 100 million U.S. households viewing the program), these extra viewers cost the network exhibiting the show nothing. But the 2 additional rating points are likely to bring in additional advertising revenue of $1.8 million for a 1-hour show. Competition between the networks to get the services of the superstar host will mean that a share of this will go to the star host as a salary premium above that of the competent host (see Rosen, 1981, if you wish to read more about this phenomenon).

To be eligible for superstar status, in terms of remuneration if not reputation, it is necessary for a movie actor or director to be based in Hollywood. The demand for stars is greater in Hollywood than anywhere else because a star in a Hollywood movie has the potential to add more to box office revenue than a star in any non-U.S. or independent movie. The greater demand in Hollywood results in greater economic rent being earned. This explains why so many British, Canadian, and Australian actors and directors spend much of their career in Hollywood. Examples, through the years, have included Charlie Chaplin (English actor), Cary Grant (English actor), Jim Carrey (Canadian actor), Dan Aykroyd (Canadian actor), James Cameron (Canadian director), Ivan Reitman (Canadian director), Mel Gibson (Australian actor), and Bruce Beresford (Australian director).

There is not the same pressure for rock bands or pop stars to relocate to the United States. Music can be recorded anywhere, and regular American tours can maintain fan interest in the largest market. This explains why the Rolling Stones can remain based in England and Shania Twain in Canada.

12.8 Summary

In this chapter, we examined competitive markets for labor occupations. Just as the price of a product is determined by the supply of and demand for a product, the wage rate and employment level for an occupation are determined by the supply of and demand for that type of labor. If the labor market is perfectly competitive, firms will be price takers, accepting the market-determined wage rate and making a decision on how much labor to employ at this wage rate.

The firm will wish to employ additional units of labor up to the level where the last unit employed adds the same to total revenue as it does to total cost. The firm's demand for labor is a derived demand, as it is not demanded for its own sake but as a means to produce goods and services and, hence, generate revenue from their sale. How much revenue is generated by employing an additional unit of labor (MRP) depends on MP (i.e., how many units of output it adds) and MR (i.e., the additional revenue from selling this output). The firm is in equilibrium at the employment level where $MRP = W$, or, substituting for MRP, where $MP \times MR = W$. The market demand curve for labor is the horizontal summation of the demand curves for labor of the firms using this type of labor.

The elasticity of demand for labor, a measure of sensitivity of demand for labor to changes in the wage rate, is calculated as the ratio

% change in the quantity of labor demanded /
% change in the wage rate

The elasticity of demand for labor will be greater the more rapidly marginal product diminishes, the more labor intensive the firm's production process, the greater the price elasticity of demand for the firm's product, and, in the long run, the easier it is to substitute capital for labor.

A change in the market demand for labor for a given occupation is caused by a change in a determinant other than the wage rate and will be reflected by a shift in the demand curve for labor. An increase in the demand for labor, shown as a shift of the demand curve for labor to the right, could be caused by an increase in demand for the product (made by this labor), an increase in labor productivity, an increase in the price of a substitute input, or decrease in the price of a complementary input. An increase in the demand for labor causes an increase in both the equilibrium wage rate and employment. A decrease in the demand for labor causes a decrease in both the equilibrium wage rate and employment.

Individuals work to earn income to buy the goods and services that provide utility. But time is scarce. Leisure is valued for its own sake and because it is necessary if consumers are going to be able to consume products. Time spent on education can lead to higher future incomes. Time allocated to nonmarket activities, such as cooking, has a return (for cooking the meal oneself saves the cost of a restaurant meal). At low and moderate income levels, the supply of labor by an individual will increase as the wage rate increases because working becomes more valuable in terms of the goods and services it enables the person to consume. However, at very high income levels, the benefits of a further increase in wage are likely to be taken in the form of more leisure time and, hence, will reduce the supply of labor. Thus we have a supply for labor curve for an individual that is backward bending at very high wage rates.

The market supply curve for a particular type of labor is the sum or, in a figure, the horizontal addition, of the supply curves for the individuals in this occupation. Even at very high wage rates, the market supply curve can be expected to be positively sloped, as additional people are attracted to this occupation. A change in market supply, represented by a shift of the market supply curve, will result from a change in a determinant of supply other than the wage rate for that occupation. For example, a decrease in supply could be caused by an increase in the wage rate, improvement in working conditions in an alternative occupation, or deterioration in working conditions in the occupation itself. A decrease in market supply (a shift of the supply curve to the left) will cause an increase in the wage rate and a decrease in employment. Similarly, an increase in market supply will decrease the wage rate and increase the employment level.

Labor market theory is able to explain the effect of the increase in the number of television channels on payments to talent, the effects of the depreciation of the Canadian dollar on wages and employment of Canadian film crews and American film crews, the effects of the formation of a union, and the effects of changes in the technology of movie projection on the wages of projectionists.

The wage rate required to induce the supply of a factor is known as transfer earnings. Any earnings over and above the transfer earnings are known as economic rent. Most of the earnings of top movie actors, TV personalities, directors, authors, and pop stars are economic rent. This is due to a very limited supply and strong demand. Superstars reduce the uncertainty surrounding the demand for the entertainment product and boost revenue at very little incremental cost (given the large economies of scale). The opportunity to obtain a much higher economic rent attracts foreign talent to Hollywood.

13

Government Intervention

Why do governments intervene in the economy? What is market failure? What are externalities, how do they relate to television programs and other media goods, and what are the implications for public policy? Why is broadcasting, but not newspaper publishing, usually regulated and sometimes subsidized? Why do most governments protect intellectual property rights through patents and copyright? What are public goods? Does off-air broadcasting qualify as a public good? What role does government have in the provision of such goods? What are the efficiency implications of advertising-funded broadcasting? What is the justification for creating a public service broadcasting organization? Why do governments enact competition (antitrust) laws? What is meant by government failure? What are the motives of politicians, bureaucrats, and voters in regard to media industries, and what role do they play in determining when, where, and how government intervention occurs in media industries? Is regulation undertaken in the interests of the public at large, or is it provided to further the interests of specific industry groups, such as producers and labor unions?

This chapter will provide answers and insights into these and other questions.

Economists have developed both normative analyses of why governments should intervene and positive theories to explain how and when governments choose to intervene.

13.1 A Normative Analysis
of Government Intervention

You may recall, from chapter 1, that normative analysis is concerned with what ought to be, whereas a positive analysis is concerned with what is.

Chapters 7 through 9 have identified a number of indicators of desirable industry performance. But sometimes the market itself cannot bring about these results—a situation termed *market failure*. Normative statements can be made that we (often the government) ought to do certain things to bring about the desired performance results. For example, we saw in chapters 7, 8, and 9 that allocative efficiency is a crucial element of the performance of an industry. It exists when resources are allocated to the goods or service produced by the industry, up to the point where the benefit to society of the last unit produced is equal to the cost to society of producing it. This analysis leads to the normative statement that governments should intervene in cases of market failure to ensure allocative efficiency.

There are three principal reasons for market failure: externalities, public goods, and monopoly power. All three are very important in media industries. In fact, they are so important that some commentators claim that economic analysis cannot adequately deal with such industries—a view with which we do not agree.

13.2 Efficient Resource
Allocation in the Absence of Externalities

There are no externalities if the person buying a good is the only one to receive a benefit and the company making the good is the only organization or individual bearing a cost.

In the absence of externalities, perfect competition will be allocatively efficient. This was demonstrated in chapter 8 but is further developed in Figure 13.1, where S represents the supply curve and D represents the demand curve of a perfectly competitive industry. Equilibrium is at price P_0 and output Q_0. A supply curve is also a marginal private cost (MPC) curve, as it shows the marginal cost borne by the supplier (remember, from chapter 8, that the supply curve is the horizontal summation of the marginal cost

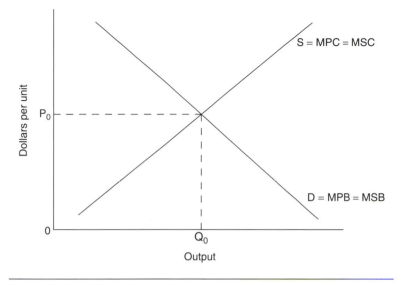

Figure 13.1   Allocatively Efficient Output in the Absence of
                    Externalities

Note: D indicates demand curve; MPB, marginal private benefit; MPC, marginal
private cost; MSB, marginal social benefit; MSC, marginal social cost; P, price; Q,
quantity (output); S, supply curve.

curves of the firms in the industry). In the absence of external costs,
the supply curve is also the marginal social cost (MSC) curve, as it
shows the cost to society resulting from an additional unit. A
demand curve is a marginal private benefit (MPB) curve because
it indicates the value or benefit attached by the purchaser of the
unit. If there are no external benefits, the demand curve is also the
marginal social benefit (MSB) curve, as it indicates the benefit of
the additional unit to society as a whole. Hence, the output is
allocatively efficicient, as

$$S = MPC = MSC$$

$$D = MPB = MSB$$

And by producing output Q_0, where $S = D$, the perfectly competitive industry is producing at the output where

$$MSC = MSB$$

13.3 Externalities

An *externality* is a cost or benefit arising from an economic transaction that falls on a third party and that is not taken into account by either of the parties (i.e., the seller [producer] or buyer [consumer]) to the transaction. Externalities may arise from the production or the consumption of goods and services.

13.3.1 External Costs

If there is an external cost (marginal external cost, or MEC) associated with an additional unit of a product, then MSC > MPC, as

$$MSC = MPC + MEC$$

External costs from production typically arise from pollution. For example, a pulp mill discharges effluent into a river, and this effluent reduces the number of fish and the catch of fishermen downstream. The MEC is the reduction in income of the fishermen.

This case, where there is an external cost but no external benefit, is illustrated in Figure 13.2. A perfectly competitive industry would supply Q_0, where D = S or MPB = MPC. As there are no external benefits, MSB = MPB. But the presence of external costs means that MSC > MPC, and hence, at output Q_0, MSC > MSB. It is in society's interest that the resources allocated be reduced and output lowered to Q_1, where MSC = MSB.

But pollution is not restricted to things like effluents and fish; television programming and feature films can, in the view of some observers, create a type of pollution all their own. Many television programs and feature films portray large numbers of violent incidents (National Television Violence Study, 1996, 1997, 1998). Viewing this violent programming may lead viewers to become hardened to violence or even to become personally violent (Paik & Cornstock, 1994). Also some viewers may come to imagine society is actually more violent than it is (Gerbner, 1990). Such viewers are likely to be more fearful than warranted and curtail their social life unnecessarily and, through reduced interaction, lessen the quality of life of others (Gerbner, 1990).

The strongest sociological evidence of a deleterious effect of violent television content on viewers exists in the case of children;

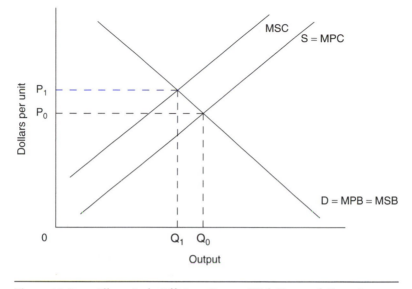

Figure 13.2   Allocatively Efficient Output With External Costs in Production

Note: D indicates demand; MPB, marginal private benefit; MPC, marginal private cost; MSB, marginal social benefit; MSC, marginal social cost; P, price; Q, quantity; S, supply.

studies (see Anderson & Bushman, 2002) have shown that children exposed to such programming exhibit higher levels of aggression and violent behavior on the playground. But violent content provision arises from a transaction between broadcasters selling advertising time and advertisers wishing to appeal to the hard-to-reach 18- to 50-year-old male and 18- to 35-year-old female segments. The exposure of children to violent content is an externality; the advertising messages on such programs are not directed at children. The portrayal of violence imposes a cost not borne, or even considered, by the producer or exhibitor. The economic concept of externalities thus provides the analytical basis for the oft-stated claim that there is too much violence on television. A competitive broadcasting market provides too many violent shows (see Hamilton, 1998).

13.3.2 External Benefits

The externalities arising from economic activity are not always bad. Sometimes producers create economic benefits for society that they are unable to capture in the prices they receive for their products. For example, external benefits from production may arise from R&D. R&D results in new knowledge embodied in new processes and products. As knowledge about innovations diffuses through the industry, other companies benefit from the technology spillover. The original R&D firm is unable to charge these other beneficiaries for what they have received.

The benefits of a company training program are similarly diffused, as some of the trained work force are subsequently hired by other companies. It is sometimes argued that a benefit of having a public service broadcasting organization is that it spends more on training than private broadcasting organizations. Certainly a number of CBC news anchors and reporters have moved on to starring roles in private broadcasting in the United States.

External benefits may also be enjoyed in consumption. If a person uses public transport rather than driving to work in his or her own car, this conveys benefits to other drivers in the form of reduced congestion and to the population at large in terms of less air pollution. If a person with a contagious infection seeks medical treatment and is cured, this is a benefit to others who might have caught the infection from the sick person. Consumption of education, besides providing the possible benefit to the recipient of a higher paying (and often more interesting) job, also provides benefits to others, as education typically leads people to become better citizens.

A similar argument is sometimes made for consumption (viewing) of some types of indigenous television programs and feature films. Here, external benefits can be thought of as positive side effects resulting from viewing. For example, current affairs, news, and documentary programs or films may promote a population more informed on national institutions, events, and issues and provide a home-grown perspective on international issues. Domestic drama and some children's programming may provide insights into the way of life of the country and reinforce the distinctiveness of that culture.

In the event of an external benefit associated with an additional unit (marginal external benefit, or MEB) then MSB > MPB, as MSB = MPB + MEB. This case is shown in Figure 13.3. The competitive industry produces output Q_0, where S = D or MPC = MPB. The allocatively efficient output, however, is the higher output Q_2, where MSC = MSB.

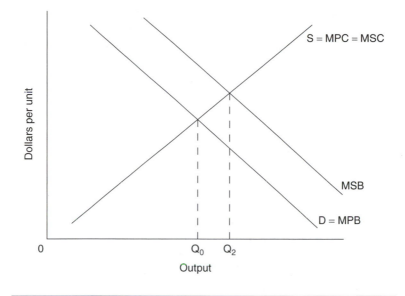

Figure 13.3   Allocatively Efficient Output With External Benefits in Production

Note: D indicates demand curve; MPB, marginal private benefit; MPC, marginal private cost; MSB, marginal social benefit; MSC, marginal social cost; Q, quantity (output); S, supply curve.

13.3.3 Public Policy for Dealing With Externalities

The most straightforward policy approach to dealing with externalities is to impose an excise tax, a per unit tax on the sale of a commodity in the case of an external cost, or a subsidy in the case of an external benefit. Variants include fees (such as effluent fees) or the auctioning of rights to pollute.

Look again at Figure 13.2. In the case it presents, an excise tax set equal to the per unit external cost would internalize this cost, and the industry's marginal private cost would now equal MSC. Imposing such a tax would cause the price to increase from P_0 to P_1 and the industry to reduce output to the optimal output of Q_1. Note that the increase in price is less than the tax per unit, which is equal to the vertical distance between the MSC and MPC curves. In effect, the industry and consumers are sharing the burden of the tax.

Although conceptually appealing, such an approach has little to offer in the case of controlling violence on television. If a tax were to be imposed on a violent television program, how large should the tax be? In other words, how large are the external costs imposed? Should the number of violent incidents be counted? Should their nature and the dramatic context be taken into account? Even if these questions could be answered, any attempt to impose, in the United States, a tax reflecting the level of violent content would be stymied by the First Amendment to the Constitution, which protects freedom of speech. Abroad, the Americans have opposed foreign taxes on U.S. television programming. They see them as covert trade restrictions rather than attempts to offset external costs.

The external benefit rationale, although subject to the same measurement problems cited in the previous paragraph, has been found to be an appealing rationale for government subsidy. If a television program is thought to have external benefits, a subsidy is appropriate. However, the level of subsidy should not exceed the level of external benefits. What program characteristics confer external benefits? How much external benefit is conferred by such characteristics? (It is important to note that the nationality of the individuals working on the production is unlikely to be related to the level of external benefit.) Determining the level of subsidy that can be justified is a problem when the external benefits are difficult or impossible to measure.

Setting standards is an alternative approach frequently used. Governments set permitted levels of pollution. Firms incur costs to reduce pollution to meet these standards. Internalizing some of what were external costs again results in a reduction of output.

Some of the activities of broadcast regulators involve setting standards. Standards with respect to portrayal of violence and sex can be thought of in terms of avoiding external costs. Content rules that require that broadcast organizations devote a certain number of hours (and/or expenditure) to news, documentaries, some children's programming, and domestic drama can be thought of as increasing provision of programming with external benefits. Such standard setting is an extremely blunt instrument, however, and it is far from clear that a benefit-cost analysis would support many of the rules and regulations found. In addition, private broadcasters, motivated by profit maximization, are adept at subverting the spirit if not the letter of requirements they find onerous and still enjoying the benefits of aspects of regulation, such as barriers to new entry, that they find appealing.

External benefits resulting from applied research and innovation have caused a dilemma within governments. The diffusion of knowledge to competitors reduces the incentive to invent and innovate. To restore this incentive, most governments provide intellectual property rights through patents and copyright. A patent or copyright is a government-sanctioned, exclusive right granted to the inventor of a good, service, or production process to produce or use the invention for a stipulated number of years. However, the disadvantage of patents and copyright is that diffusion of knowledge, and the competition that reduces prices, is delayed. Governments are thus faced with a difficult trade-off regarding the degree and length of protection provided. A further complicating factor is piracy. For example, digital technology has made unauthorized copying, of perfect quality, of video and music extremely inexpensive, and consequently, copyright laws are becoming increasingly difficult to enforce.

13.4 Public Goods

Pure *public goods* have two unusual characteristics. They are non-rival in consumption and are nonexcludable. What do these characteristics mean, and what are the implications?

Nonrivalry. People are rivals in consumption for most goods. For example, if Debbie buys and eats a chocolate bar, Deirdre cannot consume that chocolate bar. If Debbie wants frequent use of a Walkman, she will have to buy her own. She cannot rely on borrowing her friend Deirdre's Walkman whenever she wishes. Thus a separate chocolate bar or Walkman has to be bought by each person who wishes to consume.

For a few goods, this is not the case. National defense, or the protection service provided by it, can be enjoyed (consumed) simultaneously by all citizens of the country. Sailors are not rivals when consuming the benefits of a lighthouse warning of dangerous rocks. Viewing of television programs is a prime example in the area of media. Here, consumers are not rivals in consumption, as viewing by one person in no way detracts from the viewing experience of another; the same program can be viewed simultaneously by 100,000 people or 100 million people.

Nonexcludability. For most goods, it is easy to exclude people from consuming. People are excluded if the price asked is greater than they are willing to pay. If Debbie is unwilling to pay the $100 price for a Walkman, she will be excluded from consumption. Similarly, Deirdre will be excluded from eating a chocolate bar if she is not willing to pay the $0.60 price asked.

For some goods, however, exclusion is impossible or impractical. If national defense is provided, it is impossible to exclude some citizens from enjoying it. It is impossible to deny some ships the benefits of a lighthouse. Similarly, basic research is published and available to everyone. For some goods, exclusion is technically possible but is considered impractical. Fire fighting services could be supplied only to those who pay for the service. This is impractical, however, because a fire in a nonpaying household, if not acted upon quickly, might spread to a paid-up household next door. As another example, it is technically possible to scramble off-air broadcast services, but this has usually been regarded as impractical or not worth the cost.

Examples of public goods that are both nonrival in consumption and nonexcludable are national defense, basic research, and light-houses. Off-air broadcasting, given that the signal is almost invariably not scrambled, can also be regarded as a public good. Similarly, much Internet content is nonrival in consumption, and although exclusion is technically possible, it is usually not practiced.

Some goods are known as *mixed goods:* They possess one of the public good characteristics but not the other. For example, movie-goers are nonrivals in consumption (if the cinema is operating below full capacity) but are excludable. Library patrons are nonrivals for library service in general but may be rivals for a particular book.

The efficient allocation of resources to a public good again entails producing up to the point where the marginal benefit (MB) of the good is equal to the marginal cost (MC) of supplying it. But, because the same unit can be consumed simultaneously by all, the MB is the addition of the marginal benefit received by each citizen. To make the illustration simple, in Figure 13.4, we assume there are just two people in a nation and that the good is the service provided by a national public service broadcasting organization. The demand curves of person J and person K for national public service broadcasting are d_J and d_K, respectively. These demand curves indicate the value each individual attaches to each unit of national public service broadcasting. The combined value of national public service broadcasting to the citizens is given by the vertical summation of their demand curves. For example, at output Q_0, the value of this unit of service to person J is

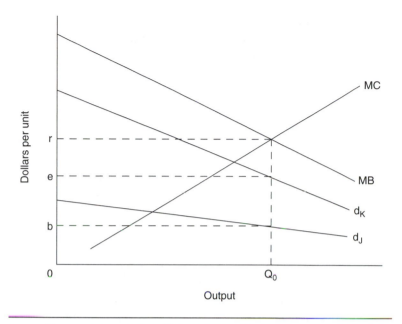

Figure 13.4   Allocatively Efficient Output for a Public Good

Note: d indicates demand curve; MB, marginal benefit; MC, marginal cost; Q, quantity (output). For b, e, and r, refer to the text.

b and the value to person K is e. The marginal benefit to the nation of the last unit of national public service broadcasting is thus r, where r = b + e. The optimal or allocatively efficient output is Q_0 because the MB of r is equal to MC at this output.

Given that public goods are nonrival in consumption and nonexcludable, who is going to supply them? In fact, there are examples of both public and private provision of such goods.

13.4.1 Public Sector Provision of Public Goods

For public goods, such as a national public service broadcasting organization, national defense, fire fighting, lighthouses, and basic research, it is the role of government to determine the optimal level of output and to finance the service from taxation (or, alternatively, for broadcasting, a television or radio license fee). Determining the optimal level of service entails benefit-cost analysis. Although quantifying the benefit is usually very difficult, it is appropriate to consider the total benefits and total costs of different levels of services and choose the level at which total benefit less total cost is greatest (that is, where MB = MC).

One policy response to the public goods issue is to have the good or service provided directly by a government department, agency, or publicly owned corporation—particularly in cases such as national defense and fire fighting services.

Free distribution of information on the World Wide Web follows the public library model. But on the Web, the library is a pure public good—there is no rivalry as long as site usage does not overload server capacity. Funding to support site maintenance must come from some public or charitable source if the information is free and there is no associated advertising.

The creation of a nonprofit public broadcasting organization (PBO) such as the BBC, the CBC, or the Australian Broadcasting Corporation also falls in this category. It may be considered a government response to two problems: the public good nature of off-air broadcasting and the related inefficiency, in terms of allocation of resources between program types, of commercial broadcasting. A public broadcasting organization can also be thought of as a way of ensuring an increased supply of the programming likely to result in external benefits (recall the earlier discussion of this subject). The purpose of the BBC is consistent with this:

> The BBC exists to enrich people's lives with great programmes and services that inform, educate and entertain. Its vision is to be the most creative, trusted organisation in the world. It provides a wide range of distinctive programmes and services for everyone, free of commercial interests and political bias. (British Broadcasting Corporation, 2004)

Sources of financing for public broadcasting organizations differ and are likely to have some impact on how successful they are at providing programming exhibiting external benefits. For example, the CBC relies on commercials for about 30% of its revenue (the remainder comes from a government grant), the BBC gets funding from TV license fees paid by households, and the Australian Broadcasting Corporation relies entirely on a government grant. The CBC's partial reliance on advertising revenue gives it an incentive, like that of private broadcasting organizations, to show programming that attracts the largest audiences.

The scale of a PBO should be determined by benefit-cost analysis. However, once established, it may not be easy to make significant changes, such as a change in mandate or reduction in size, even if new circumstances suggest this to be appropriate. (The opposition to a proposal, announced in May 2000 by the president of the CBC, to cut local programming provides a case in point.) In most countries, the increase in the number of channels, many of a subscription nature delivered by cable and satellite, has decreased the PBO's viewing share. In addition, some of these channels now exhibit programming of a type that used to be shown only by a PBO. As a consequence, benefit-cost analysis may not justify a PBO of the same scale and scope that it would have 20 years ago. Subsidizing individual programs is certainly a more flexible approach than creating a PBO.

13.4.2 Private Sector Provision of Public Goods

Private sector provision of public goods is difficult because of what is called the free-rider problem. No individual consumer will be willing to pay for the value of service received because, if others pay enough to provide the service, he or she will be able to enjoy the benefits at zero cost (a free ride).

In media industries, however, public goods such as off-air broadcasting and a lot of the digital content distributed on the Internet are supplied by the market system. Such digital content can take the form of computer software, video, audio, animation, images, or text. But how can private firms generate revenue from supplying these public goods?

One approach private sector suppliers have used is to tie the provision of these public goods to the sale of advertising, a related private good. Television broadcasters sell viewer exposures to 30-second advertising spots; many Internet sites sell banner advertisements. From the viewpoint of allocative efficiency, however, advertising is not an ideal revenue source because the advertising revenue raised depends purely on the number of viewers and takes no account of the value received from viewing. Thus a program that attracts five viewers who value that program at $1 each (MB = $5) would be chosen by a commercial broadcaster over an alternative program that attracts four viewers who value it at $3 each (MB = $12).

13.5 Monopoly

As we saw in chapter 8, monopoly does not result in allocative efficiency. To repeat the analysis, in Figure 13.5, S_{PC} is the supply curve of a perfectly competitive industry and D the demand curve. The output of the perfectly competitive industry would be Q_{PC}, sold at a price of P_{PC}. In the absence of externalities, output Q_{PC} is allocatively efficient. If the industry were instead run by a monopolist, its marginal cost would be MC_M and its marginal revenue MR_M. The monopolist would produce Q_M, where $Q_M < Q_{PC}$, at a higher price of P_M. The monopolist devotes less than the optimal amount of resources to production of the good.

One government policy approach to this form of market failure is to enact competition (antitrust) laws that give powers to the courts and government agencies that are intended to prevent monopolies from occurring. Conspiracy, or collusion, between companies to raise prices and decrease output is outlawed. Also, as we discussed in chapter 9, proposed mergers are often scrutinized to assess whether

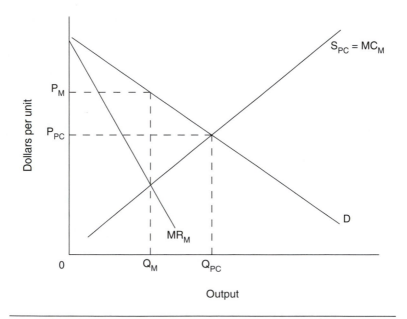

Figure 13.5   Allocatively Inefficient Output of a Monopolist

Note: D indicates demand curve; MC, marginal cost; MR, marginal revenue; Q, quantity (output); P, price; S, supply curve.

they would reduce competition unduly. For example, the regulators examined the AOL merger with Time Warner and approved it subject to the condition that AOL open up its cable lines to rival Internet service providers. Regulators recognized efficiencies from economies of scope but moved to forestall a potential source of monopoly power. In contrast, WorldCom and Sprint aborted their merger plans after opposition from EU and U.S. authorities, who ruled that a merger of the second and third largest U.S. telecommunications companies would seriously undermine competition.

However, as we saw in chapter 8, in the case of a natural monopoly, the huge economies of scale mean that only a monopolist can operate at minimum total cost; that is, be productively efficient. A common government response is regulation. Historically it has been the norm to regulate electrical and gas utilities, telephone companies, and cable TV companies. Regulation consists of rules administered by a government agency to limit the discretion of the company or industry over matters such as price, output, product, and market entry.

Figure 13.6 shows a natural monopoly with average and marginal cost declining throughout the relevant output range. A monopolist

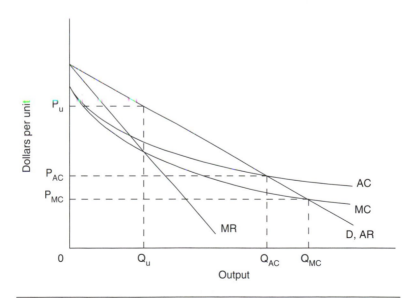

Figure 13.6   Price Regulation of a Natural Monopoly

Note: AC indicates average cost; AR, average revenue; D, demand curve; MC, marginal cost; MR, marginal revenue; Q, quantity (output); P, price.

not subject to price regulation would set a price of P_U and produce Q_U where MR = MC.

Two forms of price regulation are practiced; namely, regulation that imposes a marginal cost price and regulation that imposes an average cost price.

The marginal cost price is P_{MC} where MC cuts the demand curve. At price P_{MC}, output Q_{MC} will be demanded. Q_{MC} is the allocatively efficient output level because, at this output, marginal benefit (shown by the demand curve) is equal to marginal cost. There is a problem, however, as at output Q_{MC} the regulated company would lose money because AR < AC. Hence a subsidy would be needed to keep the company in business.

Average cost price regulation would involve price P_{AC} where AC cuts the demand curve. At price P_{AC}, output Q_{AC} will be demanded. Average cost price regulation of a natural monopoly has the disadvantage that the output is less than the allocatively efficient level, although much closer to it than the unregulated output Q_U. However, it has the advantage that zero economic profits are earned. Remember that economic costs include a normal return, equal to that available at similar risk elsewhere. Thus no subsidy is necessary.

Figure 13.7 illustrates price regulation where no natural monopoly exists. In this case, the marginal cost price, P_{MC}, would result in positive economic profits, as AR > AC at output Q_{MC}, and the company would enjoy a return greater than that available elsewhere at similar risk. Output Q_{AC}, at the average cost price of P_{AC}, where AC cuts the demand curve, is now greater than the allocatively efficient output Q_{MC}. It should be noted that if no natural monopoly exists, it is not obvious that the industry should be regulated. A more promising approach is likely to be for the government to create an industry environment in which effective competition takes place.

Governments have usually chosen to regulate an average cost price rather than a marginal cost price. They have preferred to live with a degree of allocative inefficiency associated with average cost pricing rather than deal with the below normal or above normal returns associated with marginal cost pricing.

Regulation is not without its difficulties. Regulation tends to be expensive and to delay decisions. Average cost rate (price) regulation hearings are often long, drawn-out affairs during which the debate revolves around issues such as the actual level of costs, whether the regulated company is operating efficiently, and the normal return earned elsewhere at similar risk. In addition, circumstances that led

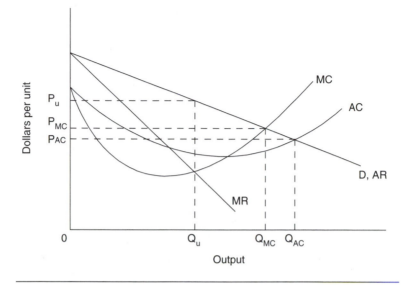

Figure 13.7   Price Regulation Where There Is No Natural Monopoly

Note: AC indicates average cost; AR, average revenue; D, demand curve; MC, marginal cost; MR, marginal revenue; Q, quantity (output); P, price.

to regulation in the first place may change, but the regulation process itself delays the technological innovation that leads to new competition. For example, in some countries, regulation delayed cable TV companies from offering telephone services and thus providing competition for the telephone companies.

13.6 Government Failure

Throughout the discussion of government intervention, we have stressed the need to weigh the benefits of intervention against the costs. If intervention is undertaken when the costs of intervention are greater than the benefits, then we have *government failure*. Thus the mere presence of market failure does not itself justify government intervention. Market failure can be viewed as a necessary but not sufficient condition for government intervention. Government failure may occur because it is too costly to set up and operate the subsidy scheme, regulation, or other form of intervention proposed. If this is the case, the resources that would be used in intervening are greater than those wasted through uncorrected market failure. Second, the intervention itself may be imperfect and do little to correct the market failure. Last, it should be noted that it is easy to exaggerate the costs associated with market failure and the benefits from intervention because externalities are so difficult to measure.

One argument that is sometimes used to justify government support of a given industry is the multiplier effect. Unfortunately, the assumptions underlying the multiplier effect are often not valid, and acting on this argument may lead to government failure.

To illustrate the multiplier effect argument, suppose there is a proposal to provide a $100 million per year subsidy to the film industry. The multiplier argument is that this government expenditure will not only increase the incomes of people in the film industry by $100 million, but this effect will be amplified. People in the film industry will spend a portion, say 80%, of their increased income on goods and services, and the incomes of people making these thus increases $80,000. The makers of these goods and services in turn spend 80% of this extra $80,000, and so on.

The first assumption underlying the multipler effect is that the money, not only from the direct subsidy to the people in the film industry but also from the portion of this they pass on through expenditures on other goods and services and so on, goes to resources that would otherwise be unemployed. Otherwise new wealth is not being created; rather, resources are diverted from one use to another. The second underlying assumption is that the government money could not be used in some other way, such as returned to tax payers (through a tax reduction) to spend as they see fit (that would provide similar multiplier benefits).

13.7 Positive Theories
of Government Intervention

Positive theories of government intervention encompass two competing theories: the public interest theory and the capture theory. Before we examine these theories, we will examine the players.

The players are the politicians, the voters, and the bureaucrats. These players interact in the political marketplace to determine public choice. As is typical in economics, it is assumed that the players pursue their own self-interest. Remember, these are positive theories about "what is," not normative statements about "what ought to be."

The politicians are elected officials at various levels of government. Politicians supply public policies. The prime objective of a politician is to get reelected. Politicians form alliances with like-minded politicians. These alliances, or coalitions, known as political parties, develop policy platforms designed to appeal to voters.

Bureaucrats are the hired officials that implement and, unofficially at least, often help initiate public policy. The BBC satirical comedy series *Yes Minister* amply illustrated the important policy determination role often played by bureaucrats. Bureaucrats are motivated by salary, job advancement opportunities, and the prestige associated with their department or agency. All of these objectives are promoted by pursuing strategies that maximize the department or agency's budget. Such strategies will involve (a) developing policy programs that will appeal to the politicians forming the government and (b) helping sell these policies to the voters.

The voters are the public (of voting age) at large. They demand policies that promote their own self-interest in their roles as consumers of goods and services, suppliers of labor and capital (through savings), and owners. In some cases, they will form alliances with like-minded voters to lobby for specific policies. For example, owners and workers in a specific industry may lobby for a subsidy for that industry. A vote is provided in exchange for the supply of desired policies.

13.7.1 Public Interest Theory of Regulation

The public interest theory is that governments, bureaucrats, and voters all believe it is in their interests that resources be allocated efficiently. This will maximize wealth and, hence, the size of the pie to be shared.

The public interest theory would predict the kind of government intervention we have identified earlier. Where benefit-cost analysis supports intervention, governments would impose an excise tax or set standards to compensate for external costs, provide subsidies for goods supplying external benefits, determine the optimal output of public goods and see that this output is supplied, maintain competition through competition (antitrust) legislation, and regulate natural monopolies.

13.7.2 Capture Theory of Intervention

The capture theory is that government intervention is provided to further the economic interests of specific groups, such as producers or labor unions. The theory has been particularly applied to intervention in the form of regulation, where it claims regulators are "captured" by the industry they are regulating and intervene in ways demanded by the industry.

Bureaucrats in the regulating agencies often stand to benefit from meeting industry demands, as this is likely to lead to employment opportunities in the private sector. In addition, they enjoy a more pleasant work environment if the relationship with the regulated industry is cooperative rather than confrontational.

Politicians will supply such intervention if they believe they will gain more votes than they lose. For politicians to gain votes they must be able to supply a group of voters with a significant benefit. Providing significant benefits may be rewarded also with campaign contributions. If the politician is not to lose votes, the costs of helping a group must be spread over a large number of people (usually in their role as consumers or taxpayers) so that no individual is aware of any significant loss.

Groups of voters will organize to lobby for intervention that furthers their interests. Cultural industry groups in many countries have been very vocal and well organized in their lobbying efforts. This activity, which we have identified before as rent seeking, is itself a deadweight loss because it diverts resources from productive activities.

13.7.3 Public Interest Theory Versus Capture Theory

Which theory best describes the pattern of intervention found? We do not believe the answer is clear cut. Regulation of natural monopolies such as electrical and gas utilities would seem consistent with the public interest theory. Some of the regulation of industries, such as in farming, trucking, taxis, and air transport, seems more consistent with the capture theory. Many of these are potentially very competitive industries, far removed from being natural monopolies.

Broadcasting has been the most heavily regulated cultural industry. Which theory best explains this regulation? The public interest theory is consistent with regulation promoting programming with external benefits. But some regulation does not appear consistent with this goal. For example, a case can be made that for a number of years the CRTC, the Canadian broadcast regulator, was captured by the cable TV industry. CRTC regulation in Canada certainly served to delay competition from satellite. With respect to broadcasting in Australia, Papandrea (2000) writes: "There is considerable evidence, over many years, that policy makers and regulators have been 'captured' by commercial and vested interests and have used this function to promote private interests ahead of the public interest" (p. 1).

In many countries, the regulation of broadcasting has lightened. The number of channels licensed has soared. This has been part of a general trend, in the 1980s and 1990s, to deregulate. This trend can be viewed as a realization by politicians that protection of industry interests through regulation had become so pervasive that consumers were beginning to recognize the costs and that the balance of votes now favored reducing or even eliminating the regulatory load.

The public interest theory does not satisfactorily explain why governments intervene in some industries but not others. For example, if there are external benefits associated with some types of television programming, it is difficult to argue that there are not similar external benefits for some newspaper articles. So why is broadcasting but not newspaper publishing regulated and subsidized in many countries? Historically, the rationale for regulating broadcasting may have been spectrum frequency scarcity, which did not apply to newspaper publishing. But most television content is delivered today by cable and satellite, which do not use spectrum frequencies at all.

13.8 Summary and Conclusion

In normative terms, government intervention in the economy may be justified on the grounds of market failure. Market failure can result from externalities, public goods, or monopoly.

An externality is a cost or benefit, arising from a transaction, that falls on a third party. Externalities may arise from the production or consumption of goods and services.

External costs from production typically arise from pollution. Violence on television and in feature films can be considered a form of pollution.

External benefits from production arise from R&D. As knowledge diffuses through the industry, other companies benefit from the technology spillover. Similar effects may be seen with company training programs. External benefits from consumption arise from goods such as public transport and education. In terms of television programs and feature films, external benefits can be thought of as positive side effects resulting from viewing.

Externalities can be internalized by imposing an excise tax in the case of external costs or a subsidy in the case of external benefits. Setting standards is an alternative that is often used. Patents and copyrights are granted to encourage R&D.

Public goods are nonrival in consumption and are nonexcludable. National defense is a prime example. It is nonrival in consumption because the protection provided can be enjoyed by all citizens simultaneously. Neither can any citizen be excluded from the benefits. Off-air broadcasting can be regarded as a public good because it is nonrival in consumption and exclusion is technically possible but not usually practiced. Commercial broadcasting organizations choose to sell viewer exposures to advertisers rather than programs to viewers.

It is the role of government to determine the optimal level of provision of public goods and to finance this through taxation. The creation of public broadcasting organizations may be viewed as a government response to the public good nature of off-air broadcasting; external benefits from viewing some programs; and the inefficiency, in terms of allocation of resources between program types, of commercial broadcasting.

Monopoly results in inefficient resource allocation, as the producer restricts output and keeps the price high. One government policy approach is to enact competition (antitrust) legislation to try to prevent monopoly from occurring. Where a natural monopoly exists, governments can regulate a marginal cost or average cost price to prevent the monopolist exploiting consumers.

Government failure occurs when the benefits of government intervention are exceeded by the costs. The mere presence of market failure does not justify government intervention. Government failure may occur because it is too costly to set up and administer a subsidy scheme, regulation, or other form of intervention proposed. The intervention itself may be ineffective and do little to correct the market failure. One should be wary of claims that a given government intervention in an industry is desirable because of its multiplier effects.

Positive theories of government intervention attempt to explain how and when governments intervene. The players are the politicians, bureaucrats, and voters, and it is assumed that each of these groups is motivated by self-interest.

The public interest theory is that government intervention is consistent with the interest of the public at large. The rival capture theory is that government intervention is supplied to further the economic interests of specific industry groups, such as producers and labor unions. Each theory is appropriate for explaining certain aspects of government intervention.

14

International Trade

Why does the United States dominate trade in movies and television programs? Why does a single country within the region dominate regional and linguistic television program markets? Should every nation strive to have a significant film industry? Is protection of cultural industries justified? Are there cultural industries or just entertainment industries? Why is trade in films and television programs so controversial? Why is the United States in a constant battle over cultural products with countries such as France and Canada at international trade negotiations? Does the United States sell television programs abroad at unfairly low prices? What are the effects of domestic content requirements for television programming? Why do most economists favor freer trade? This chapter will provide you with insights and, in some cases, answers to these questions.

This chapter discusses international trade. We start by examining why specialization and trade can benefit all participating nations.

14.1 Comparative Advantage and Trade

We will begin with an example in which the benefits of specialization and trade are fairly self-evident. To keep the example simple, suppose we have a two-product, two-nation world. The products are VCRs and videos, the nations are the United States and Japan. Their production capabilities are as follows:

If the United States allocates all its resources to producing VCRs, it will produce 200 VCRs.

If the United States allocates all its resources to producing videos, it will produce 2400 videos.

If Japan allocates all its resources to producing VCRs, it will produce 400 VCRs.

If Japan allocates all its resources to producing videos, it will produce 1200 videos.

Suppose that both nations, operating as closed economies (i.e., without trade), devote half their resources to producing both goods. This would provide the consumption levels shown in Table 14.1.

It is clear in this example that Japan is better at producing VCRs and the United States is better at making videos. It should be no surprise that the consumers in both nations can benefit from specialization and trade.

If Japan devotes all its resources to making VCRs and the United States devotes all its resources to making videos, we have the output shown in Table 14.2. As total output of both goods in Table 14.2 is greater than that in Table 14.1, it is obvious that specialization and trade can result in both nations being better off. Suppose both nations agree to an exchange rate of six videos for one VCR. This exchange rate could be arrived at through barter, but in a money economy, the rate will be determined through market transactions and prices. An example of the trade that could occur is that Japan produces 400 VCR units and trades 150 VCRs (this means that 250 VCR units will be consumed at home in Japan, and 150 will now be consumed in the United States) for 900 units of videos (note that $900 = 150 \times 6$). The United States produces 2400 videos, retains 1500 for home consumption, and trades 900 videos for the 150 VCRs. This gives the consumption levels shown in Table 14.3.

Table 14.1   Consumption of VCRs and Videos Without Trade

	VCRs	Videos
United States	100	1200
Japan	200	600
Total consumption	300	1800

Table 14.2   Output of VCRs and Videos With Complete
Specialization

	VCRs	Videos
United States	0	2400
Japan	400	0
Total output	400	2400

Table 14.3   Consumption With Specialization and Trade

	VCRs	Videos
United States	150	1500
Japan	250	900
Total consumption	400	2400

Comparing consumption with specialization and trade (as shown in Table 14.3) to consumption with closed economies (as shown in Table 14.1), we see that consumers in the United States have 50 more VCR units and 300 more videos. Consumers in Japan benefit in the same way, with 50 more VCR units and 300 more videos. (It is a coincidence that in this example the size of the additional consumption of each product is identical for both nations.)

But what happens if one country is better at producing both goods? Surely in this case the less productive country will not be willing to trade because its industries will be unable to compete. In fact this is not the case. The Theory of Comparative Advantage demonstrates that specialization and trade still increase consumption opportunities for all parties to the trade.

Before we illustrate the Theory of Comparative Advantage, we need to define some terms.

A nation has an *absolute advantage* in a good if it can produce more of the good with the same resources. In our example, Japan has an absolute advantage in VCRs and the United States has an absolute advantage in videos.

A nation has a *comparative advantage* in a good if the opportunity cost associated with producing it is less. The opportunity cost is the number of units of the other good that must be given up to produce one more unit. In our example, the opportunity costs are as follows.

For Japan, the opportunity cost for one VCR is forgoing three videos (1200:400 = 3:1). (Alternatively, it could be said that the opportunity cost for one video is one third of a VCR unit.) For the United States, the opportunity cost for one VCR is 12 videos (2400:200 = 12:1). (Alternatively, the opportunity cost for one video is one twelfth of a VCR unit.)

Thus Japan has a comparative advantage in VCRs because it only has to give up three videos to be able to produce another VCR, whereas the United States would have to give up 12 videos. On the other hand, the United States has a comparative advantage in video production because it only has to forgo one twelfth of a VCR unit to produce one more video, whereas Japan would have to give up one third of a VCR unit.

Although absolute advantage and comparative advantage coincide in our U.S. and Japan example, as we shall see, it is actually comparative advantage that explains the pattern of trade.

We will now move to the more interesting case, in which one nation has an absolute advantage in production of both goods. To keep the example simple, again suppose we have a two-product, two-nation world. The products are food and books, and the nations are Canada and Britain. Their production capabilities are as follows:

If Canada allocates all its resources to producing food, it will produce 1600 units of food.

If Canada allocates all its resources to producing books, it will produce 1600 books.

If Britain allocates all its resources to producing food, it will produce 700 units of food.

If Britain allocates all its resources to producing books, it will produce 1400 books.

Canada has an absolute advantage in both food and book production, as it can produce more of each.

To determine the comparative advantage, we must examine the opportunity costs.

For Canada, the opportunity cost for one unit of food is forgoing one book (1600:1600). (Alternatively stated, the opportunity cost for one book is one unit of food.) For Britain, the opportunity cost for one unit of food is two books (1400:700). (Alternatively, the opportunity cost for one book is half a unit of food.) Consequently, Canada has a comparative advantage in food. It only has to forgo one book to produce another unit of food, whereas Britain has to forgo two books. But Britain enjoys a comparative advantage producing books. It only has to forgo half a unit of food to produce another book, whereas Canada has to forgo one unit of food.

Operating as closed economies, if Canada chooses to devote half of its resources to producing each good, and Britain devotes three quarters of its resources to producing food and one quarter to producing books, we have the situation shown in Table 14.4.

Total output of both goods will be greater if each nation specializes in the product in which it has a comparative advantage; that is, if Canada specializes in food production and Britain in books. As we see in Table 14.5, output of food will increase by 275 units to 1600 units and output of books by 250 units to 1600 units.

At terms of trade (the rate of exchange) of food for books between 1:1 (the opportunity cost for Canada) and 1:2 (the opportunity cost for Britain), both nations can consume more of both goods if they specialize in the product in which they have a comparative advantage and trade. For example, suppose the rate is 1:1.25 (1 unit of food can be exchanged for 1.25 books) and

Canada produces 1600 units of food and trades 700 units of food (900 units are retained for domestic consumption) for 875 books.

Britain produces 1400 books (525 retained) and trades 875 books for 700 units of food.

The consumption available for both nations is now given in Table 14.6.

Table 14.4   Consumption of Food and Books Without Trade

	Food	Books
Canada	800	800
Britain	525	350
Total consumption	1325	1150

Table 14.5   Output of Food and Books With Complete Specialization

	Food	Books
Canada	1600	0
Britain	0	1400
Total output	1600	1400

Table 14.6   Consumption of Food and Books With Specialization and
Trade

	Food	Books
Canada	900	875
Britain	700	525
Total consumption	1600	1400

Comparing these consumption levels with the consumption levels for the no trade case in Table 14.4, we see that Canada is able to consume 100 additional units of food and 75 additional books; Britain is able to consume 175 additional units of food and 175 more books. Britain, which is at an absolute disadvantage in production of both goods, is still better off specializing in the good in which it has a comparative advantage and trading.

The Law of Comparative Advantage, as illustrated in this example, is the basic reason most economists favor free(r) trade. One of the great fallacies is to regard international trade as a constant-sum game. It is not; all nations can benefit.

14.2 Gains From Trade in the Real World

In the real world, there are often additional advantages of specialization. These are associated with economies of scale and the learning curve. If economies of scale are present, then the cost per unit decreases as the output rate increases. Learning by doing may lead to a decrease in per unit costs with time and cumulative output. These advantages are particularly important for small countries, where the volume of production needed to supply the domestic market is insufficient to yield such benefits. The wide variety of consumer tastes permits countries to gain economies of scale for subproduct lines. For example, there is a demand for various types of passenger plane. Although the United States and the EU dominate the market in passenger planes, Canada and Brazil have achieved economies of scale in supplying the short-haul, regional jet market niche. Similarly, although the United States dominates trade in film and television programs, Japan has had success with animation, the United Kingdom with costume dramas, and Canada with low-cost programming for cable stations.

Even with these advantages of specialization, the complete specialization implied by our illustrative numerical examples does not occur. Why is this? The reason is that the factors of production within a nation are not homogeneous; they are not all identical and equally suited for producing a given good. To illustrate, referring back to our example involving trade of food and books, as Canada expands food production it is likely to start running out of fertile land and be forced to use less suitable land. The opportunity cost of another unit of food, in terms of books forgone, will rise. Similarly, in Britain, not all labor will be equally suited to producing books. Thus, as output expands, labor that is less productive in this endeavor has to be employed. Beyond a certain level of output, the country no longer has a comparative advantage.

14.3 Sources of Comparative Advantage

An important source of comparative advantage, and the one traditionally emphasized by economists, is different factor endowments. According to the Hecksher-Ohlin Theory, countries have a comparative advantage in the production of products that are intensive in the use of factors in which they are abundantly endowed. For example, China, which has abundant cheap labor, sells labor-intensive clothing and small appliances to Canada, and Canada, which has a small population but is abundantly endowed with agricultural land, sells land-intensive wheat to China.

Natural resources and climate are part of the factor endowments. Australia is well endowed with coal and sells it to Japan. Jamaica has a tropical climate and glorious beaches and sells tourism and bananas.

In recent years, an increasing emphasis has been attached to acquired or dynamic comparative advantage. New industries, in particular, are thought to depend more on human knowledge and the competitive environment than on physical factor endowments. Michael Porter (1986) emphasizes that the characteristics of a country's demand and operating environment can be a source of comparative advantage. An optimal environment involves the presence of strong, preferably geographically concentrated, local competition and sophisticated buyers. Such characteristics ensure that the survivors will be formidable competitors in the international marketplace. An additional advantage ensues if the product attributes demanded by the commercially sophisticated domestic buyers lead to product varieties particularly well suited to the world market. Such a domestic demand and operating environment form a desirable "global platform." An example is Silicon Valley in computer software and Internet applications.

14.4 Application: Why Does the United States Dominate Film and Television Program Production?

Part of the U.S. advantage relates to factor endowments. In the early days of the film industry, the consistent sunshine of California was a plus in the industry locating there.

Another factor endowment is that the United States enjoys the unique combination of a large population with a common language and a high per capita income, which makes it much the biggest of the world's markets for television programs, feature films, and videos. Possessing the largest home market provides the United States with a crucial advantage for film and television programs, but not most other goods, because film and television are subject to a cultural discount and enjoy huge economies of scale because they are nonrival in consumption. As we saw in chapter 3, the cultural discount refers to the diminished appeal of imported film or programming because viewers have difficulty relating to the way of life, values, institutions, and language (even allowing for dubbing or subtitling) represented.

The advantage can be illustrated by a numerical example. To keep the example simple, assume a world comprising just two countries, the United States and Spain, with the U.S. market being 11 times larger than Spain's. Suppose it costs $1.15 million to produce comparable 1-hour drama programs in both countries and that in the absence of a cultural discount, both programs could recover $1.1 million in the U.S. market and $100,000 in the smaller Spanish market. If there were no cultural discount, then no advantage would be conferred on the United States by its larger domestic market. Both programs would be made, as revenue from the sale of each program to the two markets would total $1.2 million (in effect, this is the situation with a culture-free product such as a VCR). However, if a cultural discount of, say, 25% applies to a sale in the other country, the revenue earned by the two producers would be as follows:

U.S. producer: $\$1,100,000 + (1 - 0.25)\ 100,000 = \$1,175,000$

Spanish producer: $\$100,000 + (1 - 0.25)\ 1,100,000 = \$925,000$

Assuming the additional cost of making the program available in the export market is insignificant, the U.S. production would make a profit of $25,000 and the Spanish producer would make a loss of $225,000. Because of the cultural discount, domestic market size is important; only the U.S. program would get made. (This example is drawn from Hoskins et al., 1997, p. 40.)

The advantage of larger market size is accentuated by the fact that the larger market of the United States justifies a higher production and promotion budget than does Spain's market. Thus Spanish productions have to compete against larger budget U.S. productions, putting them at a further disadvantage. (For a numerical example illustrating this, see Hoskins et al., 1997, pp. 41-42.)

Another natural advantage possessed by the United States is that its TV programs, feature films, and videos are produced in English, which is, in terms of buying power, the largest language market in the world. Language is an important component of the cultural discount, and hence we would expect English-language producers to enjoy a lower discount when accessing other English-language national markets. In addition, English is the world's major second language, and English-language productions are often more acceptable than other foreign-language productions in non–English-language markets.

In terms of acquired comparative advantage, U.S. producers of films and television programs have long operated in a competitive industry concentrated in Hollywood. Los Angeles is the single physical location in the world where all the necessary ingredients for a successful feature film are readily accessible. These ingredients include the agents, who often act as deal makers; producers; production skills and infrastructure; stars; directors; financial and distribution expertise; entertainment lawyers; script editors; and so on. They operate in a melting-pot society that rewards broadly based, popular programming. It should not be surprising that movies and drama programs that are successful in the competitive, polyglot, U.S. domestic market are also successful in most foreign markets. In the case of feature films, much of the competition from countries such as France is from highly subsidized producers who often appear to cater more to the art circuit than the commercial cinema. The vertically integrated nature of the major studios, which are distributors as well as producers, also provides advantages, especially in film.

Although the United States dominates trade in film and television programs, as we have noted earlier, other countries enjoy a comparative advantage in some program types: Japan in animation, the United Kingdom in costume drama, and Canada in low-cost programming for cable channels. In addition, regional linguistic markets have developed where the dominant trader is from within the region. For example, Brazil and Mexico are very successful in exporting programs to the rest of Latin America. Similarly, Egypt dominates film and television programming in the Arab region. The reason is that similarities in way of life and language mean that producers within a region face a lower cultural discount than those, including those in the United States, from outside the region. Finally it should be noted that the cultural discount for some programming genres, notably domestic news, is so great that domestic producers have a comparative advantage when it comes to supplying the home market.

If you wish to learn more about the U.S. comparative advantage in producing movies and TV programs, see Hoskins et al. (1997, chapters 4 and 5).

14.5 The Case for Protection

Arguments used to justify protecting given industries include the following.

To protect against "unfair" trading practices. An example is dumping, where a product is exported at an artificially low price. In Section 14.6, we will examine the allegation that the U.S. dumps television programs in foreign markets. Similarly, protection of national film industries has been justified by allegations that vertically integrated U.S. majors use their market power in distribution to reduce exhibition opportunities for films from other sources.

To protect infant industries. An infant industry is a new or undeveloped industry that would enjoy a comparative advantage if it could become established. This argument is more likely to be persuasive if there are very substantial economies of scale or learning by doing. Protection is provided in an attempt to establish the industry. Some of the arguments made by countries protecting fledgling film industries have been consistent with the infant industry argument. But note that protection provided on these grounds should be short term and should be withdrawn when the industry is established. Almost invariably, this has not happened, which suggests other motives.

To ensure national security. The usual argument is that domestic suppliers of strategic goods need to be protected, as foreign suppliers could not be relied on at a time of conflict. A variant of this is the argument that flourishing cultural industries are necessary to a nation's well-being and even long-term survival. This contention is open to debate. For a dissenting view, see Collins (1990).

Risks of over-specialization. Where a country is extremely dependent on one product, often an agricultural product, it becomes very vulnerable to changes in the price of the product, changes in consumer tastes, and changes in technology that render the product obsolete. In such cases, protection may be justified to diversify the economy.

You will notice that the list of rationales for protection does not include an increase in employment (the converse of arguing that freer trade increases unemployment). This is because there is no evidence that protection increases jobs in the aggregate. However, it may well increase job opportunities in the protected industries. Although freer trade is a nonconstant sum game at the national level, as all nations benefit, there are groups of people who are worse off in each country. These groups are the producers and workers in industries that are at a comparative disadvantage.

14.6 Application: Does the United States Dump Television Programs?

As we have seen, protection is sometimes justified as a response to unfair trading practices by others. One broadcasting example often cited is dumping of television programs by the United States. The allegation is that U.S. producers sell their programs at unfairly low prices in foreign markets to drive out competitors.

Dumping is usually defined as occurring if either of the following conditions apply:

- The price charged in the foreign market is below cost.
- The price the producer charges in the foreign market is less than the price in the home market.

Taken at face value, both of these conditions would appear to be met. For example, an hour of U.S. drama programming costing $1.5 million to produce might be sold to a U.S. network for $1 million; a Canadian network for $70,000; and a broadcasting organization in Trinidad and Tobago for $400. This makes it difficult for producers based elsewhere to compete with U.S. programming in their domestic market.

However, when it is said that U.S. export prices are "low" and below cost, this is relative to the "high" production cost in the United States or the "high" cost to the foreign producer (often the broadcasting organization) of producing an indigenous substitute. But a comparison to production cost is not appropriate because this cost is not attributable to a sale to an additional export market. The relevant cost is the low marginal cost of making an additional copy and distributing it to that export market. In most markets, the price paid for U.S. programming is far in excess of this incremental cost of supplying the market.

With respect to the second condition, it is true that the prices of U.S. television programs in foreign markets are invariably below the U.S. domestic price. This is because the U.S. market is uniquely large and wealthy and because there is a cultural discount applied to U.S. programming in foreign markets but not in the U.S. domestic market.

The charge of dumping is, in fact, virtually meaningless for a good that is nonrival in consumption. If the United States is guilty, so is every other exporting country. For example, if France sells a program to a Belgian broadcasting organization, it does so at a price that is below production cost. If an independent producer in the United Kingdom sells a program to the Australian Broadcasting Corporation, it does so at a lower price than it charges the BBC. In fact, other countries generally sell programs abroad at prices that are even lower than U.S. prices because their programs are less popular.

If you wish to learn more about the export pricing of television programs, see Hoskins et al. (1997, chapter 6).

14.7 Application: Protection of Cultural Industries

As we have seen, the Theory of Comparative Advantage suggests that a nation should specialize in making products or supplying services in which it has a comparative advantage. Thus the United States should specialize in producing, for example, films and television drama. The converse is that a nation should not be producing goods in which it is at a comparative disadvantage. This suggests that many countries should not expect to have, for example, a significant film industry. It suggests that many nations should be concentrating television program production in areas such as domestic news (where it will have a comparative advantage) rather than in big-budget drama programs.

But is there any reason for rejecting this conclusion when it comes to films, television drama, newspapers, books, and other cultural goods?

Many countries argue that flourishing cultural industries are essential to the preservation of their own distinctive values and way of life and hence the well-being of the nation state and even its long-term survival (as we saw earlier, a variant of the national security argument). This can also be classified as an external benefits argument, for protection. In contrast, the United States does not even recognize the existence of cultural industries; instead, it considers these industries to be entertainment industries producing a commercial product no different from any other. The United States views cultural arguments as rhetoric used as a smokescreen to promote protection (a protection demanded by industry lobby groups).

This difference in philosophy has led to an ongoing battle in trade negotiations. The 1947 General Agreement on Tariffs and Trade (GATT) was primarily concerned with trade in goods but did include an article permitting nations to impose quotas on feature film imports. Restrictions on television program trade also became widespread, and the United States made an unsuccessful attempt in 1961 to amend the GATT to prevent such impediments. Canada succeeded in exempting cultural industries from its Free Trade

Agreement with the United States in 1988 and fought to maintain this exemption under the North American Free Trade Agreement (NAFTA).

The importance of trade issues related to cultural industries became particularly apparent in the closing stages of the Uruguay Round of GATT in 1993-1994. The treatment of service sectors under the General Agreement on Trade in Services is complex, but, through exemption or noninclusion of audiovisual industries, nations that choose have been able to maintain bilateral coproduction treaties, apply quotas, and subsidize domestic producers and distributors.

For more on the international trade regime for cultural industries, see Acheson and Maule (1996).

14.8 Tariffs and Quotas

Protection takes various forms. The most common are tariffs and quotas. A *tariff* is a tax imposed by the importing country when a good crosses its border. The tax may be expressed as a percentage of the import price or as a given dollar amount per unit. A *quota*, on the other hand, is a restriction on the quantity of a good; in this context, the quantity that can be imported from abroad.

The supply curve S_H and demand curve D shown in Figure 14.1 are those for the domestic market. In the absence of trade, product price P_1 and quantity Q_1 would be determined by domestic supply and demand. With free trade, the world price P_0 would apply. This world price is itself determined by the interaction of the world supply and demand for the product (not shown). The country can buy as many units of the product as it wishes at this price (P_0), so the supply curve it faces for foreign goods is S_F. The world price P_0 is below P_1 (otherwise, imposing a tariff or quota would make no sense). At P_0, quantity Q_0 is demanded. The quantity supplied by domestic producers at this price is Q_2 and by foreign producers is $Q_0 - Q_2$.

If a tariff of T per unit were imposed, the supply curve for foreign goods would shift upward to S_{F+T}, and foreign goods would be sold at a price of $P_0 + T$. If T was great enough that $P_0 + T > P_1$, then no trade would take place, and the price would be P_1 for a domestic output of Q_1. This would be equivalent to a foreign quota of zero units.

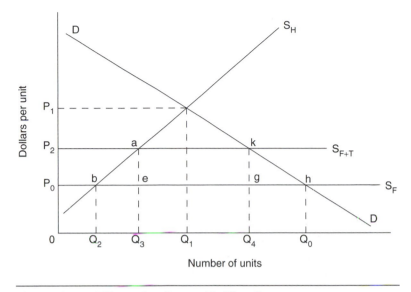

Figure 14.1 Effects of an Import Tariff or Quota

Note: D indicates domestic market demand curve; P, price; Q, quantity; S, supply curve. Points a, b, e, g, h, and k are used in the discussion in the text.

The more usual case is that T is not large enough to negate all trade, or the foreign quota is not zero.

Let us suppose that $T = P_2 - P_0$ so that after a tariff, consumers pay P_2, where $P_2 < P_1$, as in Figure 14.1. At price P_2, the quantity demanded is Q_4. The supply of domestic goods is Q_3, so $Q_4 - Q_3$ is imported.

Alternatively, an equivalent quota of $Q_4 - Q_3$ units from foreign suppliers would have the same result. Only at price P_2 would the restricted supply equal demand. At any price below P_2, the quota would result in an excess demand for foreign goods and a resulting upward pressure on price. An example often cited is the increase in the price of Japanese cars in the United States and Canada from 1983 to 1986, after the Japanese had acquiesced to voluntary, quotalike restrictions.

In the absence of a compelling reason for protection, applying a tariff or quota is not in the overall interests of the country. Compared to the unfettered trade case, if a tariff is imposed, domestic suppliers gain producer surplus equal to the area of the trapezoid

P_2abP_0. The government collects revenue from the tariff totalling the area of rectangle akge. But these gains are more than offset by the loss of consumer surplus, represented by trapezoid P_2khP_0 (P_2kgP_0 is lost due to the payment of a higher price for the Q_4 units still bought at the higher price; the remainder of khg is loss of consumer surplus on the $Q_0 - Q_4$ units no longer consumed). The net domestic loss is aeb + khg.

If a quota is imposed rather than a tariff, then foreign producers, instead of the domestic government, capture akge, and the net domestic loss is correspondingly greater at aeb + khg + akge.

14.9 Application: Domestic
Content Rules for Television Programming

Domestic content requirements are common in broadcasting and are sometimes found, for example in France, for theatrical exhibition of films. Domestic content regulations are usually expressed in terms of a required percentage of domestic programming. The remaining percentage of total programming can be foreign. This is equivalent to imposing a percentage quota on imported programming and hence can be regarded as an unusual form of foreign quota. For example, an Australian requirement that domestic programming comprise at least 55% of a station's air time between 6:00 a.m. and midnight is equivalent to an import quota of 45%. Some countries, Australia again being a case in point, also stipulate domestic content requirements for specific genres of programming. Although a domestic content requirement is a form of quota, the market for television programming differs from the market for many commodities in one important aspect: The total quantity of programming that can be broadcast in any one day is limited to 24 hours. As will be seen, this peculiarity prevents the price for imported programming from falling to a common world price, as it did in our general analysis for quotas.

In Figure 14.2, D is the domestic demand curve for television programming for a season and S_H is the domestic supply curve. In the absence of trade, Q_1 would be the quantity supplied and demanded at a price of P_1. The foreign supply curve, showing the marginal cost to foreign producers of supplying a copy of a program to this market, is S_F.

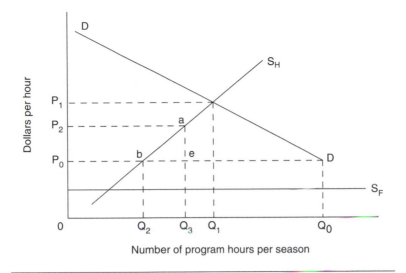

Figure 14.2   Effects of Domestic Content Rules for TV Programs

Note: D indicates domestic demand curve; P, price; Q, quantity (number of program hours per season); S, supply curve. Points a, b, and e are used in the discussion in the text.

   With free trade and competitive conditions, the price would normally be equal to marginal cost. However, the demand for television programs is truncated at the quantity Q_0, which represents the total broadcast hours available in the season (broadcasting organizations cannot exhibit programs beyond 24 hours per day). (Note that if imports were banned, the quantity of programs shown, Q_1, would be less than Q_0, indicating that broadcasting organizations would choose to be on air for less than 24 hours a day.) This permits foreign program suppliers to price at P_0, the price at which domestic demand equals Q_0. (Note that as the location of the demand curve will vary from market to market, the export price will vary from market to market. This is consistent with our analysis in chapter 10.) P_0 would also apply to domestic programs. Q_2 domestic programs would be supplied and $Q_0 - Q_2$ programs imported.

   However, if a domestic content requirement of 50% is in place, the quantity of domestic programming exhibited must be Q_3, where $Q_3 = .5Q_0$. To induce a supply of Q_3 units of domestic programming, broadcasting organizations must pay price P_2 for domestic programs. The price for foreign programs remains at P_0. Unlike the case for Japanese cars, there will be no excess demand for foreign programs and consequently no upward pressure on foreign price because the broadcasting organizations have a finite number of hours to fill and must buy an hour of domestic programming for each hour of foreign programming purchased.

What are the welfare effects of domestic content rules? Domestic suppliers of television programs gain producer surplus equal to the area of trapezoid P_2abP_0 as a result of the higher price for domestic programming. Consumers (broadcasting organizations) lose surplus of the area of the rectangle P_2aeP_0. The net loss is aeb. But this ignores any external benefits from domestic programming. If there are external benefits and these are greater than aeb, the domestic content rules may increase welfare (although there may be superior policy alternatives, such as a subsidy for programming providing external benefits).

14.10 Summary

A nation has an absolute advantage in a good if it can produce more of that good than some other nation using the same resources.

A nation has a comparative advantage in a good if its opportunity cost is less. The opportunity cost is the number of units of the other good that must be given up to produce one more unit.

The Theory of Comparative Advantage shows that every nation is better off specializing in goods in which it has a comparative advantage and trading some of these goods for others in which it possesses no such advantage. This applies even when one nation has an absolute advantage in all goods. A common fallacy is to regard international trade as a constant-sum game in which one nation can only benefit at the expense of another. All nations benefit.

In the real world, specialization may lower unit costs if there are economies of scale or learning. These advantages are particularly important for small countries and, together with the wide variety of consumer tastes, promote specialization in subproduct lines. An example is Japan, with its animated films and television programs. But complete specialization does not occur because all factors within a country are not identical or equally suited for producing a given good.

An important source of comparative advantage is different factor endowments. Nations specialize in production of goods that are intensive in the use of factors in which they are abundantly endowed.

In recent years, an increasing emphasis has been attached to acquired or dynamic comparative advantage. Advantage is conferred by an environment that promotes human knowledge and competition. Such an environment is more likely if an industry is geographically concentrated. An example is Silicon Valley for computer software.

The United States has a comparative advantage in films and television programs stemming from its market size, language, climate, and a geographically concentrated (in Hollywood) and competitive industry environment. But other countries possess a comparative advantage in some genres, an example being the United Kingdom in costume drama. In addition, regional and linguistic markets have arisen in which a nation within the region has a comparative advantage due to a common language and similar culture. An example is Egypt in the Arab region.

Various arguments are made for protection. Protection is supported to offset "unfair" trading practices by foreign governments or foreign competitors. Temporary protection for an infant industry is sought so that a viable industry can be established. Protection is demanded in the interests of national security. Protection is sought to diversify the economy and avoid the risk associated with a very heavy dependence on one good.

The Theory of Comparative Advantage suggests that nations should not protect industries in which they are at a comparative disadvantage. Is there any reason that this conclusion should not apply to cultural goods? Many countries argue that flourishing cultural industries are essential to the preservation of their distinctive way of life and hence the well-being of the nation-state and even its long-term survival. This argument can be regarded as a variant of the national security argument or, alternatively, as an external benefit argument for government intervention. However, some other nations, notably the United States, say that this cultural argument is without merit and serves merely as a smokescreen for unjustifiable protection. Indeed, the United States does not even recognize the existence of cultural industries, regarding them simply as entertainment industries. This difference has led to ongoing battles at international trade negotiations.

The most common forms of protection are quotas, tariffs, and subsidies. Supply and demand analysis can be used to examine the effects of these measures. Domestic content requirements for television programming were examined as an application.

References

Acheson, K., & Maule, C. (1996). *International agreements and the cultural industries.* Ottawa, ON: Centre for Trade Policy and Law.

Adams, W., & Yellen, J. (1976). Commodity bundling and the burden of monopoly. *Quarterly Journal of Economics, 90,* 475-498.

Ad Resource. (2004). *Sample ad rate guide: Sample rates as of June, 2000.* Retrieved February 24, 2004, from http://adres.internet.com/adrates/article/0,1401,00.html

Albarran, A. (1996). *Media economics: Understanding markets, industries and concepts.* Ames: Iowa State University Press.

Albarran, A., & Dimmick, J. (1996). Concentration and economics of multiformity in the communication industries. *Journal of Media Economics, 9*(4), 41-50.

Albon, R., Hardin, A., & Dee, P., with McCalman, P. (1997, March). *Telecommunications economics and policy issues* (Cat. No. 9609504). Canberra: Productivity Commission, Government of Australia. Retrieved February 13, 2004, from http://www.pc.gov.au/ic/research/information/teleeco/teleeco.pdf

Anderson, C., & Bushman, B. (2002, March 29). The effects of media violence on society. *Science, 295,* 2378-2379.

Barnard, B. (1994-1995, December-January). Newspaper wars. *Europe,* p. 30.

Barrett, M. (1995). Direct competition in cable television delivery: A case study of Paragould, Arkansas. *Journal of Media Economics, 8*(3), 77-94.

Bart, P. (1999, February). The shrinking studio. *Daily Variety.* Retrieved April 29, 2000, from http://www.variety.com.

Besen, S., & Farrell, J. (1994). Choosing how to compete: Strategies and tactics in standardization. *Journal of Economic Perspectives, 8*(2), 17-131.

Blackstone, E. (1975). Restrictive practices in the marketing of Electrofax copying machines and supplies: The SCM Corporation case. *Journal of Industrial Economics, 23,* 189-202.

Boardman, A., & Hargraves-Heap, S. (1999). Network externalities and government restrictions on satellite broadcasting. *Journal of Cultural Economics, 23*(3), 167-181.

Braddon, R. (1965). *Roy Thomson of Fleet Street.* London: Colliers.

British Broadcasting Corporation. (2004). *About the BBC: Purpose and values.* Retrieved February 9, 2004, from http://www.bbc.co.uk/info/purpose/

Broadcasting Act, 38-39 Elizabeth II, C11 Pt 1 § 3.1.m (1991).

Bureau of Economic Analysis. (2004). *National economic accounts: 2003 comprehensive revision of the national income and product accounts.* Retrieved February 14, 2004, from http://www.bea.doc.gov/bea/dn1.htm

Cabletelevision Advertising Bureau. (2003, February 26). Ad-supported cable scores double-digit percentage gains in primetime viewership for February sweeps (Press release). Retrieved February 13, 2004, from http://www.cabletvadbureau.com.

Cairncross, F. (1997). *The death of distance: How the communications revolution will change our lives.* Boston: Harvard Business School Press.

California to lure film back. (1997, December 23). *Globe and Mail,* p. A14.

Cave, M., & Williamson, P. (1991, Autumn). Make or break strategy: The great channel 3 licence race. *Business Strategy Review,* pp. 53-89.

Christopherson, S., & Storper, M. (1986). The city as studio; the world as backlot: The impact of vertical disintegration on the location of the motion picture industry. *Environment and Planning D: Society and Space, 4,* 305-320.

Chysi, H., & Sylvie, G. (1998). Competing with whom? Where? And how? A structural analysis of the electronic newspaper market. *Journal of Media Economics, 11*(2), 1-18.

Coase, R. (1937). The nature of the firm. *Economica, 4,* 386-405.

Collins, R. (1990). *Culture, communication and national identity: The case of Canadian television.* Toronto,ON: University of Toronto Press.

Controlling Britain's news. (1993, September 4). *The Economist,* p. 19.

Crain Communications, Inc. (2004a). *AdAge.com: Coen's spending totals for 2002.* Retrieved February 14, 2004, from http://www.adage.com/page.cms?pageId=1010

Crain Communications, Inc. (2004b). *AdAge.com data center: Marketers/ advertisers.* Retrieved February 7, 2004, from http://www.adage.com/datacenter.cms?dataCenterId=1

Crandall, R. (1990). Elasticity of demand for cable service and the effect of broadcast signals on cable prices. In *TCI reply comments* (FCC Mass Media Docket 90-4). Washington, DC: United States Federal Communications Commission.

Cusumano, M., Mylonadis, Y., & Rosenbloom, R. (1992). Strategic maneuvering and mass-market dynamics: The triumph of VHS over Beta. *Business History Review, 66*(1), 51-80.

Douglas, E. (1992). *Managerial economics: Analysis and strategy* (4th ed.). Englewood Cliffs, NJ: Prentice-Hall.

Eberts, J., & Ilott, T. (1990). *My indecision is final: The spectacular rise and fall of Goldcrest Films, the independent studio that challenged Hollywood.* New York: Atlantic Monthly Press.

El Ibiary, R. (1996). Film pirates run aground. *Middle East Times, 33.* Retrieved January 21, 1998, from http:// www.metimes.com/issue33/ bus/2piracy.htm.

Fraser, R. (1986). *Innovation: The attacker's advantage.* New York: Summit.

Gerbner, G. (1990, October 4-5). Violence and terror in and by media. Paper presented at the Colloquium on Media and Crisis, University of Laval, Quebec City, Quebec.

Globerman, S., & Stanbury, W. (1986). Changing the telephone pricing structure: Allocative, distributional and political considerations. *Canadian Public Policy, 12*(1), 214-226.

Graham, A. (1998). Broadcasting policy in the digital age. In C. Firestone & A. Korzick Garmer (Eds.), *Digital broadcasting and the public interest* (pp. 151-192). Retrieved February 7, 2004, from http://www. aspeninstitute.org/index.asp?s=0&bid=642

Guback, T. (1982). Film as international business: The role of American multinationals. In G. Kindem (Ed.), *The American movie industry: The business of motion pictures* (pp. 336-350). Carbondale: Southern Illinois University Press.

Hamilton, J. (1998). *Channelling violence: The economic market for violent television programming.* Princeton, NJ: Princeton University Press.

Hewitt, M. (1994, June 30). A cut-throat war. *Marketing,* p. 16.

Hoskins, C., & McFadyen, S. (1996). The mandate, structure and financing of the CBC. In H. Holmes & D. Taras (Eds.), *Seeing ourselves* (2nd ed., pp. 285-301). Toronto, ON: Harcourt Brace Canada.

Hoskins, C., McFadyen, S., & Finn, A. (1997). *Global television and film.* Oxford, England: Oxford University Press.

Hoskins, C., McFadyen, S., & Finn, A. (1999). International joint ventures in the production of Australian feature films and television programs. *Canadian Journal of Communication, 24*(1), 127-139.

Hoskins, C., & Mirus, R. (1988). Reasons for the US dominance of the international trade in television programmes. *Media, Culture and Society, 10,* 499-515.

Hoskins, C., Mirus, R., & Rozeboom, W. (1989). US television programs in the international market: Unfair pricing? *Journal of Communication, 39*(2), 55-75.

Hotelling, H. (1929). Stability in competition. *Economic Journal, 39,* 41-57.

Jarvie, I. (1992). *Hollywood's overseas campaign: The North Atlantic movie trade, 1920-1950.* Cambridge, England: Cambridge University Press.

Kalita, J., & Ducoffe, R. (1995). A simultaneous-equation analysis of pricing, circulation, and advertising revenue for leading consumer magazines. *Journal of Media Economics, 8*(4), 1-16.

Katz, M., & Shapiro, C. (1994). Systems competition and network effects. *Journal of Economic Perspectives, 8*(2), 93-115.

Lacy, S., & Noh, G. (1997). Theory, economics, measurement, and the Principle of Relative Constancy. *Journal of Media Economics, 10*(3), 3-16.

La Franco, R. (1998, September 21). Starbucks. *Forbes Magazine.* Retrieved February 8, 2004, from http://www.forbes.com/forbes/1998/0921/6206220a.html

Lewis, R. (1995). Relation between newspaper subscription price and circulation, 1971-92. *Journal of Media Economics, 8*(1), 25-41.

Lorinc, J. (1999, September 21). Dispute with publishers sparks probe. *Globe and Mail,* p. C1.

Ludwig, J. (2000). The essential economic problem of the media: Working between market failure and cross financing. *Journal of Media Economics, 13*(3), 187-200.

MacCentral staff. (1999, January 21). iMac top Q4 US retail/mail order PC sales. Retrieved February 3, 2001, from www.maccentral.com/news/9901/21.imacs.shtml

MacKie-Mason, J., & Varian, H. (1994). Economic FAQs about the Internet. *Journal of Economic Perspectives, 7*(3), 75-96.

Mayer, I. (1990). Batman boffo in video rescue. *Channels Field Guide, 10,* 85.

McClennan, S. (1998, July 6). Disney stock dips. *Broadcasting & Cable,* p. 24.

McCombs, M. (1972, August). Mass media in the marketplace. *Journalism Monographs, 24.*

Nagle, T., & Holden, R. (1995). *The strategy and tactics of pricing* (2nd ed.). Englewood Cliffs, NJ: Prentice-Hall.

NationalGeographic.com. (1996). *Birth of the society.* Retrieved February 2, 2004, from http://www.nationalgeographic.com/birth/

National Television Violence Study (Vol. 1). (1996). Thousand Oaks, CA: Sage.

National Television Violence Study (Vol. 2). (1997). Studio City, CA: Mediascope.

National Television Violence Study (Vol. 3). (1998). Santa Barbara: Center for Communication and Social Policy, University of California.

Neuman, W., McKnight, L., & Solomon, R. (1997). *The Gordian knot: Political gridlock on the information highway.* Cambridge: MIT Press.

Newspaper Association of America. (1994). *Facts about newspapers.* Reston, VA: Author.

Nua Internet Services. (2004). *How many online?* Retrieved January 27, 2004, from http://www.nua.ie/surveys/how_many_online/

Oi, W. (1971). A Disneyland dilemma: Two-part tariffs for a Mickey Mouse monopoly. *Quarterly Journal of Economics, 85*, 77-96.

Owen, B., & Wildman, S. (1992). *Video economics.* Cambridge, MA: Harvard University Press.

Oxford Concise Dictionary of Quotations (3rd ed.). (1997). Oxford, England: Oxford University Press.

Paik, H., & Cornstock, G. (1994). The effects of television violence on antisocial behavior. *Communication Research, 21*, 516-546.

Papandrea, F. (2000, February). *Broadcasting planning and extended protection for incumbent broadcasters* (IPA Policy Paper 2000/1). Canberra, Australia: University of Canberra.

Peacock Committee. (1986, July). *Report of the committee on financing the BBC.* London: Her Majesty's Stationery Office.

Picard, R. (1993). Economics of the daily newspaper industry. In A. Alexander, J. Owers, & R. Caveth (Eds.), *Media economics: Theory and practice* (pp. 181-204). New York: Lawrence Erlbaum.

Picarelli, L. (1996). Win 95 just one in a bushel of woes at Apple. *Computerworld, 30*(35), 15.

Porter, M. (1986). Competition in global industries: A conceptual framework. In M. Porter (Ed.), *Competition in global industries* (pp. 15-60). Boston: Harvard Business School Press.

Prasad, A., Mahajan, V., & Bronnenberg, B. (2003). Advertising versus pay-per-view in electronic media. *International Journal of Research in Marketing, 20*(1), 13-30.

Prindle, D. (1993). *Risky business: The political economy of Hollywood.* Boulder, CO: Westview Press.

Pye, J. (1999, April 10). Murdoch's record bid turned down. *Globe and Mail*, p. A32.

Record CD seizures in the US. (1996, October). *One to One*, p. 12.

Robinson, G. (1998). Spectrum property law 101. *Journal of Law and Economics, 41*(2), 609-625.

Roseman, D. (1999, February 15). How to protect Canadian magazines. *Globe and Mail*, p. A13.

Rosen, S. (1981). The economics of superstars. *American Economic Review, 75*(1), 845-857.

Ryan, B. (1999). *Making capital from culture.* Berlin: Aldine de Gruyter.

Schmalensee, R. (1982). Product differentiation advantages of pioneering brands. *American Economic Review, 72*(3), 349-365.

Schnol, J. (1991, August 23). VSDA in Las Vegas. *Publishers Weekly*, p. 38.

Schumpeter, J. (1950). *Capitalism, socialism, and democracy* (3rd ed.). New York: Harper & Row.

Shapiro, C., & Varian, H. (1999). *Information rules: A strategic guide to the network economy.* Boston: Harvard Business School Press.

Signorielli, N., & Morgan, M. (Eds.). (1990). *Cultivation analysis: New directions in media effects research.* Newbury Park, CA: Sage.

Soley, L., & Craig, R. (1992). Advertising pressures on newspapers: A survey. *Journal of Advertising, 21*(4), 1-10.

Steiner, P. (1952). Program patterns and preferences, and the workability of competition in radio broadcasting. *Quarterly Journal of Economics, 66,* 194-223.

Stigler, G. (1963). United States v. Loew's Inc.: A note on block-booking. In P. Kurland (Ed.), *The Supreme Court review* (pp. 152-157). Chicago: University of Chicago Press.

Television Business International Yearbook 95. (1995). London: FT Media and Telecoms.

Theater Enterprises, Inc., v. Paramount Film Distribution Corp., 346 U.S.C. 537 (1954).

Throsby, D. (1994). The production and consumption of the arts: A view of cultural economics. *Journal of Economic Literature, 23*(1), 1-29.

Tracy, M., & Redal, W. (1995). The new parochialism: The triumph of the populist in the flow of international television. *Canadian Journal of Communication, 20*(3), 343-366.

Tribune Wire Services. (2002, July 13). Sprint, WorldCom scrap ill-fated merger worth $129 billion. *Chicago Tribune,* p. 3.

Vogel, H. (1998). *Entertainment industry economics: A guide for financial analysis* (4th ed.). Cambridge, England: Cambridge University Press.

Waxer, C. (1998, November 5). Indies cut their own record deal. *Globe and Mail,* p. B5.

Wells, W., Burnett, J., & Moriarty, S. (2002). *Advertising: Principles and practice* (6th ed.). New York: Prentice Hall.

Wenders, J. (1987). *The economics of telecommunications: Theory and policy.* Cambridge, MA: Ballinger.

Index

About the Authors

Colin Hoskins, Ph.D., is Professor Emeritus of Business Economics in the School of Business at the University of Alberta, Canada. He was awarded a McCalla Research Professorship by the University for 1989-1990. Teaching awards include the MBA Students Award, 1981-1982, and the J. Douglas Muir Award for Teaching, 1982-1983. He has published widely, often with Stuart McFadyen and Adam Finn, in media economics on topics that include reasons why U.S. producers dominate trade in television programs and films, the role of public service broadcasting, regulation of broadcasting, evaluation of subsidy and other incentives for film producers and distributors, and corporate strategies such as international coproductions. Book publications include *Global Television and Film: An Introduction to the Economics of the Business* (with S. McFadyen and A. Finn, 1997). He currently owns and operates EconoMedia Consulting.

Stuart McFadyen is Professor Emeritus in the School of Business at the University of Alberta in Canada. He has conducted research on the television and feature film businesses with Colin Hoskins and Adam Finn since the 1980s. Their work has focused on international joint ventures in film and television production, new product development, public broadcasting, and, most recently, new media. Stuart McFadyen and Adam Finn executive produced the 1-hour television special *Television Canada*, which was shown nationally on the CBC network. The show deals with U.S. domination of the world's television and film markets and suggests ways of dealing with the problems raised.

Adam Finn is the R. K. Banister Professor of Business and Professor of Marketing at the University of Alberta School of Business, where from 1995 to 2000 he was also Academic Director of the Canadian

Institute of Retailing and Services. He has published more than 50 articles in academic journals, books, and proceedings. His research has appeared in journals such as *Journal of Marketing Research, Marketing Science, Journal of Retailing, Journal of Cultural Economics,* and *Canadian Journal of Communication.* This published research has addressed such issues as advertising effectiveness, store and mall patronage and choice, measurement of service quality, new product development and performance in the cultural industries, and the use of tradeoff methods for public policy research. Recent projects funded by grants from the Social Sciences and Humanities Research Council of Canada include developing a scale to assess e-tailer website quality, valuing the Canadian Broadcasting Corporation, and examining the impact of government support for new media content and broadband delivery infrastructure in Canada.